In wildness is the preservation of the world.

—*H.D. Thoreau*

Sierra South

100 Back-country trips
in California's Sierra

Thomas Winnett, Jason Winnett,
Kathy Morey and Lyn Haber

WILDERNESS PRESS
BERKELEY

iv

FIRST EDITION May 1968
Second printing January 1969
Third printing March 1970
Fourth printing January 1971
Fifth printing June 1971
Sixth printing March 1973
Seventh printing April 1974
SECOND EDITION March 1975
Second printing July 1977
Third printing April 1978
THIRD EDITION May 1980
Second printing September 1981
Third printing July 1983
Fourth printing April 1984
FOURTH EDITION April 1986
Second printing August 1988
FIFTH EDITION June 1990
Second printing August 1991

SIXTH EDITION August 1993
Second printing April 1995

Photos by the authors except as noted
Front-cover photo by Lyn Haber
Back-cover photo by Lyn Haber
Design by Thomas Winnett, Jason Winnett and Kathy Morey
Map by Jeff Schaffer

Library of Congress Card Number 93-30454
ISBN 0-89997-162-8
Manufactured in the United States of America
Published by   **Wilderness Press**
      2440 Bancroft Way
      Berkeley, CA 94704
      Phone (510) 843-8080/FAX (510) 548-1355
      Write for free catalog

Library of Congress Cataloging-in-Publication Data

Sierra south : 100 back-country trips in California's Sierra / Thomas Winnett ... [et al.].
  -- 6th ed.
          p.   cm.
      Previous eds. entered under: Winnett, Thomas.
      Includes index.
      ISBN 0-89997-162-8
        1. Backpacking--Sierra Nevada (Calif. and Nev.)--Guidebooks. 2. Hiking-
-Sierra Nevada (Calif. and Nev.)--Guidebooks. 3. Backpacking--California--Guide-
books.   4. Hiking--California--Guidebooks.   5. Sierra Nevada (Calif. and
Nev.)--Guidebooks. 6. California--Guidebooks. I. Winnett, Thomas.
GV199.42.S55W564   1993
796.5'1'097944--dc20   93-30454
                                              CIP

Acknowledgments

I want to acknowledge the lifelong help of my wife, Lu, in the wilderness and out. For inspiration, I have been fortunate enough to live in the same time as David Brower. Karl Schwenke did most of the fieldwork and most of the writing for the first edition of this book, and his mark is still upon it. Jeff Schaffer has always been quick to give me help with maps, natural history, and everything else that makes a guidebook. Noelle Imperatore has been picking up the loose ends I have left around for the last 25 years.

T.W.

There is so much that came together to make this book possible. The four main ingredients are the four co-authors—thank you Tom, Kathy and Lyn. Also, I thank Wilderness Press. In particular I thank you, Tom—editor and father—for your dauntless guidance, patience and coordination that allowed all of us to combine our gifts into one endeavor. I also thank my mother, Lu, and the Great Spirit for making me and all things possible.

J.W.

I shall always be indebted to those who encouraged me, shuttled me around the Sierra, and generally put up with me. In particular, alphabetically: Barbara Dallavo, Christina O'Keefe, Ed Schwartz, and Thomas Winnett. Working with my co-authors on this sixth edition has been a privilege; my thanks to each of you.

K.M.

Ralph Norman Haber has accompanied me on every trail into the wilderness. Tom Winnett encouraged me however far I went.

L.H.

Preface to the Sixth Edition

Our intention in *Sierra South* is to help you explore and enjoy the wilderness in the southern High Sierra. The book seeks to provide you with the most accurate and up-to-date information possible. Therefore, *Sierra South* is an ongoing process, and this sixth edition is a report on the progress so far.

This edition has a new format, the same one that is in the sixth edition of *Sierra North*, the companion book. This format makes it easier to choose a trip because you can quickly compare things such as distance and type—e.g., loop. And there are many new trips to choose from. We now also have four co-authors—one for each of the four directions. Never before has *Sierra South* enjoyed so many different talents or such extensive revision.

Because change is the only real constant in the mountains (as it is anywhere else) we tend to emphasize process rather than form. Experiencing change in the wilderness can help you better feel your connection with all life, including your own. By feeling more alive you will find that it's easier to care—both for the earth and for yourself. Indeed, respect for the earth is really self-respect, because no one is separate from the whole of creation. Everyone and everything share one destiny, one life. Enjoy it.

Contents

Introduction 1
The Care and Enjoyment of the Mountains 4
Safety and Well Being 8
    Health Hazards 8
    Wildlife Hazards 10
    Terrain Hazards 11
The Bear Problem 12
    Backcountry Bear Box Locations in Sequoia and Kings
        Canyon National Parks 16
    A Word About Cars, Theft and Car Bears 18
Maps and Profiles 19
    How to Acquire Your Maps 20
Wilderness Permits and Quotas in the Sierra 21
    Wilderness Permit Application (sample form) 28
The Trailheads 29
Mono Creek to Glacier Divide 32
    1   Bear Dam Junction to Twin Falls 36
    2   Bear Dam Junction to Upper Bear Creek 38
    3   Bear Dam Junction to Vermilion Campground 40
    4   Bear Dam Junction to Lake Italy 42
    5   Bear Dam Junction to Lake Italy 45
    6   Bear Dam Junction to Medley Lakes 48
    7   Bear Dam Junction to Florence Lake 50
    8   Bear Dam Junction to Vee Lake 54
    9   Bear Dam Junction to Second Recess 57
    10   Mosquito Flat to Gem Lakes 60
    11   Mosquito Flat to Fourth Recess 62
    12   Mosquito Flat to Second Recess 65
    13   Pine Creek Roadend to Honeymoon Lake 67
    14   Pine Creek Roadend to Moon Lake 70
    15   Pine Creek Roadend to Lake Italy 72
    16   Pine Creek Roadend to Medley Lakes 74
    17   North Lake to Piute Lake 78
    18   North Lake to Humphreys Basin 80
    19   North Lake to Hutchinson Meadow 82
    20   North Lake to Lamarck Lakes 84
    21   Lake Sabrina to Emerald Lakes 86
    22   Lake Sabrina to Midnight Lake 88
    23   Lake Sabrina to George Lake 90
    24   Lake Sabrina to Tyee Lakes 91

25	Lake Sabrina to Baboon Lakes	93
26	Florence Lake to Lost Lake	94
27	Florence Lake to Courtright Reservoir	96

Glacier Divide to Bubbs Creek 98

28	Courtright Reservoir to Post Corral Meadows	102
29	Courtright Reservoir to North Fork Kings	104
30	Courtright Reservoir to Rae Lake	106
31	Courtright Reservoir to Devils Punchbowl	108
32	Courtright Reservoir to Guest Lake	110
33	Courtright Reservoir to Devils Punchbowl	112
34	Courtright Reservoir to Portal Lake	114
35	Courtright Reservoir to Florence Lake	116
36	Courtright Reservoir to Crown Valley Trailhead	119
37	Wishon Reservoir to Halfmoon Lake	121
38	Wishon Reservoir to Portal Lake	124
39	Wishon Reservoir to Crown Lake	125
40	Crown Valley Trailhead to Cabin Creek	127
41	Crown Valley Trailhead to Crown Creek	129
42	Crown Valley Trailhead to Blue Canyon	131
43	South Lake to Treasure Lakes	134
44	South Lake to Treasure Lakes	136
45	South Lake to Dusy Basin	138
46	South Lake to Chocolate Lakes	140
47	South Lake to Palisade Basin	142
48	South Lake to North Lake	146
49	Big Pine Creek to North Fork Big Pine Creek	153
50	Big Pine Creek to Sixth Lake	156
51	Sawmill Creek Roadend to Sawmill Lake	159
52	Sawmill Creek Roadend to Twin Lakes	161
53	Sawmill Creek Roadend to Taboose Creek Roadend	163
54	Sawmill Creek Roadend to Oak Creek	166
55	Lewis Creek to Kennedy Lakes	170
56	Lewis Creek to Volcanic Lakes	173
57	Cedar Grove to Granite Lake	175
58	Cedar Grove to State Lakes	177
59	Cedar Grove to South Lake	179
60	Cedar Grove to Vidette Meadow	184
61	Cedar Grove to Charlotte Lake	187
62	Cedar Grove to Sixty Lake Basin	189
63	Cedar Grove to Rae Lakes	191
64	Cedar Grove to Lake Reflection	196
65	Cedar Grove to Upper Kern River	199
66	Onion Valley to Flower Lake	203

67   Onion Valley to Charlotte Lake 205
68   Onion Valley to Rae Lakes 207
69   Onion Valley to Symmes Creek Trailhead 209
Bubbs Creek to Lower Kern 214
70   Whitney Portal to Outpost Camp 216
71   Whitney Portal to Crabtree Ranger Station 218
72   Whitney Portal to Wallace Lake 221
73   Whitney Portal to Milestone Basin 223
74   Whitney Portal to Kern-Kaweah River 226
75   Whitney Portal to Symmes Creek Trailhead 228
76   Lodgepole Campground to Ranger Lake 231
77   Lodgepole Campground to Roaring River......................233
78   Lodgepole Campground to Crescent Meadow 235
79   Crescent Meadow to Whitney Portal 238
80   Crescent Meadow to Mt. Whitney 245
81   Cottonwood Lakes Trailhead to South Fork Lakes 249
82   Cottonwood Lakes Trailhead to Upper Rock Creek......251
83   Cottonwood Lakes Trailhead to Upper Rock Creek......253
84   Cottonwood Lakes Trailhead to Whitney Portal 255
85   Cottonwood Lakes Trailhead to Mineral King 258
86   Cottonwood Lakes Trailhead to Symmes Creek
       Trailhead 263
87   Horseshoe Meadow to Rocky Basin Lakes 266
88   Horseshoe Meadow to Mt. Whitney 269
89   Horseshoe Meadow to Whitney Portal 274
90   Mineral King to Upper Cliff Creek.................................276
91   Mineral King to Little Five Lakes 278
92   Mineral King to Nine Lake Basin 280
93   Mineral King to Hamilton Lakes 282
94   Mineral King to Spring Lake 285
95   Mineral King to Lost Canyon 288
96   Mineral King to Upper Rattlesnake Creek 290
97   Mineral King to Little Claire Lake 293
98   Mineral King to Little Five Lakes 295
99   Mineral King to Big Five Lakes 298
100 Mineral King to Crescent Meadow 301
Trip Cross-Reference Table 303
Co-authors 306
Index 307

Introduction

Backcountry travelers know the exhilaration of the out-of-doors in a rich, personal way that is beyond the ken of the ordinary car camper. Far from the crowds that infest the roadside campgrounds, they come to realize the value of solitude, and they learn the calmness of spirit that derives from a fundamental relationship with the mountains. They come to know the simple satisfaction of deep breaths, strong muscles and a sound sleep under brilliant stars. But, above all, in renewing their bond with the wilderness they rekindle that cherished spark of childlike innocence that is so easily extinguished by the pressures of city life. It is these pressures that account for the dramatic increase in the demand for wilderness experiences. The Sierra, offering some of the finest and most spectacular wilderness in the United States, has drawn more than its share of the demand.

Together with the companion volume *Sierra North,* this book is a discriminating effort to meet the needs of both the newcomer and the "old hand." Taking up where *Sierra North* leaves off, this book describes backcountry trails between Mono Creek and the southern end of Sequoia National Park. Here are trips ranging in length from overnighters to two-week expeditions; trips that will sate the appetite of the most avid angler, naturalist or camera bug.

These trips were chosen after considerable screening. The authors interviewed rangers, packers and mountaineers, and—most importantly—hiked each potential trip. The final selections were made on the basis of (1) scenic attraction, (2) wilderness character (remoteness, primitive condition), and (3) recreational potential (fishing, swimming, etc.).

After walking a trip, the authors decided how long it should take if done at a leisurely pace, how long at a moderate pace, and how long at a strenuous pace. They considered not only distance but also elevation change, heat, exposure, terrain, availability of water, appropriate campsites and finally, their subjective feeling about the trip. For each trip, then, we suggest how many days you should take to do it at the pace ("Leisurely," "Moderate" or "Strenuous") you prefer. Some trips simply don't lend themselves to a leisurely pace—

maybe not even a moderate pace. Such trips have a blank in the number-of-days spot for the corresponding pace at the beginning of the trip. Some are not strenuous unless you do the whole thing in one day. Such trips have the word "Day" or "½ Day" after "Strenuous."

Since this book is written for the average backpacker, we chose to describe most trips on either a leisurely or a moderate basis, depending on where the best overnight camping places were along the route. The exceptions were the trips that involve a initial climb of more that 3000 feet—as much as 6500 feet—to climb the eastern escarpment of the Sierra or to climb out of the deep canyons of the Kings and Kaweah rivers. We deemed all such trips strenuous.

Campsites are labeled "poor," "fair," "good" or "excellent." The criteria for assigning these labels were amount of use, immediate surroundings, general scenery, presence of vandalization, availability of water, kind of ground cover and recreational potential—angling, side trips, swimming, etc.

Angling, for many, is a prime consideration when planning a trip. The reports in this book are the result of (1) on-the-trail sampling, (2) on-the-trail observation of fish populations and feeding habits, (3) on-the-trail interviews with other anglers, (4) research into California Department of Fish and Game's trout program, and (5) reading other literature, such as Charles McDermand's *Yosemite and Kings Canyon Trout* and *Waters of the Golden Trout Country*. An up-to-date book on fishing in the High Sierra is Ralph Cutter's *Sierra Trout Guide*. Like the campsites, fishing was labeled "poor," "fair," "good" or "excellent." These labels refer to the quantity of fish in the stream or lake and the fishes' inclination to take the hook. Experienced anglers know that the size of their catch relates not only to quantity, type and general size of the fishery, which are given, but also to water temperature, feed, angling skill, and that indefinable something known as "fisherman's luck." Generally speaking, the old "early and late" adage holds: fishing is better early and late in the day, and early and late in the season.

Deciding when in the year is the best time for a particular trip is a difficult task because of altitude and latitude variations. Low early-season temperatures and mountain shadows often keep some of the higher passes snowbound until well into August. Snows can whiten alpine country in July and August. Some of the trips described here are low-country ones, designed specifically for the itchy hiker who, stiff from a winter's inactivity, is searching for a "warm-up" excursion. These trips are labeled "early season," a period that extends roughly from late May to early July. "Midseason" is here considered to be from early July to late August, and "late season" from then to mid-October. These divisions are arbitrary and can vary from year to year.

Most of the trails described here are well maintained (the exceptions are noted), and are adequately signed. If the trail becomes indistinct, look for blazes (peeled bark at eye level on trees) or "ducks" (two or more rocks piled one atop the other). Two other significant trail conditions have also been described in the text: (1) degree of openness (type and degree of forest cover, if any, or else "meadow," "brush," or whatever; and (2) underfooting (talus, granite, pumice, sand, "duff"—deep humus ground cover of rotting vegetation—or other material).

Bridgeless stream crossings are designated either (1) "Wet in early season," indicating that at high water a particular ford is likely to require wading—sometimes through water several feet deep—or (2) "Difficult in early season," indicating that a crossing may be dangerous due to fast, deep water, or falls and rapids downstream. A dangerous ford should be attempted only by someone with a rope and the experience to use it properly.

Mt. Whitney from Mt. Barnard

The Care and Enjoyment of the Mountains

Be a good guest. The Sierra is home—their only home—to a spectacular array of plants and animals. We humans are merely guests—uninvited ones at that. Be a careful, considerate guest in this grandest of Nature's homes.

The mountains are in danger, particularly the High Sierra. About a million people camp in the Sierra wilderness each year. The vast majority of us care about the wilderness and try to protect it, but it is still threatened with destruction.

Litter isn't the only issue. Increasingly, wilderness campsites, even when free of litter, have that "beat out" look of over-crowded roadside campgrounds. The fragile high-country sod is being ground down under the pressure of too many feet. Lovely trees and snags are being stripped, scarred, and removed altogether for firewood. Dust, charcoal, blackened stones and dirty fireplaces are accumulating. These conditions are spreading rapidly, and in a few years *every* High Sierra lakeshore and streamside may be severely damaged.

The national park service and the forest service are faced with the necessity for reservations systems, designated campgrounds, restrictions on fire building, increased ranger patrols, and even rationing of wilderness recreation. Not only the terrain but the wilderness experience is being eroded. Soon conditions may be little different from those we wanted to leave behind at the roadend.

The solution depends on each of us. We can minimize our impact. It's a fine art that develops as we deepen our relationship with the wilderness. The saying, "Take only memories (or photos), leave only footprints," sums up the minimum-impact attitude. To leave no trace of one's passing is a skill that Native Americans practiced and that we can learn through conscious intent and experience.

Learn to go light. This is largely a matter of acquiring wilderness skills, of learning to be at home in the wilderness rather than in an elaborate camp. The "free spirits" of the mountains are those experts who appear to go anywhere under any conditions with neither encumbrances nor effort but always with complete enjoyment. John Muir, traveling along the crest of the Sierra in the 1870s with little more that his overcoat and his pockets full of biscuits, was the archetype.

Modern lightweight equipment and food are a convenience and a joy. The ever-practical Muir would have taken them had they been available in his day. But a lot of the stuff that goes into the mountains is burdensome, harmful to the wilderness, or just plain annoying to other people seeking peace and solitude. Anything that is obtrusive or that can be used to modify the terrain should be left at the roadend: gigantic tents, gas lanterns, radios, saws, hatchets, firearms (except in the hunting season), etc.

Carry *all* your trash out. You packed those cans and bags in full; you can pack them out empty. Never litter or bury your trash.

Sanitation. Eliminate feces at least 100 feet from lakes, streams, trails, and campsites. Bury feces at least 6 inches deep wherever possible. Intestinal pathogens can survive for years in feces when they're buried, but burial reduces the chances that critters will come in contact with them and carry pathogens into the water. Your object is to keep them from getting into the water, where they could infect others. Where burial is not possible due to paucity of soil or gravel, as at some places above the treeline, leave feces where they will receive maximum exposure to heat, sunlight, etc., to hasten the destruction of pathogens. Where safe to do so, burn used toilet paper so that it can't be uncovered by animals and blown into the water. Otherwise, pack toilet paper out.

Pick "hard" campsites, sandy places that can stand the use. The fragile sod of meadows, lakeshores and streamsides is rapidly disappearing from the High Sierra. It simply cannot take the wear and tear of campers. Its development depends on very special conditions. Once destroyed, it does not ordinarily grow back. Camp at least 100 feet from water unless that's absolutely impossible; in no case camp closer that 25 feet. Don't make campsite "improvements" like rock walls, bough beds, new firerings and tent ditches.

Spare the trees: use a backpacking stove. Throughout popular places in the Sierra, especially in treeline country, thoughtless campers are burning up wood faster that it is being produced. Wood is a precious resource; use it sparingly or, better still, not at all.

Trees, both live and dead, are not only part of the scenery but are food and shelter to many creatures. Fallen, they return essential nutrients to the soil. Standing trees, live or dead, should never be cut or broken. The exquisite, golden trunks left standing after lightning strikes should be left completely alone. Sadly, in some popular areas they have already been destroyed for firewood, and you would never know they had been there.

We encourage the use of modern, lightweight backpacking stoves. They free you of campfire chores. With a stove, you won't have to waste time gathering wood, wondering why in heck your fire won't get going, and dousing the coals till they're dead out. Food spilled on the coals while cooking over a campfire is a fragrant invitation to bears. Using a stove means your eyes won't be so blinded by campfire flames that you can't enjoy the stars. And your and your gear won't stink from campfire smoke. You greatly increase your choices for campsites with a stove, because you won't be limited to sites with wood. A stove works just fine in the rain—no more problems with wet wood.

At the same time, the use of stoves leaves precious downed wood to replenish fragile soils, to shelter small animals, and to provide that essential stick for bear-bagging as well as that fine log to sit on for stargazing or to lean against for a worthwhile afternoon of critter-watching.

Always use a stove when you are above 10,000 feet or in a place where wood is scarce. If you use a stove that requires fuel cartridges, be sure to pack out all the cartridges you bring in.

Or don't cook at all. If you don't want to use a stove, let your next choice be to take food that doesn't need cooking. What a great way to reduce camp chores!

If you must have a campfire, try to camp in established, regularly used campsites where a single, small, substantial fireplace can serve each group of campers for both cooking and warming. If kept scrupulously clean it should last for many years. Unfortunately, fireplaces (and campsites) tend to become increasingly dirty and to multiply. There are now, by actual survey, a hundred times as many fireplaces as are needed in the High Sierra. The countless dirty fireplaces should be eradicated. Many campsites situated at the edge of water should be entirely restored to nature and not used again. It is a noble service to use and clean up established campsites where they are present, and to restore them to nature where called for.

Elsewhere build a small fireplace, if one is legal. A fireplace 6 inches wide internally is enough for 1–2 people to cook on. Please eradicate your fireplace and restore your campsite to a natural condition before you leave. This is facilitated if you build with restoration in mind: two to four medium-sized stones along the sides of a shallow trench in a sandy place. When the camp is broken the stones are returned to their places. Never build a fire against a boulder; it disfigures the boulder and thus the scenery with ugly black scars.

Extinguish fires ½ hour before you leave by adding water and stirring the ashes until the entire bed of coals and the ground beneath it are thoroughly saturated and cold. It is the only way to be sure that a fire and the organic matter in the soil beneath it are dead out. Do not add dirt, as this fills in the fireplace and will lead to its becoming needlessly enlarged.

Never leave fires unattended, even for a second. Many disastrous forest fires have begun from unattended campfires and campfires that weren't adequately put out. Fire is part of the natural course of events, but only when it's caused by Nature.

Protect the water from soap and other pollution. In many areas the water is unsafe to drink, even apart from the *Giardia* it may contain.

Drinking in the good old days

Safety and Well Being

Hiking in the high country is far safer than driving to the mountains, and a few precautions can shield you from most of the discomforts and dangers that could threaten you.

Health Hazards

1. **Altitude Sickness.** If you normally live at sea level and come to the Sierra to hike, it may take your body several days to acclimate. Starved of your accustomed oxygen, for a few days you may experience shortness of breath with even minimal activity, severe headaches, or nausea. The best solution is to spend time at altitude before you begin your hike, and to plan a very easy first day.

2. **Giardia.** Giardiasis is a serious gastrointestinal disease caused by a waterborne protozoan, *Giardia lamblia.* Any mammal (which includes humans) can become infected. It will then excrete live *Giardia* in its feces, from which the protozoan can get into even the most remote sources of water, such as a stream issuing from a glacier. *Giardia* can survive in snow through the winter and in cold water as a cyst resistant to the usual chemical treatments. Giardiasis can be contracted by drinking untreated water. Symptoms appear 2–3 weeks after exposure.

Since giardiasis can be very debilitating and difficult to treat, prevention is best. And prevention is easy. First, assume that all open sources of water are contaminated. Second, treat all water you take from open sources, like lakes and streams. Boiling for 5 minutes is the preferred method and is easy to do when cooking. Or use filters. To be effective, the filter must be sturdy and reliable and must filter at least down to 2 microns to catch both protozoans and cysts. Before you run out to buy a filter, see *Cryptosporidium,* below.

Chemicals like the popular iodine tables are hard to use properly against *Giardia*—but better than no treatment at all. Consider chemicals a back-up system to be used only when boiling or filtering isn't possible. To kill with chemicals, first bring the water temperature to about 70° F so that the cysts will open and the protozoans will be vulnerable to the poison. Then use the chemicals as directed.

Cryptosporidium. A new pest, *Cryptosporidium,* lurks in the wings: It's several times smaller than *Giardia lamblia* and causes a similar disease. It's been found in the streams of the San Gabriel Mountains of Los Angeles, and is spreading throughout Southern California. Probably it will eventually infest Sierran waters. It's resistant to any known chemical treatment. Boiling and filtering are the only known defenses at this time (spring 1993). To be effective, the filter needs to filter at least down to 0.4 micron.

3. **Hypothermia.** Hypothermia refers to subnormal body temperature. More hikers die from hypothermia than from any other single cause: it represents the greatest threat to your survival in the wilderness. Caused by exposure to cold, often intensified by wet, wind and weariness, the first symptoms of hypothermia are uncontrollable shivering and imperfect motor coordination. These are rapidly followed by loss of judgment, so that you yourself cannot make the decisions to protect your own life. To prevent hypothermia, stay warm: carry wind-and-rain-protective clothing, and put it on as soon as you feel chilly. Stay dry: carry or wear wool or a suitable synthetic (not cotton) against your skin; bring raingear even for a short hike on an apparently sunny day. If weather conditions threaten and you are inadequately prepared, flee or hunker down. Protect yourself so you remain as warm and dry as possible.

Treat shivering at once—remember, hypothermia acts quickly and destroys judgment. Get the victim out of the wind and wet, replace all wet clothes with dry ones, put him or her in a sleeping bag and give him or her warm drinks. If the shivering is severe and accompanied by other symptoms, strip him or her and yourself (and a third party if possible), and warm him or her with your own bodies, tightly wrapped in a dry sleeping bag.

4. **Lightning.** Although the odds of being struck are very small, almost everyone who goes to the mountains thinks about it.

An afternoon thunderstorm may come upon you rather quickly, but not so fast that you can't get to a safer place if you are exposed. All exposed places are dangerous: a mountain peak, a mountain ridge, an open field, a boat on a lake. But so are a small cave and an overhang.

Then where should you shelter if the thunderstorm catches you? The safest place is an opening or a clump of small trees in a forest. But one is not always handy. If you are above treeline, and can get next to any pinnacle, do so, taking a position no farther from the pinnacle than its height. Lacking any pinnacles, position yourself atop a small boulder that is detached from bedrock. If caught in an open area, get to the lowest place that is not wet.

Wherever you position yourself, the best body stance is one that minimizes the area your body covers. You should drop to your knees and put your hands on your knees. This is because the more area your body covers, the more chance that ground currents will pass through it.

Most people believe that metal as such attracts lightning, but the actual danger from your packframe, tent poles, etc. is due to induced currents. We won't explain them here, but just be sure to get all your metal away from you as fast as you can.

And what if lightning strikes you anyway? There isn't much you can do except pray that someone in your party is adept at CPR—or at least adept at artificial respiration if your breathing has stopped but not your heart. It may take hours for a victim to resume breathing on his or her own. If it's your companions who are victims, attend first to those who are not moving. Those who are rolling around and moaning are at least breathing. Finally, a victim who lives should be evacuated to a hospital, because other problems often develop in lightning victims.

Wildlife Hazards

1. **Rattlesnakes.** They occur at lower elevations (they are rarely seen above 7000 feet) in a range of habitats, but most commonly near riverbeds and streams. Their bite is rarely fatal to an adult. If you plan a trip below 6000 feet along a watercourse, you may want to carry a snake-bite kit. If you hear a snake rattle, stand still long enough to determine where it is, then leave in the opposite direction.

2. **Marmots** (see the photo on page 79). They live from about 6000 feet to 11,500 feet. Because they are curious and always hungry, and like to sun themselves on rocks in full view, you are likely to see them. Marmots enjoy many foods you do, including cereal and candy (especially chocolate). They may eat through a pack or tent when other entry is difficult. Marmots cannot climb trees or ropes, so you can protect your food by hanging it.

3. **Mosquitoes.** If you have no protection against mosquitoes, they can ruin your trip. However, protection is easy. Any insect repellent containing *N, N diethylmeta-toluamide* ("DEET") will keep them off. Don't buy one without it. Clothing is also a bar to mosquitoes—a good reason for wearing long pants and a long-sleeved shirt. If you are a favorite target for mosquitoes (they have

their preferences) you might take a head net—a hat with netting suspended all around the brim and a snug neckband. Planning your trip to avoid the height of the mosquito season is also a good preventive.

4. **Bears.** We've devoted a separate section to bears; please see "The Bear Problem" below.

Terrain Hazards

1. **Snow bridges and snow cornices.** Stay off them.

2. **Stream crossings.** In early season, when the snow is melting, crossing a river can be the most dangerous part of a backpack trip. Later, ordinary caution will see you across safely. If a river is running high, you should cross it only if 1) the alternatives to crossing are more dangerous than crossing, 2) you have found a suitable place to ford, and 3) you use a rope.

As for #1, obviously it's better to turn back than to risk accident. As for #2, it may take considerable looking around to find a suitable place to ford. If you can find a viewpoint high above the river, you can better check out the river's width, speed and turbulence, any obstructions in it, and the nature of its bottom.

Whichever method you use to cross a stream, you should:

- If the water is at all high, wait till morning to cross, when the level will be at its daily low.
- Unfasten the hip belt of your pack, in case you have to jettison it.
- Keep your boots on. They will protect your feet from injury and give your feet more secure placement.
- Never face downstream. The water pushing against the back of your knees could cause them to buckle.
- Move one foot only when the other is firmly placed.
- Never allow your legs to cross; keep them apart.
- Use a stick as a support on the upstream side.

The Bear Problem

What bears? The bears of the Sierra are American black bears; their coats range from black to light brown. They're relatively unaggressive unless provoked, and their normal diet consists largely of plants. The suggestions in this section apply only to American black bears. These suggestions *don't* apply to dealing with the more aggressive grizzly bear, which is extinct in California.

American black bears run and climb faster than you ever will, they are immensely stronger, and they are very intelligent. Long ago they learned to associate humans with easy sources of food. Now, keeping your food away from the local bears is a problem. Remember, though, that all they want is your *food*. They aren't interested in inedible *you*. They will try to avoid you whenever possible. So don't let the possibility of meeting a bear keep you out of the Sierra. Respect these magnificent creatures—sighting one is a rare privilege. Learn what you can do to keep yourself and your food safe. Some suggestions follow.

Bears: any time, anywhere. Bears are normally daytime creatures. But they've learned that our supplies are easier to raid when we're asleep, so they're working the night shift, too. *Bears are active at all times of day and night.* Also, it used to be that you rarely saw bears above 8,000–9,000 feet. As campers moved into the higher elevations, the bears followed. *You can't rely on altitude to help protect your food against bears.*

To avoid bears while hiking, make noise as you go. Some hikers tie cowbells or clanking hardware—pots, pans, Sierra cups—to their packs; others sing, talk or just hike noisily. American black bears are shy and will scramble off to avoid meeting you if they hear you coming.

In camp, store your food properly and always scare bears away immediately—see the suggestions under **Food storage**, below.

***You* are responsible for protecting your food.** Backcountry management policies now hold campers responsible for keeping their food away from bears. *If a bear gets your food, it is your fault.* The bear is just being a bear. You, however, can be fined. You're also responsible for cleaning up the mess once you're sure the bear has had its fill and won't be back for seconds. You also have an ethical responsibility for your part in the process that leads to that bear becoming a repeat-problem bear, maybe a bear that has to be killed.

Plan ahead. Think and plan to avoid problems. Avoid taking smelly foods and fragrant toiletries; they attract bears—bears have a superb sense of smell. Check the hypoallergenic section of the drugstore for fragrance-free toiletries; use baking powder instead of toothpaste. Ask rangers where there are bear problems, and avoid those areas. Ask rangers and other backpackers what measures they take to safeguard food and chase bears away; maybe some of their ideas will work for you. Consider camping where you can use a bear box (below). If you need to counterbalance your food bags (also below), practice the skill before you need it. Cook and clean up afterward in a way that doesn't leave food residues to attract bears. Clean any food out of your gear and store it with the rest of your chow; otherwise, you could lose a pack to a bear who went for the granola bar you forgot in a side pocket. Don't take food into your tent or sleeping bag unless you want ursine company. Store your garbage just as carefully as you store your food.

Food storage. Here are some food-storage suggestions:

1. **Bear boxes.** A number of well-used backcountry sites offer food storage lockers, popularly called bear boxes. These are large steel lockers intended for storage of food only, and they will hold the food bags of several backpackers. Everyone shares the bear box; you may not put your own locks on one. It's designed so that its latches, simple for humans, are inoperable by bears. Food in a properly fastened bear box is safe from bears; however, some boxes have holes in the bottom through which, if the holes aren't plugged, mice will squeeze in to nibble on your goodies.

An open bear box is a fragrant temptation for any bears in the vicinity, so don't leave the box open even when there are people around. Open it, use it, close it and latch it promptly. The presence of a bear box attracts campers as well as bears, and the area can become overused. However, it isn't necessary for *everyone* to cluster right around the box. A campsite a few hundred yards away may be more secluded and pristine; the stroll to and from the bear box is a pleasant way to start and end a meal.

Bear-box "don'ts." Never use a bear box as a garbage can! Rotting food is smelly and very attractive to bears; it takes up room and fouls the box for other users. Never use a bear box as a food drop; its capacity is needed for people actually camping in its vicinity. Never leave a bear box unlatched; it's literally an open invitation to raiding bears and other critters.

There is a list of the current bear-box sites and the one remaining cable site, all within Sequoia and Kings Canyon, at the end of this section. The national forests do not offer bear boxes yet.

2. **Bearproof food canisters** are lengths of sewer pipe fitted with a bottom and a lid only a human can open. You'll see them advertised in various outdoor publications. They weigh 3–5 pounds empty and hold 3–5 days' worth of food. You carry the filled canister in your pack. It's very heavy, rigid, and bulky. Our experience is that it's suitable only for a very short trip on a route that lacks bear boxes.

3. **Counterbalance bear-bagging.** If bear boxes aren't available, counterbalance your food. It's best to get to camp early enough to get your food hung while there's light to do it by. This technique slows the bear down but is not secure all by itself. It gives you time to hear the bear going after your food and time to scare it away. When you get a permit, you typically get a sheet on counterbalance bear-bagging. Here's the technique as we use it; practice it at home before you go:

• Find a tree with a live, down-sloping branch that's well off the ground but that you can throw a rock over. Make sure there are no objects below the branch—like another branch—that could support a bear.

• Divide your food and anything else with an odor, like toiletries and garbage, into two bagged, approximately equal loads of not more than 8–10 lbs. each—they'll counterbalance each other. Or, if you have only one bag, counterbalance it with a rock. The bags should be heavy duty nylon stuff sacks.

• Use enough rope to go over the branch and back to the ground. Use *strong, thin* ($\frac{1}{8}''$–$\frac{1}{4}''$) rope, like parachute cord.

• Tie a rock to the rope's end and toss it over the branch as far out as will support the weight of your food but not a bear cub.

• Tie things like pots or Sierra cups to one or both bags—things that will make a lot of noise to alert you if a raiding bear disturbs the bags.

• Tie the first sack onto the rope and hoist it up to the branch.

• Tie the second sack (or the counterbalancing rock) as high as you can on the other end of the rope. Put the excess rope in the sack, or wrap it around the counterbalancing rock, leaving a loop out for retrieval.

• With a stick, push the second sack up until the sacks are about at the same height and they balance each other. Both bags should rest far enough off the ground that you can't touch them even when you're on tiptoe—even higher if you're short.

• To retrieve your food, use a stick to push up one bag until the other descends to where you can reach it or at least the loop of rope. When you free the first bag, remember to keep hold of the rope so the other doesn't come crashing down.

- Sleep a couple of dozen feet or so away from your properly-hung food—close enough that you can hear a raiding bear and scare it away as quickly as possible.
- If a bear goes after your food, jump up and down, make a lot of noise, wave your arms—anything to make yourself seem huge, noisy and scary to a bear. Have a stash of throwing rocks at hand and throw them at trees, boulders, etc., to make more noise. Bang pots together. Blow whistles. The object is to scare the bear away. *Never directly attack the bear itself.*

4. **Cables** are lengths of steel cable strung high between two trees. You counterbalance your food over a cable as you would over a branch. Cables used to be as common as bear boxes are now, but there's only one cable left in the area of this book, at Horse Creek on the Hockett Plateau.

5. **Above treeline, there are no trees to hang your food bags from.** But there are still bears—as well as mice, marmots, and ground squirrels—anxious to share your chow. Look for a tall rock with an overhanging edge from which you can dangle your food bags high off the ground and well away from the face of the rock. (Unlike bears, marmots, etc., have not learned to get your food by eating through the rope suspending it.) Or try the stash-in-a-crack technique below.

6. **Stash-in-a-crack.** One of us has had good luck with this technique; use it only above treeline. Bag your food and push it deep into a crack in the rocks too small and too deep for a bear to reach into—but be sure *you* can still retrieve it. You may lose a little food to mice or ground squirrels, but it won't be much.

7. **When dayhiking from a base camp where you can't bear-box your food,** it's safer to take it with you instead of leaving it hanging or stashed in a crack.

Once a bear gets your food, never try to get it back. It's the bear's food now, and the bear will defend it aggressively against puny you. You may hear that there are no recorded fatalities in bear-human encounters in recent Sierra history. Of course, this isn't true: plenty of *bears* have been killed as a result of repeated encounters. And there have been very serious, though not fatal, injuries to humans in these encounters.

If, despite your best efforts, you lose your food to a bear, it may be the end of your trip but not of the world. You won't starve to death in the maximum 3–4 days it will take you to walk out from even the most remote Sierra spot. Your pack is now much lighter. And you can probably beg the occasional stick of jerky or handful of gorp from your fellow backpackers along the way. So cheer up, clean up the mess, get going and plan how you can do it better on your next trip.

Backcountry Bear Box Locations in Sequoia and Kings Canyon National Parks*

General area	Specific area (number of boxes)
Woods Creek	Lower Paradise Valley (2) Middle Paradise Valley (1) Upper Paradise Valley (1) Woods Ck. Crossing/John Muir Trail jct. (2) Rae Lakes (3, one at each main lake)
Copper Creek	Lower Tent Meadow (1)
Bubbs Creek	Sphinx Creek (2) Charlotte Creek (1) Lower Junction Meadow (2) Vidette Meadow (2) 9900′ elev. on John Muir Tr. in this area (1) Center Basin Creek/John Muir Tr. jct. (1) East Lake (2) East Creek (1)
Charlotte/ Kearsarge Lakes	Charlotte Lake (1) Kearsarge Lakes (3)
Tyndall/ Crabtree Area	Tyndall Creek Frog Ponds (1) Tyndall Creek/John Muir Trail jct. (1) Lower Crabtree Meadow (1) Crabtree Ranger Station (1) Wallace Creek/John Muir Trail junction (1)
Rock Creek	Lower Rock Ck. crossing/Pacific Crest Tr. (1) Lower Rock Creek Lake (1) Lower Soldier Lk. (Upper Rock Creek Lk.) (1)

*No other agency in *Sierra South*'s area of coverage provides bear boxes.

Backcountry Bear Box Locations (continued)

General area	Specific area (number of boxes)
Kern Canyon	Junction Meadow (1) Kern Hot Springs (2) Upper Funston Meadow (2) Lower Funston Meadow (1)
Hockett Plateau	Hockett Meadow (1) South Fork Meadow (1) Hidden Camp (1) Rock Camp (2) Horse Creek CABLE (1)
Mineral King Area	Monarch Lake (2) Franklin Lake (3)
Little Five Lakes/ Cliff Creek	Big Arroyo Crossing (1) Big Five Lakes (1) Little Five Lakes (1) Cliff Creek Crossing (1) Pinto Lake (1) Columbine Lake (1)
Lodgepole Backcountry	Mehrten Ck. Crossing/High Sierra Tr. (1) Nine Mile Ck. Crossing/High Sierra Trail (1) Bearpaw Meadow/High Sierra Trail (4) Hamilton Lake/High Sierra Trail (2) Emerald Lake (2) Pear Lake (2) Clover Ck. So. Crossing/Twin Lks. Tr. (1) JO Pass Trail/Twin Lakes Trail jct. (1) Twin Lakes (2) Buck Creek Crossing/High Sierra Trail (1)
Sugarloaf Valley/ Roaring River	Ranger Lake (2) Seville Lake (2) Lost Lake (1) Rowell Meadow (1) Sugarloaf Meadow (1) Roaring River Ranger Station (3) Comanche Meadow (1)

A Word About Cars, Theft and Car Bears

Stealing from and vandalizing cars are becoming all too common at popular trailheads. You can't ensure that your car and its contents will be safe, but you can increase the odds. Make your car unattractive to thieves and vandals by disabling your engine (your mechanic can show you how), hiding everything you leave in the car, closing all windows and locking all doors and compartments. Get and use a locking gas-tank cap. If you have more than one car, use the most modest one for driving to the trailhead.

Bearproof your car by not leaving any food in it and by hiding anything that looks like a picnic cooler or other food carrier—bears know what to look for. To a bear, a car with food in it is just an oversized can waiting to be opened.

Maps and Profiles

As a backcountry traveler you may already be familiar with maps, knowing both how to use them and where to get them. For some, however, maps may yet present some mysteries. Rest assured that most hikers find maps valuable and easy to use.

There are many different maps available for the Sierra Nevada. Each one provides different information. In this book you will find an overview map inside the back cover. On this map trails and trailheads are indicated in red, and access roads are delineated in brown. This map is very general, meant only for trip planning purposes. Another kind of "map" in this book is the simple trip profile at the beginning of each trip. These profiles give you a quick picture of the ups and downs of each route. The vertical scale shows elevation, and the horizontal scale distance. Keep in mind that the vertical scale has been exaggerated 25 times, which might make some trips look ridiculous. Since carrying a pack uphill can be very grueling, this exaggeration may be appropriate.

In the backcountry it is very useful to have a basic, working knowledge of topographic maps. Topographic maps (topos) are the standard for use in the field because they provide the most detailed and accurate information about landforms, waterways, vegetation, place names and trails. If you don't yet know how to use topos, you can learn, and it's well worth the effort. You can ask a friend to teach you, or take a class. There are also several books on the subject. Once you learn the meaning of the basic symbols you will be able to just look at a topo and get a mental picture of the landscape it represents.

For the *Sierra South* backcountry there are several kinds of topos. The traditional standard is the United States Geological Survey (USGS) fifteen minute (15′) quadrangle (quad) series. They are called 15′ because they cover an area that spans 15 minutes of longitude and 15 minutes of latitude. They cover an area about 14 x 17 miles at a scale of about 1 inch=1 mile, or 1:62,500. The USGS is letting this series go out of print. But, fortunately, Wilderness Press now publishes updated versions of the 15′ quads for most of the *Sierra South* area. These quads are well above the USGS standards for accuracy. They are more up-to-date, have an index of place names, and are printed on waterproof, tear-resistant plastic. If any of these maps covers all or part of a given trip, its title(s) appear in boldface at the beginning of the trip. So far Wilderness Press publishes the following 15' quads: *Mt. Abbot* (including part of Mount Tom), *Mt. Goddard* (including part of Big Pine), *Triple Divide Peak*, *Mineral King* and *Mt. Whitney*.

The other pertinent USGS topos are the 7½' series. These quads cover an area about 7 x 8 miles, at a scale of 1:24,000. These topos are more detailed, as they cover a smaller area. It takes four of these to cover one 15' quad. Each trip in *Sierra South* is entirely covered by quads in the 7½' series and their titles are also listed at the beginning of each trip.

Another useful topo is the US Forest Service map entitled *John Muir Wilderness and Sequoia-Kings Canyon Backcountry*. This map covers all of the *Sierra South* area at a scale of 1 inch = 1 mile, or 1:63,360. This map comes on three sides of two very large sheets of paper, and is less accurate than the USGS topos. Although it may be a little inconvenient for trail use, it is good for trip planning purposes.

How to Acquire Your Maps

Wilderness Press maps and books, as well as USGS and Forest Service maps, compasses and many other useful products, are available in person or by mail order from:

The Map Center
2440 Bancroft Way
Berkeley, CA 94704
(510) 841-MAPS
Mon.-Sat. 10–6

The Map Center
63 Washington
Santa Clara, CA 95050
(408) 296-MAPS
Mon.-Sat. 10–5

Closer to the trailheads you can find topos at National Forest and National Park ranger stations as well as some of the other locations where wilderness permits are issued.

A topographic map index for California, and the regular USGS topos are available from:

345 Middlefield Rd
Menlo Park, CA 94025
(415) 329-4390

Forest Service maps are available from:

USDA Forest Service
630 Sansome St
San Francisco, CA 94111
(415) 705-2874

Wilderness Permits and Quotas in the Sierra

Overuse has become a serious problem in our Sierra national parks and wilderness areas. To help combat this, the agencies responsible for these areas—national parks and national forests—have set up a system of quotas and permits for overnight stays in the backcountry. You do not need a permit to dayhike in the area of this book. Issuing permits helps agencies not only to control use of the backcountry but also to find out who's using it, how, and how many users there are. It also gives them a way to educate backcountry users, thanks to safety and minimum-impact technique information typically included with the permit.

The information below applies to overnight trips covered in this book. Elsewhere, policies may vary—and probably do.

Overview. Here's a simplified overview of how the permit/quota system works:

- **Quotas** determine the total number of people and of stock that can start an overnight trip on the same day from the same trailhead.
- **Quota periods** determine the time period—usually summer—when quotas apply. *You still need a permit before and after the quota period*; the difference is that there's no quota for the number of people and stock. Limits on group sizes still apply.
- **Limits on group size** determine the maximum number of people and stock in any one group traveling and camping together. These limits are in effect year-round. See below.
- **Permits** are issued by these agencies to help enforce the above policies. Permits can be *reserved in advance by mail* (not actually issued) or *issued on demand in person*—except for Whitney Portal. Some agencies charge a small fee per person for permit reservations by mail to cover the cost of the paperwork.

  Agencies set aside part of a trailhead's daily permit quota for permits to be reserved by mail, and only a part of those may be reserved by large parties (10 or more people). Another part of a trailhead's daily permit quota is set aside for permits to be issued on demand—except for Whitney Portal. See below for more about getting permits on demand.

If your trip crosses more than one contiguous administrative area, you still need only one permit. Get that permit from the agency in charge of the trailhead where you'll start (see below). The other agencies will honor it.

• **Permit-reservation issuing period.** There is a limited period each year during which you can *apply* for permits by mail. It varies by agency; see below. Requests are processed in order of postmark dates. Allow up to 5 weeks for a written response. Permit applications postmarked before or after this period, or lacking a check or money order for the paperwork fee (also see below), will not be processed.

You may or may not get the permit you apply for. To improve your chances, specify alternate starting dates and/or alternate trailheads, and avoid starting on weekends or holidays.

• **A permit reservation is *not* a permit.** If you apply for a permit in advance by mail, you will be issued a permit *reservation*, not a real permit. *Read it!* Your permit reservation will tell you where and when you can pick up the real permit in advance of your trip. Frequently, you'll pick up the real permit at an entrance station nearer your trailhead than the ranger station that issued your permit reservation. Unclaimed reserved permits are added to the day's allocation of on-demand permits.

• **If you are caught in the backcountry without a permit,** you are subject to fines and expulsion from the wilderness. We've seen it happen.

Who's in charge. The agencies responsible for the parts of the Sierra this book covers are Sequoia and Kings Canyon national parks (two contiguous parks handled as one administrative unit), Sierra National Forest, and Inyo National Forest.

Limits. These agencies have been working with nearby Yosemite National Park and Sequoia, Toiyabe, and Stanislaus national forests to establish common limits on maximum group (party) size, number of pack/riding stock per party, and a maximum party size per campsite in the wilderness areas this book covers. The final policy, which takes effect throughout the central and southern Sierra in 1993, sets these limits:

• **Maximum group size:** 15 persons
• **Maximum at a campsite:** 15 persons (backpacker and/or stock parties)

- •**Maximum number of pack and saddle stock:** 25 head per party.

Individual agencies can establish lower limits in sensitive areas, or grant exceptions in special circumstances.

To apply for a permit in advance by mail, fill out a Wilderness Permit Application—one for each trip—like the one at the end of this section. Or write a letter containing the same information. Enclose the necessary paperwork fee if any, and send it to the appropriate agency during the period when they accept permit applications by mail. Here's a list of agencies to apply to *for trips in this book*, their permit application periods, and their fees if any:

- •*West side:*

Sierra National Forest:

Permit application period: Postmarked March 1 to August 15
Fee with permit application: $3 per person
Period when quotas are in effect: Last Friday in June to September 15

For Vermilion Campground (Lake Edison), Bear Dam Junction, and Florence Lake trailheads:

Sierra National Forest
Pineridge Ranger District
P.O. Box 300
Shaver Lake, CA 93664
(209) 841-3311

For Courtright Reservoir/Maxon, Wishon Reservoir, and Crown Valley trailheads:

Sierra National Forest
Kings River Ranger District
34849 Maxon Road
Sanger, CA 93657

Sequoia and Kings Canyon National Parks:

Permit application period: Postmarked March 1 to September 20 and at least 15 days before the start of your trip
Fee with permit application: None
Period when quotas are in effect: May 20 to September 20

For Lewis Creek, Cedar Grove Roadend, Lodgepole Campground, Crescent Meadow, and Mineral King trailheads:

Wilderness Permit Reservations
Sequoia and Kings Canyon National Parks
Three Rivers, CA 93271

• *East side:*

Inyo National Forest controls all east-side trailheads in this book:

Permit application period: March 1 to May 31
Period when quotas are in effect: Last Friday in June to September 15, except for Whitney Portal (below)
Whitney Portal quota period: May 22 to October 15
Fee with permit application: $3 per person

For Mosquito Flat, Pine Creek Roadend, North Lake, Lake Sabrina, South Lake, and Big Pine Creek trailheads:

Inyo National Forest
White Mountain Ranger District
798 N. Main St.
Bishop, CA 93514
(619) 873-4207

For Sawmill Creek Roadend, Oak Creek Roadend, Onion Valley, Symmes Creek, Whitney Portal, Cottonwood Lakes/ Cottonwood Creek, and Horseshoe Meadow trailheads:

Inyo National Forest
Mt. Whitney Ranger District
P.O. Box 8
Lone Pine, CA 93545
(619) 876-5542

Other restrictions. In addition to the trailhead restrictions above, there are places in the backcountry that are closed to all camping, places where you are restricted to a one- or two-night stay, and places where wood fires are forbidden. These restrictions help protect damaged areas against more abuse, so please respect them. You'll find out what and where they are in the trip write-ups in this book and in the literature you'll get with your permit.

Permits on demand. Identify the trailhead you want to start from and then call or write the appropriate office listed above to find out where (location and how to get there) and when (dates, days of the week, and hours) you can get a permit on demand for that trailhead. On-demand permits are issued *only* for the day on which you will start your trip. If you get a permit, you must start on that day; otherwise, your permit will be invalid. If you don't make that trailhead's quota for that day, you will have to try again.

Exception: All Whitney Portal permits must be reserved in advance. None are *set aside* to be issued on demand, though chance may make one available.

Your chances of getting an on-demand permit are better if you apply on a weekday and get into the queue very early. It also helps if you pick one of the less popular trailheads—for example, Cottonwood Pass instead of Cottonwood Lakes. The office you call or write can advise you which trailheads are less popular.

Here, by trailhead, are the stations where you can get permits on demand. Some stations are open only in summer; they're noted as "seasonal":

● *West side:*

For Vermilion Campground (Lake Edison), Bear Dam Junction, and Florence Lake trailheads:

Seasonal: High Sierra Ranger Station (on Kaiser Pass Road between Kaiser Pass and the turnoff to Florence Lake; (209) 877-3138)

Year-round: Pine Ridge Ranger Station (on Highway 168 in Shaver Lake; (209) 841-3311)

For Courtright Reservoir/Maxon, Wishon Reservoir, and Crown Valley trailheads:

Seasonal: Dinkey Creek Ranger Station (on Dinkey Creek Road—accessible from Highway 168 at Shaver Lake—just north of the junction with McKinley Grove Road; (209) 841-3404)

Year-round: Pine Ridge Ranger Station (on Highway 168 in Shaver Lake; (209) 841-3311)

For Lewis Creek and Cedar Grove Roadend:

Seasonal: Cedar Grove Roadend Ranger Station (at the east end of Highway 180; no telephone)

For Lodgepole Campground and Crescent Meadow; for general information:

Year-round: Lodgepole Visitor Center (just off the General's Highway (Highway 198) at Lodgepole; (209) 565-3456)

For Mineral King:

Seasonal: Mineral King Ranger Station (in Mineral King, about 1 mile west of the end of Mineral King Road. Telephone: call Sequoia-Kings Canyon at (209) 565-3761 or -3766 first to find out if the Mineral King station is manned yet; if it is, they'll tell you how to telephone Mineral King Ranger Station)

● *East side:*

For Mosquito Flat (Little Lakes Valley):

Seasonal: Rock Creek Entrance Station (take the Rock Creek exit from Highway 395 at Tom's Place; the station is a short distance west along the road to the trailheads)

Year-round: Inyo National Forest, White Mountain Ranger District (798 N. Main St., Bishop, CA 93514; (619) 873-4207)

For Pine Creek Roadend:

Year-round: Inyo National Forest, White Mountain Ranger District (798 N. Main St., Bishop, CA 93514; (619) 873-4207)

For North Lake, Lake Sabrina, and South Lake:

Seasonal: Bishop Creek Entrance Station (on Highway 168 west of Bishop and east of the turnoff to South Lake)

Year-round: Inyo National Forest, White Mountain Ranger District (798 N. Main St., Bishop, CA 93514; (619) 873-4207)

For Big Pine Creek:

Seasonal: From campground host at Upper Sage Flat Campground (near the end of the road to the Big Pine Creek trailheads; permits issued between 7:00–7:30 and 11:00–11:30 A.M. only)

Year-round: Inyo National Forest, White Mountain Ranger District (798 N. Main St., Bishop, CA 93514; (619) 873-4207)

For Sawmill Creek Roadend, Oak Creek Roadend and Symmes Creek:

Year-round: Inyo National Forest, Mt. Whitney Ranger District (on Highway 395 in Lone Pine; (619) 876-6200)

For Onion Valley:

Seasonal: Onion Valley Entrance Station (on the road to Onion Valley, west of Highway 395) from 7–9 A.M. only. After that, Inyo National Forest, Mt. Whitney Ranger District (on Highway 395 in Lone Pine; (619) 876-6200).

Year-round: Inyo National Forest, Mt. Whitney Ranger District (on Highway 395 in Lone Pine; (619) 876-6200).

For Whitney Portal:

All Whitney Portal permits are reserved in advance, normally by mail (see above). If you're very lucky, you may get one on demand, but only if someone with a reserved permit has canceled it or failed to pick it up on time.

For Cottonwood Lakes/Cottonwood Creek and Horseshoe Meadow (Cottonwood Pass):

Year-round: Inyo National Forest, Mt. Whitney Ranger District (on Highway 395 in Lone Pine; (619) 876-6200)

Note: At least for 1993, the Mt. Whitney Ranger Station will be open only from 7:30–3:30 (closed during lunch hour).

Call or write ahead! The information above will almost certainly change over time. We recommend you call or write ahead for the very latest information on quotas, quota periods, fees, etc., for the trailhead you're interested in. The offices listed above should be able to answer your questions or refer you to someone who can. For the sake of completeness, here are the national forest and park main offices:

> Sierra National Forest
> 1600 Tollhouse Road
> Clovis, CA 93612
> (209) 487-5155
>
> Inyo National Forest
> 873 N. Main St.
> Bishop, CA 93514
> (619) 873-4207
>
> Visitor Information
> Sequoia and Kings Canyon National Parks
> Three Rivers, CA 93271
> (209) 535-3134 (visitor information, 8:00–4:30 daily)
> (209) 565-3708 (backcountry information, 8:00–4:30
>   Monday–Friday)

On the next page, there's a sample Wilderness Permit Application for your use *(not valid for Mt. Whitney Ranger District beginning in 1994)*.

Wilderness Permit Application

(Invalid for Mt. Whitney Ranger District beg. in 1994; see below.)

To: [name of agency] _____

Areas to be visited: [names of wildernesses, park backcountry]

_____

Number of people in party: _____

Number of stock in party: _____

Method of travel (foot, horse, ski, snowshoe) _____

Itinerary

Entry date: _____   Exit date: _____

Entry trailhead: _____   Exit trailhead: _____

Overnight camp areas (list):   Nights in each camp:

1. _____   _____

2. _____   _____

3. _____   _____

(Etc., for every night you plan to be in the backcountry)

Alternate Itinerary

[Same format as above. It's recommended that you propose at least two alternate itineraries, even if they differ only by having different start/end dates.]

Organization/Group Name: _____

Applicant's name: _____

Address: _____

City: _____   State: _____ Zip: _____

Phone (include area code):

(_____)_____

I will insure that my party and I follow all wilderness rules and regulations while on this trip.

Applicant's signature: _____

Date: _____

- Write to Mt. Whitney Ranger District (address above) for their special application form and instructions.
- Send the completed application to the appropriate agency/office listed above during the period when they accept applications.
- Don't forget to enclose the fee, if any is required.
- Make as many copies of this form as you wish.

The Trailheads

Here are descriptions for driving to all the trailheads used in trips in this book. At the beginning of each trip are a trailhead name and number, keyed to the numbers here. Shuttle trips have two trailheads, so the starting trailhead is given first in the trip, followed by the ending trailhead.

1. **Mosquito Flat** (10,230'). From Tom's Place (25 miles north of Bishop on U.S. 395) go 11 miles on paved road to road's end at Mosquito Flat beside Rock Creek.

2. **Pine Creek Roadend** (7400'). Go 10 miles northwest from Bishop on U.S. 395 and then 10 miles on paved road through Rovana to a signed parking area beside Pine Creek.

3. **Lake Sabrina** (9130'). Go 18 miles southwest from Bishop on State Highway 168 to the backpackers' parking area below the lake, at the North Lake turnoff.

4. **North Lake** (9360'). Go 18 miles from Bishop on State Highway 168 almost to Lake Sabrina and turn right on a dirt road. After a few hundred feet turn right again and go 2 miles to a backpacker's parking area just west of North Lake. You must walk the last ½ mile to the trailhead beyond the campground.

5. **Vermilion Trailhead** (7650'). Go east from Clovis (near Fresno) on State Highway 168. Just before Lakeshore at Huntington Lake, turn right, by the Eastwood Forest Service Center. The road becomes very steep, narrow and bumpy before Kaiser Pass and remains so; allow time to travel slowly. 36 miles from Shaver Lake is the High Sierra Ranger Station; permits issued here. One mile beyond is the Lake Edison/Florence Lake **Y** junction. Go left 9 miles to Vermilion Valley Resort. Continue past the campground, staying to the right, and in 0.7 mile from the resort arrive at the trailhead parking loop.

6. **Bear Dam Junction** (7010'). From the Lake Edison/Florence Lake **Y** junction (see above) go 2½ miles toward Lake Edison to the Bear Diversion Dam road junction, on the right. A high-clearance 4WD can travel this road 2½ miles to the trailhead above the reservoir (7450').

7. **Florence Lake** (7350'). From the Lake Edison/Florence Lake **Y** junction (see above) go right 6 miles to the overnight parking area.

Beyond, the boat taxi is to the left, by the store, and the trailhead is to the right.

8. **South Lake** (9760'). Go 15½ miles southwest from Bishop on State Highway 168 to the South Lake turnoff, and then 7 miles to the South Lake parking area.

9. **Big Pine Creek** (7700'). From the middle of the small town of Big Pine on US 395 south of Bishop, go west on Crocker Street 11 miles to the trailhead turnoff on the right. The trailhead is 0.2 mile up this road.

10. **Taboose Creek Roadend** (5460'). Turn west on a dirt road that leaves U.S. 395 12 miles south of Big Pine. Go right at a fork at 1.7 miles, pass through a gate at 2.4 miles, and continue to the roadend at 5.8 miles. The last ¼ mile is very rough.

11. **Sawmill Creek Roadend** (4600'). Turn west on a dirt road marked "Black Rock Springs Road" that leaves U.S. 395 17.5 miles south of Big Pine. Go west 0.8 mile to a junction. Turn north and follow Old U.S. 395 1.2 miles to Division Creek Road, leading west. Follow this road 2.1 miles to the trailhead.

12. **Oak Creek Roadend** (6040'). Turn west from U.S. 395 2.3 miles north of Independence onto paved Fish Hatchery Road and go 1.3 miles to a junction. Go right here, passing Oak Creek Campground, 5.8 miles to the roadend.

13. **Onion Valley** (9200'). Go west from Independence 15 miles to the roadend parking lot.

14. **Courtright Reservoir** (8200'). Go northeast 42 miles from Clovis (near Fresno) on State Highway 168 and in Shaver Lake turn right onto Dinkey Creek Road. Follow this 26 miles to the Courtright/Wishon **Y**. Courtright Reservoir is 7½ miles north. From the junction above the reservoir, cross the dam, and in ⅔ mile the road ends at a paved parking lot signed MAXON TRAILHEAD.

15. **Wishon Reservoir** (6720'). Follow the directions above to the Courtright/Wishon **Y** and from there go south 4 miles, crossing the dam, to a parking lot on the east side of the road (the "Woodchuck Trailhead").

16. **Crown Valley Trailhead** (6750'). From the Woodchuck Trailhead (see above), continue south 2.4 miles to a junction signed for the Crown Valley Trailhead. Go right 1 mile to the trailhead.

17. **Lewis Creek Trailhead** (4580'). Go 77 miles east from Fresno on State Highway 180, to a parking area about ¼ mile east of the national park boundary (and 1½ miles west of Cedar Grove).

18. **Cedar Grove Roadend** (5035'). Go 85 miles east from Fresno on State Highway 180 to the roadend 6 miles east of Cedar Grove.

19. **Lodgepole Campground** (6800′). From the north, go 50 miles east from Fresno on State Highway 180 to a junction with State Highway 198, then 26 miles southeast on 198 to Lodgepole Village; turn east and go to a parking area near the Lodgepole Nature Center. From the south, take 198 east through Visalia and Three Rivers. Continue northeast on it to Lodgepole, passing Giant Forest Village, about 63 miles.

20. **Crescent Meadow** (6800′). Go about 2 miles south and east of Giant Forest Village (see above) on a road running past Moro Rock to the road's end.

21. **Mineral King** (7830′). Go 37 miles east from Visalia on State Highway 198, turn east, and go 23 miles on a mostly paved road. This narrow, winding 23 miles takes more than an hour to drive. Marmots were reported to have eaten parts of parked cars here a few years ago. Check with the ranger station for the current situation.

22. **Symmes Creek Trailhead** (6250′). Go 4½ miles west from Independence on Onion Valley Road, turn left on Foothill Road and go 1.3 miles to a fork. Take the right-hand fork and go past an old corral on the left, then immediately cross Symmes Creek. In ½ mile take the right fork, and take the right fork again at the next two forks. Then proceed ½ mile to the trailhead near Symmes Creek. Some of these forks may have small signs.

23. **Whitney Portal** (8360′). Go 13 miles west from Lone Pine on Whitney Portal Road. A special permit situation exists for the Mt. Whitney Trail. For details, see "Wilderness Permits and Quotas in the Sierra" in this book.

24. **Cottonwood Lakes/Creek Trailhead** (10,040′). From the center of Lone Pine on U.S. 395 go 3.5 miles west on Whitney Portal Road, turn left, and go south 20 miles on Horseshoe Meadow Road past the old Cottonwood Lakes trailhead. Turn right at the sign for Cottonwood Lakes and go about 1 more mile to the parking lot. There are restrooms, potable water and a one-night campground here.

25. **Horseshoe Meadow** (9920′). (Labeled "Kern Plateau" in 1986 USDA *Golden Trout Wilderness and South Sierra Wilderness* map.) Follow the directions to the Cottonwood Lakes Trailhead above, but don't turn right for Cottonwood Lakes. Instead, follow the road about ½ mile more to its end at a large parking lot where there are restrooms, potable water and a one-night campground.

26. **South Lake Road** (9000′). Go 15½ miles southwest from Bishop on State Highway 168 to the South Lake turnoff, and then 5 miles to the Tyee Lakes/South Lake Road parking area.

Mono Creek to Glacier Divide

Part of the 540,000-acre John Muir Wilderness, this region towers between Mono Creek and the northern boundary of Kings Canyon National Park. It is a roadless vastness of incredibly rugged alpine beauty, a wilderness that beckons to all who hear of it. Barren summits rise above a dense mat of green conifers, and the landscape is stippled with a thousand blue-green lakes bound by connecting silver ribbons of mountain streams. Encompassing an area of roughly 500 square miles, this section nevertheless contains enough trails and cross-country routes to entice the most dedicated backcountry traveler for many summer seasons.

The profile of this region is classic. It boasts the typical short, steep eastern escarpment, and the typical long, gradual western slope. The west side is cut by the drainages of Mono, Bear and Piute creeks—all tributaries of the South Fork San Joaquin. And the east side is cleft by the precipitous, hurrying waters of Rock Creek, Pine Creek and the North Fork Bishop Creek—all tributaries of the Owens River. These watersheds are separated by spectacular divides, which, together with the main Sierra crest—if one uses a little imagination—form an interesting plan view. Seen from the air, the main crest and ancillary divide spurs of this section take on the aspect of a very large frog: the head centers on Mt. Mills; Mono Divide and the Mt. Morgan/Wheeler Ridge make the forelegs; and the Mt. Hooper/Mt. Senger complex and the Mt. Tom/Basin Mountain divide are the two hind limbs. Naturalists would hasten to render this absurd analogy more "authentic" by pointing out that the frog's back is covered with warts (17 summits exceeding 13,000′), and that this mountainous region should therefore be analogized to a toad. You can make your own Rorschach of the topography, but in any case it is vitally important—particularly in cross-country travel—for you to have a working map knowledge of the country and its terrain.

However, map knowledge never does justice to the country. This awareness comes with one's first glimpse of the majestic prominences and the awesome, blue-hazed canyons. With awareness comes wonder—a pause to ponder the colossal forces required to move, pluck and sculpt the rock on such a scale. Clarence King, a member of the famous Brewer Survey party of 1864, was among the first Europeans to look at this part of the Sierra and record his thoughts: "I believe no one can study from an elevated lookout the length and depth of one of these great Sierra canyons without asking himself some profound geological questions." Indeed, how did it happen?

The answer has much to do with water, in both liquid and solid forms. The deep canyons were carved primarily by stream erosion, but they have been scoured out and widened periodically by glaciers during many "ice ages" in the Pleistocene Epoch, from 2 million to 10,000 years ago. In this part of the Sierra, glaciers covered over 1500 square miles at different times during the Pleistocene. The small glaciers that exist today were all formed within the last few hundred years. Glaciers are very sensitive to changes in climate: a major "ice age" could be initiated by worldwide cooling of only 2–3° C.

The huge U-shaped valleys mark the courses of the main glaciers, while the smaller side valleys mark the flows of tributary glaciers. Usually suspended high above the main valleys, they are called *hanging valleys.* At the head of a side valley is a *cirque* where a glacier originated. In cirques and just below them are where you typically find lakes in the Sierra.

Other glacial features include glacial polish, where bedrock (especially granitic) was wet-sanded to a smooth sheen by grains of pulverized rock in the base of a glacier. In these scoured areas one also finds grooves and crescentic marks where rocks in the glacier base gouged the bedrock. Rocks—from huge boulders to particles of silt—that a glacier picks up along the way are deposited as moraines at the glacier's margins.

The landscape here is still changing. Streams have cut through sediments left by glaciers. Avalanche chutes flute near-vertical peak facades, and accumulations of scree and talus slope away at their feet. Subtler forms of weathering continue to attack the talus, reducing that rock to granules, which then provide a suitable habitat for hardy plants. One can observe this ecological progression while walking the trails around timberline.

The presence of an ample and healthy plant life is necessary to animals, and one is sure to see many animals in this region's heavily wooded drainages. Birds are particularly plentiful, and the lakes and streams abound with fish. Among the most commonly seen mammals are mule deer. Early-season hikers working their way up Bear Creek are almost sure to come upon a grazing doe, and with some luck, perhaps a pair of brand-new, spotted-back fawns. In early and mid-season, both does and bucks have reddish coats, which are replaced in the fall with longer, gray hair. Because the buck is much warier, a sighting of him is rarer.

It should be noted that any wild-animal observation requires "freezing"—not necessarily stealth, but quietness and immobility. There isn't a naturalist observer worth his or her salt who hasn't experienced the dilemma of a hovering mosquito and a "once in a triptime" wild-animal observation opportunity.

One will also make trailside, passing acquaintance with the numerous squirrels that populate the heavily wooded areas, especially the fir belt. Easily recognizable because of the dual stripes running down its coppery-red back is the tiny golden-mantled ground squirrel. It is, perhaps, the most often seen squirrel, found in both the lodgepole and subalpine belts. Its less distinguished cousin, the California ground squirrel, will be seen near the trailheads—generally below 8000 feet—and the Belding ground squirrel, or "picketpin," is seen in most of the meadows of this section. Constant companions to the high-country hiker are the cony, a small, rabbitlike creature, and the beaverlike marmot. Found in talus and other rocky areas, these somnolent rodents arouse themselves and pipe and chirp excitedly whenever approached.

Other, less common, but consequently more exciting, sightings that one may make are of black bear, mountain coyote, porcupine, flying squirrel and mountain lion. The black bear, contrary to impressions one might well have gathered in heavily camped national-park areas, is not often observed in the backcountry. The notable exception to this rule occurs when one leaves food lying about untended.

The mountain lion, the coyote and the flying squirrel are more often heard than seen, and the happy occasion of hearing one of these animals usually occurs when one is busy setting up camp, bedding down or cooking a daybreak breakfast. A coyote's "singing" is a familiar sound to anyone who has watched a western movie, but the habitual birdlike whistling of a mountain lion is usually unrecognized because it seems totally out of character. This cat rarely screams, but it does meow, spit and growl in unmistakable feline fashion. Hearing a flying squirrel, contradictory as it may seem, is a fairly common occurrence. It takes place at night (the squirrel is nocturnal), usually with a *whhhist...splat* sound that characterizes its "flight" from one tree to another.

The most commonly seen animals in this region are your fellow hikers. They're usually quite domesticated and exceedingly easy to approach. A query like, "Where've you been?" can bring forth a stream of information and friendly advice. In the perspective of geologic time, we've been on the scene but a moment, and our written history consumes only a fraction of a second. But despite our relative newness, our effect has been great, and the marks of our passage are on the land—temporarily.

In this area, humans' trails, usually following those of other animals, are plentiful, clearly marked and well maintained. The trail following Mono Creek and crossing Mono Pass, and the one following the South Fork San Joaquin River and branching over Piute Pass are old trade routes of the Mono Indian tribes. Paralleling these ancient trails is the relatively newer Italy Pass trans-Sierra crossing, and bisecting all three of these routes is the renowned John Muir Trail, which traverses the west slopes in a north-south direction.

Enjoy your trips in this climax High Sierra.

1

Bear Dam Junction to Twin Falls

Trip	From Bear Dam Junction to Twin Falls
Distance	11 miles
Type	Out and back trip
Best season	Early or late
Topo maps	**Mt. Abbot** 15′; Mt. Givens, Florence Lake 7½′
Grade (hiking days/recommended layover days)	
Leisurely	2/0
Moderate	—
Strenuous	Day
Trailhead	Bear Dam Junction (6)

HIGHLIGHTS   Few creeks in the Sierra possess the simple, primitive appeal of Bear Creek. Never constant, it cascades, chutes and then tumbles down its rocky course, interrupted at graceful intervals by deep, slow-moving, sandy-bottomed pools. Golden, brook, and brown trout inhabit this stream.

DESCRIPTION (Leisurely trip)

1st Hiking Day (**Bear Dam Junction** to **Twin Falls**, 5½ miles): From the paved road, the unmaintained 4WD road to Bear Dam heads east through lichen-covered granite outcrops. This bedrock was glaciated during the Pleistocene epoch, from 2 million to 10 thousand years ago. Judging from the rounded shapes of the rocks it's clear that it's been a long time since glaciers were here. Actually, it was about 13 thousand years. Today, our steps will retrace the path of a glacier that once flowed down Bear Creek Canyon.

Since a glacier retreats up canyon as it slowly melts, we will take a journey through time as we follow a path of retreat. The higher we go, the more recent is the landscape, because less time has passed since the glacier did its work there. Starting our hike in the oldest terrain, we see the effects of longstanding weathering: rocks have become darker due to oxidation and lichen growth, and they have eroded to become sand and gravel. Where soil can form, it gets deeper and richer over time. Thus, you can tell the progress of glacial history at different locations just by looking. There are also places that have never experienced glaciers, such as the densely forested ridges you can see.

Our road descends to cross shadeless slabs before climbing 2 miles to its end. This stretch can be very hot and dry. At road's end is the trailhead above Bear Diversion Dam (7450') and with relief we begin hiking on a trail. Here we enter a rare and valuable space, a canyon without roads or dams: wilderness. We pass the John Muir Wilderness boundary, the political line that signifies the priority of Congress to keep this canyon wild. Humans created this arbitrary boundary, a line on a map. The other animals and plants know not of its existence, but they do know that they need habitat to live. We humans protect this area called John Muir Wilderness because we also need wild places. As a species we evolved in wilderness. Must it not also be a part of us?

The first mile of trail is gentle, and one can find beautiful pools and fine campsites by venturing over to the creek. Beyond the cutoff to the Bear Ridge Trail, branching left, our trail steepens and spends more time near the creek, which alternates between falls, rapids and long pools. Along the way we cross a section of dark-colored metamorphic rock and the last of the canyon live oaks, at the upper end of their elevation range.

Nearing Twin Falls, we cross some wet areas and pass through some inviting aspen groves. Twin Falls (8000') can be seen as two cascades rushing down granite slabs, with a wide pool at the base. On a summer day you can take a refreshing dip and then crawl onto the rocks or the beach to sun-dry yourself. There is a well-used campsite several hundred feet up the trail, near a grove of aspens. Other campsites are across the creek below the falls.

2nd Hiking Day: Retrace your steps, 5½ miles.

Snow plant blooms only in early season and only in mid-elevation

2

Bear Dam Junction to Upper Bear Creek

Trip	From Bear Dam Junction to Upper Bear Creek
Distance	21 miles
Type	Out and back trip
Best season	Early or late
Topo maps	**Mt. Abbot** 15′; Mt. Givens, Florence Lake, Mt. Hilgard 7½′

Grade (hiking days/recommended layover days)

Leisurely	4/1
Moderate	3/1
Strenuous	—

Trailhead	Bear Dam Junction (6)

HIGHLIGHTS   Following the path of the ancient glaciers, this trip takes in much of Bear Creek canyon above where it spills into the valley of the South San Joaquin River. Part of this route follows the famous John Muir/Pacific Crest Trail, but it's easy to get off that beaten path for some seclusion. This trip is fairly easy for most hikers, but there is one very steep section of trail.

DESCRIPTION (Leisurely trip)

1st Hiking Day: Follow Trip 1 to **Twin Falls**, 5½ miles.

2nd Hiking Day (**Twin Falls** to **Upper Bear Creek**, 5 miles): Today's first 2 miles are steep, followed by much gentler ground. Leaving Twin Falls and the creek, we climb a section of trail rebuilt in 1992 by the California Conservation Corps and the Forest Service. Designed for livestock and low maintenance, this trail is extremely wide, with much clearing. This sturdy trail shows us that even though we are far from the city, we haven't necessarily left our industrial ways of thinking behind.

Climbing steadily, our route alternates between steep, rocky areas and shady aspen groves. The glacial terrain here is jumbled, with many steep ravines, domes and cliffs. Since it's so difficult to build a trail through such a landscape, we continue climbing high above the creek in order to avoid the maze-like terrain in the valley. After 1000 feet of climbing, the views open up and we cross a ridge before heading back down toward Bear Creek. Our route follows the bend in the canyon from northeast to south. Note the vegetation changes: Jeffrey pine, aspen and juniper are all but gone, and the ubiquitous lodgepole pines are all around. The most common tree worldwide, the lodgepole covers much of two continents.

Our route levels off near the creek and we pass the first of many overused camping areas. Beyond a wet, muddy area we reach Old Kip Camp—a poor, sloping camping area. Just above is the John Muir/Pacific Crest Trail, where we turn right. The shaded trail stays near dashing Bear Creek for most of a mile. Beyond a narrow canyon the grade eases, and for the next ½ mile the trail is again away from the creek. Anytime now you can veer right to one of several good campsites on either side of Bear Creek (9100′). Golden trout enjoy the waters, and there are nice slabs for sunbathing by the creek.

3rd and 4th Hiking Days: Retrace your steps, 10½ miles.

3   Bear Dam Junction to Vermilion Campground

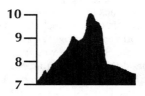

Trip	From Bear Dam Junction to Vermilion Campground via Quail Meadows
Distance	21 miles
Type	Shuttle trip
Best season	Early or late
Topo maps	**Mt. Abbot** 15′; Mt. Givens, Florence Lake, Graveyard Peak, Sharktooth Peak 7½′

Grade (hiking days/recommended layover days)

Leisurely	4/1
Moderate	3/1
Strenuous	2/0
Trailhead	Start at Bear Dam Junction (6), end at Vermilion Campground (5)

HIGHLIGHTS   This U-shaped route circumnavigates massive Bear Ridge by ascending Bear Creek canyon, crossing Bear Ridge and then descending Mono Creek. Accordingly, the trip has a big feel for the distance traveled. The option of the boat-taxi across Lake Edison makes this trip a reasonable weekend choice.

DESCRIPTION (Moderate trip)

1st Hiking Day: Follow Trip 1 to **Twin Falls**, 5½ miles.

2nd Hiking Day (**Twin Falls** to **Quail Meadows**, 10 miles): Follow the 2nd hiking day, Trip 2, to the John Muir Trail and turn left. Our route follows the Muir Trail as we traverse northward toward Bear Ridge. The trail soon makes a steady climb to top Bear Ridge. Views back into the Bear Creek drainage are excellent, including Recess Peak, Mt. Hilgard and Seven Gables. At the rocky summit of Bear Ridge, we pass a trail that goes west to Lake Edison.

As the trail begins the steep series of 70 switchbacks that drop into the Mono Creek watershed, the traveler is treated to excellent views of the Silver Divide, the immediate Mono Creek watershed, and Lake Thomas A. Edison. When the trail finally levels off, we ford a tributary of Mono Creek and soon reach a bridge crossing of the creek. Several good campsites line the north side of Mono Creek near Quail Meadows (7760'), several hundred yards west. Additional campsites can be found along the south side of the creek.

3rd Hiking Day (**Quail Meadows** to **Vermilion Campground**, 5½ miles): From the junction near the bridge we head down-canyon, passing small, overgrazed Quail Meadows. Our varied descent stays away from Mono Creek and we pass the John Muir Wilderness boundary, where a message board from the Wilderness Ranger says good things. Now, near the high-water mark of Lake Edison, we wind through quaking aspen, Jeffrey pine, juniper and lodgepole pine. When we actually get very close to the high-water mark, we meet the signed lateral to the boat taxi pick-up point. Since this point varies from year to year with the lake level, you may have yet another ⅔ mile to hike if you want to take the boat taxi. It depends on how far along the shore they are able to cruise. They leave here at 9:45 A.M. and 4:45 P.M. It's about $6 one way. For more information write Vermilion Valley Resort, Box 258, Lakeshore, CA 93634 (enclose a SASE).

Those choosing the trail back will first climb over a ridge far above this reservoir that drowned Vermilion Valley. Descending gradually past a small creek, we level off before climbing past the Goodale Pass Trail. Once across Cold Creek bridge, our trail becomes more dusty, until the unsigned trail to the pack station veers right. From here we climb gently a bit more and ease into the parking loop at Vermilion Trailhead (7700').

Recess Peak over Lake Edison

4 Bear Dam Junction to Lake Italy

Trip	From Bear Dam Junction to Twin Falls, Hilgard Meadow, Lake Italy
Distance	34 miles
Type	Out and back trip
Best season	Mid or late
Topo maps	**Mt. Abbot** 15′; Mt. Givens, Florence Lake, Mt. Hilgard 7½′

Grade (hiking days/recommended layover days)

Leisurely	6/1
Moderate	4/1
Strenuous	3/1
Trailhead	Bear Dam Junction (6)

HIGHLIGHTS   This spectacular hike offers a wide variety of High Sierra delights. From the forested depths of Bear Creek Canyon to breathtaking and secluded Lake Italy, this hike even has a touch of cross country. The route follows the path of ancient glaciers, taking us past classic glacial features.

DESCRIPTION (Leisurely trip)

1st Hiking Day: Follow Trip 1 to **Twin Falls**, 5½ miles.

2nd Hiking Day (**Twin Falls** to **Hilgard Meadow**, 7 miles): First, follow the second hiking day, Trip 2, to Upper Bear Creek. From the camping areas along the creek, the gentle ascent continues up the east side of Bear Creek. The trail parallels the creek as it turns into a narrow section of canyon. Soon it levels off away from the creek and you reach the Italy Pass Trail junction. Here you leave the John Muir/ Pacific Crest Trail and head east up slabs. The trail may be faint here, but it becomes quite definite under the trees. You pass a drift fence and a welcome sign announcing that Hilgard Meadow is closed to grazing. From here you stroll gently under lodgepole pines ⅔ mile to the grassy expanses of Hilgard Meadow (9600'). Mt. Hilgard looms almost 4000 feet above, and at your feet the meadow supports thousands of purple Indian paintbrush plants in mid season. Excellent campsites border the northwest side of this subalpine meadow.

3rd Hiking Day (**Hilgard Meadow** to **Lake Italy**, 4½ miles): Skirting the north side of Hilgard Meadow, our trail soon climbs moderately over slabs and crosses the outlet of Hilgard Lake. Then you pass another drift fence and come near purling Hilgard Branch. After you quickly cross several very small creeks, the trail leaves tree cover. Here the route may become confusing, so veer left beyond some aspens, climb away from Hilgard Branch, and cross an open, rocky slope. Next comes a wet meadow where the trail becomes very faint. Descend a little before meeting the edge of the forest, where the trail resumes climbing. You then pass a nice campsite near the main creek before crossing another spring-fed rill.

Now far from the main creek, you climb up steep slabs, following the curve in the canyon as it turns east, steepens and narrows. Downstream, the canyon is wide and gently sloping, and beyond the narrow gorge the canyon again becomes a meadow, wide and gently sloping. This variation in form is due to differences in the structure of the bedrock.

Although stream erosion has done most of the work in carving this canyon, glaciers have recently modified its shape. Before glaciers come, canyons usually have a V-shaped cross section. After the passing of glaciers, the canyons usually have a pronounced U-shaped cross section. Glaciers, then, tend to do most of their erosion horizontally. This happens for several reasons. One is that Sierra glaciers are wet-based: they ride along on a thin layer of water between the ice and the rock. Water occurs there due to heat and pressure trapped under the heavy, insulating river of ice. With this kind of lubrication, the ice tends to slide over, rather than dig deeply into, the bedrock. However, out at the margins of the glacier, colder air and thinner ice allow the glacier to stay frozen to the ground. Being "glued" to the sides of the valley, the passing glaciers tear out pieces of bedrock and carry them away. This action is called glacial quarrying.

Now, in order to account for the variations in canyon slope and width, we can look at how erosion reflects bedrock structure. In this canyon, the primary variable of structure is joints—cracks in the bedrock. Since joints are planes of weakness, then the more there are, the faster the rock is weathered (broken down) and carried away. Where joints are mostly in a vertical orientation, glaciers break off column-like pieces from the valley sides, thereby undermining the canyon walls above. In such a place, the valley will be exceptionally flat-bottomed and steep-sided, like Yosemite Valley. Where jointing is primarily horizontal, the glaciers of course flow parallel to the joints. In such a place, glaciers tend to just slide along the surface, eroding less and leaving more of the original V-shaped profile. That's what happened in the narrow, steep sections of Hilgard Branch canyon.

Continuing along this beautiful meadow, the trail then climbs over smooth bedrock, becoming faint. You swing near the creek, which has carved a mini, gorge-like channel since the glaciers left. Don't follow the trail across the creek. Rather, go 200 yards up this channel to Teddy Bear Lake's outlet, which comes in on the other side. Cross just above this confluence and climb east across slabs and meadow.

The route then veers north across slabs into the canyon below Lake Italy, where the trail becomes more obvious. Your sudden arrival at Lake Italy (11,154') is heralded by vistas of Mt. Gabb, Mt. Abbot, Bear Creek Spire and Mt. Julius Caesar. This large lake (124 acres) gets its name from its similarity in shape to the European peninsula. You will find some illegal campsites by the outlet, but camping is legal across the outlet and up the hill a bit.

More regal camps can be made near the creek from Jumble Lake, which comes into Lake Italy 1 mile along the south shore. Since campsites are merely places where you spend a lot of time, anywhere in this incredible basin can be a sublime campsite. The best way to get to the toe of Lake Italy is via the north shore. There are golden trout in the nearby lakes, and alpine wildlife is all around you.

4th, 5th, and 6th Hiking Days: Retrace your steps, 17 miles.

Glacial erratic

Bear Dam Junction to Lake Italy   5

Trip	From Bear Dam Junction to Lake Italy via Hilgard Branch, return via Vee Lake, East Fork Bear Creek
Distance	39 miles
Type	Semiloop trip
Best season	Mid or late
Topo maps	**Mt. Abbot** 15′; Mt. Givens, Florence Lake, Mt. Hilgard 7½′

Grade (hiking days/recommended layover days)

Leisurely	—
Moderate	6/1
Strenuous	4/0

Trailhead   Bear Dam Junction (6)

HIGHLIGHTS   For experienced hikers only, this route involves some cross-country travel. It follows the path of ancient glaciers to their birthplace high among the peaks of spectacular Lake Italy basin. Here you can find solitude and exceptional alpine splendor.

DESCRIPTION (Moderate trip)

1st, 2nd, and 3rd Hiking Days: Follow Trip 4 to **Lake Italy**, 17 miles.

4th Hiking Day (**Lake Italy** to **Vee Lake**, 5 miles, part cross-country): Today promises to be glorious, as you will visit some very high and wild places. Following the rocky south shore of Lake Italy, you reach the meadowy inlet from Jumble Lake. Here, at the heel of Italy you head south, ascending the west side of the inlet. Near some rocky slabs, veer left, picking up the now-distinct Italy Pass Trail at the base of the moraine that dams Jumble Lake. The Italy Pass Trail climbs east around this moraine. Staying far above the chaotic north shore of aptly-named Jumble Lake, the trail crosses a sandy bench. There is a nice rest area here, especially if the meadowy little creek is flowing just beyond. Pause to look south to the high point of this trip at the saddle between Peaks 12756 and 12710.

From this bench the trail climbs straight up the hill toward a sandy gully to the left of some bedrock slabs. You, however, leave the trail at the base of those slabs and go right. Heading southeast, climb steadily in order to get above the steep slope above Jumble Lake. You may encounter much snow up here. Leveling off at the saddle, you can feel the thin air here at 12,000 feet as you ponder whether to make the short ascent northwest to Peak 12756. Going south, a trail becomes distinct as you pass a seasonal pond. Shortly, you arrive at the lip of East Fork Bear Creek basin. This is a great place to take in the awesome glacial scenery. This lip is the upper limit of glaciers that flowed over the top of the dome to the south and then through the pass to the right of White Bear Lake, just below. Most of this basin was under ice many times during the Pleistocene Epoch, 2 million to 10 thousand years ago. Indeed, ice caps covered most of the High Sierra from Mt. Whitney to Lake Tahoe. To tell which areas remained above the ice, note the jagged or pointed peaks and ridges. These high points protruded above the glaciers, which eroded them from several sides, leaving them very steep but not smoothed over. Conversely, total glacial cover produces round, domelike peaks and ridges. The sandy, bouldery areas behind you were never glaciated (or at least, not recently), and they show no clean or fresh bedrock, such as glaciers uncover in places where they scrape away surface debris. If glaciers never come, then over hundreds of thousands of years the rock cracks into angular boulders which, in turn, weather into gravel and sand.

To see where you are going later today, look beyond the outlet of White Bear Lake. You'll see a shallow valley with two ponds that runs in a line of sight connecting you and the outlet of White Bear Lake. This valley is your route to Vee Lake. The descent to White Bear Lake follows the steep, sandy gully below you. Skirt the west shore and follow the trail down the west side of the outlet to Big Bear Lake. If you want a nice lunchtime stroll, Ursa and Bearpaw lakes are easy to reach, as these three lakes virtually make one.

If there is not a lot of snow or water, then it's easiest to follow the outlet of Big Bear Lake through a gorge to Little Bear Lake. Otherwise stay several hundred feet north of the gorge and then veer left through a small gap to the east end of Little Bear Lake. Either way, follow the south shore of Little Bear Lake from its inlet, climbing over a small outcrop by the water. A sort of meadowy corridor veers left away from the lake, heading toward Seven Gables. Follow this and descend to cross a wet area where the corridor continues away from the lake to a low saddle. Now on a faint trail, you pass two ponds. By now this corridor has become a small valley, and it turns left toward Vee Lake. The last pond above Vee Lake offers good camping with wonderful views. From the seasonal outlet of this pond go east a short distance to find a cleft down through the cliff below and descend it to the meadowy shore of the north arm of Vee Lake (11,163′). Feather Peak (13,242′, north of Royce Peak) dominates the eastern skyline, and hikes in that direction are full of opportunities to find secret places in this secluded glacial wonderland.

5th Hiking Day (**Vee Lake** to **Upper Bear Creek**, 6½ miles): Follow the trail along the north shore to the bedrock dam of Vee Lake. From the outlet turn right and descend a grassy swale several hundred feet. The small dome that is separated from the ridge in front of you has great views, as the existence of a trail up it testifies. Go to the right of this viewpoint and climb down the gully that cuts through this ridge. If there is too much snow, simply return to the outlet, descend it, and turn right at the bottom. Otherwise follow the trail below the gully to the east shore of the lowest of the Seven Gables Lakes below. Turning right, the twisting trail follows the outlet, passes a pond and fords the outlet of Little Bear Lake. Several hundred feet beyond is a small gorge. Cross the creek to a small stand of whitebark pines. Staying on the south side of the creek, the trail is usually far from it until it turns left and descends steeply under the northern ramparts of Seven Gables. The trail becomes indistinct at times but doesn't cross the creek for about ¾ mile. It crosses at the base of a long cascade down slabs. Once on the north side, the trail is more distinct as it continues to another gorge. Part way down this gorge you'll cross the creek and then recross it at the lower end of the gorge.

The grade eases now as the shady trail winds northwest, away from the creek. Soon you may notice campsites and a scarcity of downed wood: you are close to the John Muir/Pacific Crest Trail. At the signed junction you turn right and stroll through open stands of lodgepole pine for 1½ miles to the bridge and rock crossings of Hilgard Branch. Just beyond is Italy Pass Trail junction, where you complete the loop part of this trip. You are now back on familiar trail and you soon arrive at the campsites on Upper Bear Creek. They may look different to you since your adventure in the land above the trees.

6th Hiking Day (**Upper Bear Creek** to **Bear Dam Junction**): Retrace the 1st and 2nd hiking days of Trip 2, 10½ miles.

6   Bear Dam Junction to Medley Lakes

Trip	From Bear Dam Junction to Bear Creek, Medley Lakes
Distance	33 miles
Type	Out and back trip
Best season	Mid or late
Topo maps	**Mt. Abbot** 15′; Mt. Givens, Florence Lake, Mt. Hilgard 7½′

Grade (hiking days/recommended layover days)

Leisurely	5/1
Moderate	4/1
Strenuous	3/1
Trailhead	Bear Dam Junction (6)

HIGHLIGHTS   In two days you can follow a major Sierra stream—Bear Creek—from nearly one end to the other. While partly using the John Muir Trail, this trip still offers a chance to avoid its heavily used campsites. The headwaters of South Fork Bear Creek provide plenty of rugged and remote side-trip possibilities.

DESCRIPTION (Strenuous trip)

1st Hiking Day: Follow Trip 1 to **Twin Falls**, 5½ miles.

2nd Hiking Day (**Twin Falls** to **Medley Lakes**, 11 miles): Follow Trip 4 to the Italy Pass Trail junction, but continue on the John Muir/ Pacific Crest Trail, immediately crossing the multiple channels of Hilgard Branch. The bridge here was built by Sierra Club volunteers. Unfortunately, the Forest Service wilderness budget continues to play second fiddle to resource extraction, especially clearcutting of ancient forests.

Nearly level now, the trail gently ascends wide Bear Creek canyon for 1½ miles to the signed junction with the Seven Gables and

Vee Lake Trail. The Muir Trail then fords Bear Creek (wet in early season) and begins a more shaded ascent that steepens until you're close to Rosemarie Meadow. At the foot of the meadow you cross the West Fork Bear Creek. Part way around the east side of the meadow you turn left onto the signed trail to Sandpiper Lake. Now off the main drag, your trail climbs over a low ridge to the west shore of shallow Lou Beverly Lake. This lake has golden trout (to 10″), and being marshy it supports a variety of marsh species such as Brewer's blackbird, a small bird that feeds among the reeds.

Proceeding around the south side of the lake you can boulder-hop the inlet. The trail then heads straight uphill toward Seven Gables. The grade eases as the trail veers right. Nearing some falls you take a sharp left and climb steeply to the lip of the glacial bench just above. Now in open country, you turn south and soon you arrive at the outlet of Sandpiper Lake (10,450′). Ford the outlet and skirt the northwest shore to avoid the overused campsites in this area. On the west side of the lake the trail turns right and climbs up through a small cleft in the bedrock. A short distance southwest the trail passes two small Medley Lakes and then disappears near the westernmost lake. These three lakes are fishless but there are some secluded campsites here, especially by the last lake. The other Medley Lakes to the south have golden trout, and you can find your own secret place among these jewels. Views from the ridge to the west are well worth the climb.

3rd Hiking Day: Retrace your steps, 16½ miles.

Seven Gables over Vee Lake

7   **Bear Dam Junction to Florence Lake**

Trip	From Bear Dam Junction to Florence Lake via Sandpiper Lake, Selden Pass, Blayney Meadows
Distance	34 miles
Type	Shuttle trip
Best season	Mid or late
Topo maps	**Mt. Abbot** 15′; Mt. Givens, Florence Lake, Mt. Hilgard, Ward Mountain 7½′

Grade (hiking days/recommended layover days)

Leisurely	5/1
Moderate	4/1
Strenuous	2/0

Trailhead	Begins at Bear Dam Junction (6), ends at Florence Lake (7)

HIGHLIGHTS   This popular shuttle trip circumnavigates the Mt. Hooper complex and has many unusual features. The most special one is at Blayney Meadows, where you will find that rare and delicate jewel, a wilderness hot spring.

Some cross-country skills are needed.

DESCRIPTION (Moderate trip)

1st and 2nd Hiking Days: Follow Trip 6 to **Medley Lakes**, 16½ miles.

3rd Hiking Day (**Medley Lakes** to **Blayney Hot Springs**, 8 miles): The first 2 miles today are cross country. You will climb over or around the prominent ridge between Sandpiper Lake and Marie Lake to the west. Southwest of Sandpiper Lake you will find three of the Medley Lakes group. From between the two nearest the ridge, head northwest several hundred feet to a low point between the ridge and the low dome just west of Sandpiper Lake. There is a small pond here where you can turn left and climb slabs to gain the ridgeline. Climb only as far as you need to avoid the cliffs at the north end of the ridge; if you go too far up it's difficult to go down the other side to Marie Lake. If this way doesn't seem good, you could go below the cliffs and climb a gully to get to the east side of Marie Lake. The views, however, are worth the climb. You can see the wide range of terrain found in the Bear Creek country: densely forested Bear Ridge rises above the wide valley of Bear Creek, while fractured granite peaks loom well above 13,000 feet.

On the east side of Marie Lake you will find a faint trail. Follow it south past the many bays and peninsulas that give this lake so much beautiful shoreline. Here, more than at Sandpiper Lake, you are likely to see sandpipers (killdeers), small birds with long legs. Look for nests hidden near the water. From the south end of Marie Lake it is an easy climb to the John Muir/Pacific Crest Trail.

Climbing moderately now on the well-designed trail, you soon reach Selden Pass (10,873'). From here you can see that Marie Lake sits on a glacial bench. Glaciers crossed the divide here as they curved south after starting north of the divide. These glaciers produced the basins of Heart and Sallie Keyes lakes. You can see Heart Lake below as you switchback down to the little creek that feeds it. Skirting the east shore, you may pause in order to seek Heart Lake gold—the golden trout that live here.

The descent to the upper Sallie Keyes Lakes is a winding tour through delightful little meadows and flower gardens. After crossing the short creek that joins the first two lakes, the trail parades along the beautiful, treelined west shore of the second lake. Now amid dense lodgepole pines, the trail crosses the outlet of the second lake but bypasses the third. Soon you swing east and descend, crossing several small creeks. A short climb around a moraine brings you to the edge of the South San Joaquin River canyon, where you can go a few yards off the trail to a splendid overlook. Once filled with glaciers thousands of feet thick, this deep valley has characteristic glacial features, such as a U-shaped cross section and a lot of freshly exposed bedrock. The dark, overlying rocks are "roof pendants"—the metamorphosed remains of ancient seabeds, seas that once covered the area where the Sierra is now. When the body of molten rock that eventually became the Sierra granite we see lay deep underground, these old sedimentary rocks overlay it like a roof. Over the past 5–6 million years the Sierra region has been uplifted rapidly, and erosion has stripped away most of the older rocks, including the "roof" rocks, exposing the white granite you see today. But here, a few dark fragments of the old roof remain, "hanging" down into the newer rock—hence their name, "roof pendants."

Resuming the descent, you cross a meadow and make long switchbacks to Senger Creek. Soon you're on the open, sunny side of the canyon and the trail is well landscaped with dry-area species, like manzanita and sagebrush. Far below at the base of the opposite canyon wall you can see a small lake by a meadow. Blayney Hot Springs lies just north of the lake.

Very long switchbacks lead into a forest of aspen, juniper and Jeffrey pine. Then the trail becomes steep and dusty. At a junction you go right, leaving the John Muir/Pacific Crest Trail. Eventually, this long descent eases and you meet and turn right on the San Joaquin River Trail. Shortly you meet the lateral to the hot springs, just east of private Muir Trail Ranch. Turn left and wind ¼ mile past some overused campsites to a wide ford of the South San Joaquin (dangerous in early season). On the other side are some more overused campsites, beyond which is a trail that crosses the meadow to the public hot pool at Blayney Hot Springs. Since this muddy pool is very susceptible to erosion, please enter and exit it carefully. Just beyond the willows is a magical little lake where you can go swimming. "Warm Lake" is a mysterious little gem, a result of an unlikely combination of beaver dams, moraines and springs which have all come together here far below the usual elevation where lakes are found in this part of the Sierra. This area is very fragile, so please minimize your impact. You are the steward of this healing place; enjoy it well.

4th Hiking Day (**Blayney Hot Springs** to **Florence Lake**, 10 miles, or 5 miles via ferry): Today's hike begins (after a soak, perhaps) by returning to the trail to Florence Lake. Turning left, you shortly go through a gate onto Muir Trail Ranch property, which you will be on for the next 1¼ miles—please don't camp here. The mass of dusty livestock trails may be confusing but just follow the main drag, which often coincides with the road to the ranch. This road leads to Florence Lake, making a private corridor through the John Muir Wilderness. It exists because the Muir Trail Ranch was here long before the 1964 Wilderness Act. The Muir Trail Ranch generously provides a food drop service, and they can be reached at Box 176, Lakeshore, CA 93634. For information, send a SASE.

The second creek you cross is Senger Creek, where you leave the road for a while, only to rejoin it near the gate on the west end of the private land. Back on public land you pass a lateral to "Lower Blayney Public Camp." Weaving in and out of dense forest, you gently ascend, crossing the outlet of Sallie Keyes Lakes. Leveling off, you then skirt Double Meadow, rejoining the road. An ancient Jeffrey pine has fallen across the path, and a cross section of the trunk has a chronology of human events placed upon the corresponding growth rings. According to the display, this tree was born in 1492. Five hundred years later, Turtle Island (North America) continues to lose indigenous species, ecosystems, and cultures.

The route continues west, wandering farther and farther away from the valley bottom. Winding across dry slabs and sandy gullies, you meet a signed trail going right to the ferry landing. Should you choose to use this excellent service, you will descend slabs where rock markers and arrows point the way. Now back on the road, you veer right, descending steeply before you arrive at the buildings where there is a radio phone. Instructions are included, and your boat taxi is just a phone call away, for it runs throughout the day as needed. The good folks at Florence Lake Store provide this service from Memorial Day through mid-October. It costs about $6, one way. For more information, contact the Florence Lake Store, Box 176, Lakeshore, CA 93634. In winter you can call them at (209) 966-3195. During drought, however, you may yet have to hike a while longer, but the way to the boat landing will be well marked.

Those hiking to the trailhead will continue from the last junction to the bridge across the South Fork San Joaquin River. Then, once over a low ridge, you cross Boulder Creek and pass the trail to Thompson Lake. Now high above Florence Lake, the trail undulates up and down to the Southern California Edison Co. road. This private road soon gives way to the public trailhead at Florence Lake (7350').

In the pool at Blayney Hot Springs

8   Bear Dam Junction to Vee Lake

Trip   From Bear Dam Junction to Vee Lake via Medley
                            Lakes, cross-country to Vee Lake, return via cross-
                            country route to Lake Italy, Hilgard Branch
Distance   45 miles
Type   Semiloop trip
Best season   Mid or late
Topo maps   **Mt. Abbot** 15′; Mt. Givens, Florence Lake, Mt.
                            Hilgard 7½′
Grade (hiking days/recommended layover days)
   Leisurely   —
   Moderate   7/2
   Strenuous   5/2
Trailhead   Bear Dam Junction (6)

HIGHLIGHTS   A fine fishing trip including a rugged cross-
country segment, this route shouldappeal to the
skilled backpacker who likes to eat trout.

DESCRIPTION (Moderate trip)

1st and 2nd Hiking Days: Follow Trip 6 to **Medley Lakes**, 16½
miles.

3rd Hiking Day (**Medley Lakes** to **Vee Lake**, 5 miles cross
country): Our rugged cross-country hike begins by rounding the west
side of Sandpiper Lake (10,500′) and fording the inlet stream. From
here the route ascends southeast by means of granite ledge systems.
Following the south fork of the east inlet stream of the labeled Medley
Lake, your route ascends steeply over smoothed, barren granite slabs
and grassy pockets to reach the upper drainage of the north fork of the
east inlet stream. Climbing eastward, you cross a saddle at 12,000
feet+, pass the lakelet east of it and then reach another saddle directly
east of the lakelet. Views during the course of this climb include

Medley Lakes, Mts. Senger and Hooper, and Seven Gables.

At the saddle one has unmatched views to the north and east. Besides the immediate summits of Seven Gables and the twin spires of Gemini, one can see Mts. Hilgard, Abbot, Gabb, Dade, Julius Caesar, Royce and Humphreys and Bear Creek Spire. Every one of these peaks towers over 13,000 feet. Also from this saddle, one can spy out the natural route to the southernmost of the Seven Gables Lakes. Though steep, this descent is made mostly over glacially smoothed rock. Route-picking, however, is sometimes made difficult by interruptions of talus and scree slides.

The upper lakes of the Seven Gables chain are talus-bound, shallow bodies of water having no fish, but anglers will want to try the good fishing on the lower lakes (golden trout to 12″) before making the final ascent to Vee Lake. These lower lakes and the intersecting stream are a fly fisherman's paradise. The ascent to Vee Lake is made over granite and talus along the outlet stream from that lake. The ascent terminates at the turfy east end (11,120′), where there are fair campsites. (Hikers who do not care for the high, alpine kind of camping should plan on ending their day at the lowest of the Seven Gables Lakes, where there are several good campsites.) Fishing on large Vee Lake (50 acres) is good to excellent for golden (to 15″).

4th Hiking Day (**Vee Lake** to **Lake Italy**, 4 miles part cross-country): From the outlet of Vee Lake follow the trail ¼ mile along the north shore of Little Bear before turning left and climbing over steep ledges to a pond. The trail resumes on the northwest side of the pond and ascends the shallow valley past more ponds. This small valley narrows to a swale before it descends to Little Bear Lake. Well short of the lake you will veer right and follow another natural corridor toward the inlet. Unless there is too much snow or water, follow this inlet to Big Bear Lake. An alternative follows the north shore of Little Bear a few yards, to where you can hike up to the right and circle around to the west shore of Big Bear. Turning north along the west shore of Big Bear Lake you will find a sandy trail ascending the west side of the creek from White Bear Lake, which is just beyond a notch in the skyline to the north. This trail becomes quite steep before you suddenly arrive at the outlet of White Bear Lake. Across the lake is a steep slope that leads to the high point of this hike. While skirting the west shore of the lake, you might take a look to the left down at the canyon below Lake Italy where you'll be tomorrow (unless you lay over at Lake Italy).

Several hundred feet above White Bear Lake the slope levels off abruptly. Here is an excellent viewpoint where you can visualize the massive glaciers that once filled this basin. About 13 thousand years ago, ice flowed within spitting distance of where you now stand. Behind you is an area that has not felt glaciers for at least a million years. You can see that glaciers did not scrape away the surface rocks and gravel. What makes the rocks and the gravel? Over time, bedrock fractures into angular boulders, which in turn crumble into sand, accumulating in deep layers. This area is probably a remnant of the surface of the ancient Sierra before the ice ages, some 2–3 million years ago. At that time the Sierra had risen to something approaching its present height, but the mountains were very rounded, with more gently sloping ridges and valleys.

Beyond the pass, the trail disappears but the route is fairly straightforward. Descend north and then northeast in order to stay above the steep slope above Jumble Lake. Keep your elevation until you are due east of Jumble Lake, then descend northwest across rocky ledges to the Italy Pass Trail. You should meet the trail where it comes down a steep, sandy slope, just before it turns west and crosses a bench. The trail stays high above the north side of Jumble Lake, going around the moraine that dams the lake. The outlet creek flows out from underneath this moraine. Follow the creek down to the south shore of Lake Italy (11,154'). The meadowy areas near this inlet provide breathtaking camping, where you can have dinner with some of the locals, such as Mts. Hilgard, Gabb, Abbot, Dade and Julius Caesar, and Bear Creek Spire. Your hosts are very tall, three of them being over 13,700 feet.

5th, 6th and 7th Hiking Days: Reverse the steps of Trip 4, 17 miles.

Northern ramparts of Seven Gables

Calvin Lee

Bear Dam Junction to
Second Recess

9

Trip	From Bear Dam Junction to Second Recess via Hilgard Branch, Lake Italy, cross-country to Lower Mills Creek Lake, Second Recess, return via Fish Camp, Quail Meadows
Distance	47 miles
Type	Semiloop trip
Best season	Late
Topo maps	**Mt. Abbot** 15′; Mt. Givens, Florence Lake, Mt. Hilgard, Mt. Abbot, Graveyard Peak 7½′

Grade (hiking days/recommended layover days)

Leisurely	—
Moderate	7/2
Strenuous	5/2
Trailhead	Bear Dam Junction (6)

HIGHLIGHTS   For those who really want to get off the beaten path, this trip is a classic. The route from Lake Italy to Second Recess is probably used most by climbers, which gives you some idea of how high and wild it is. Climbing to over 12,200 feet you will come within a mile of three peaks over 13,700 feet. For experienced cross-country hikers only.

DESCRIPTION (Moderate trip)

1st, 2nd and 3rd Hiking Days: Follow Trip 4 to **Lake Italy**, 17 miles.

4th Hiking Day (**Lake Italy** to **Second Recess**, 5 miles cross-country): This scenic cross-country route rounds the granite-bound north side of Lake Italy to Toe Lake, and then ascends the increasingly steep north cirque wall to 12,250-foot Gabbot Pass (the saddle between Mt. Gabb and Mt. Abbot). The ascent involves a strenuous workout, but does not require rock-climbing skills. As a reward, the hiker obtains some of the finest views in this part of the Sierra. This route is generally considered a climber's access route for ascents of Mts. Gabb and Abbot, and is seldom used by casual hikers. Parts of it are slippery in early summer. Peaks in line of sight during the ascent and at the pass include, to the west, Mts. Hilgard and Gabb; to the south, Mt. Julius Caesar, Royce Peak and "Feather Peak," to the east, Mts. Dade, Abbot and Mills, and Bear Creek Spire; and to the north, the crest of the Silver Divide.

From the pass, this ducked route descends just east of the Mt. Gabb glacier to the steep headwall of the Upper Mills Creek Lake cirque. Traversing the east side of this cirque, the route becomes a trail as it continues down the east side of the cascading creek between the lakes to the good campsites at the timberline outlet of Lower Mills Creek Lake (10,840'), an outstandingly pretty lake. Both Upper and Lower Mills Creek lakes are meadow-fringed, though mostly rockbound, and offer good-to-excellent golden-trout fishing (to 13"). Views from the campsites are excellent of the Mono and Silver divides.

5th Hiking Day (**Lower Mills Creek Lake** to **Quail Meadows**, 9½ miles): Staying on the east side of the creek, a faint trail descends to a small lake. Beyond, the trail disappears on granite slabs, but it reappears on the east shore of the pond below. Soon, the grade steepens and the trail veers away from the creek before the extremely steep and rocky descent into awesome Second Recess. Once down on the valley floor, the trail is nearly level for a mile, crossing a beautiful meadow and then a grove of lodgepole pines that are all broken off. None of these broken trunks stands higher than about 12 feet, which was the snow depth at the time the avalanche hit, in February, 1986.

Continuing down the valley, the trail again leads away from the creek and crosses another avalanche-flattened section of forest. Soon, the trail descends steeply to cross Mono Creek on a log and arrives at Fish Camp (8550').

At Fish Camp this route passes several overused campsites and turns left (west) onto the Mono Creek Trail. This creekside trail descends moderately, offering between-the-trees views into First Recess, and of the abrupt, dark north face of Volcanic Knob. Frequent groves of quaking aspen line this route, and late season sees the banks of Mono Creek clad in golden hues. At the point where the canyon walls appear to be closing in, about 3 miles below Fish Camp, the trail veers away from the creek on a steep, switchbacking ascent that crosses the long-nosed ridge that separates the North Fork from the main canyon of Mono Creek. On the west side of this ridge, the route descends a short distance to the John Muir Trail junction, and turns left along the east side of North Fork Mono Creek. The trail then switchbacks down steeply to ford the North Fork a few yards above its confluence with the main stream. Now gently descending through mixed forest, the trail soon arrives at a signed junction above Quail Meadows. Good campsites are on the south side of Mono Creek. Just beyond the bridge, turn left and then veer right for about 200 feet to a shady grotto campsite. For a more open feeling, there is a flat area closer to the creek about 200 yards above the Muir Trail bridge.

6th and 7th Hiking Days: Reverse the 2nd and 1st hiking days, Trip 3, 15½ miles.

Aerial view of Lake Italy and Mt. Hilgard looking west

E.P. Pister

10 Mosquito Flat to Gem Lakes

Trip	From Mosquito Flat to Gem Lakes
Distance	8 miles
Type	Out and back trip
Best season	Mid or late
Topo maps	**Mt. Abbot** 15'; Mt. Morgan, Mt. Abbot 7½'
Grade (hiking days/recommended layover days)	
Leisurely	2/0
Moderate	Day
Strenuous	—
Trailhead	Mosquito Flat (1)

HIGHLIGHTS   Majestic scenery dominates this short, popular trip. Because of its moderate terrain and high country "feel," this route through the Little Lakes Valley has been a long-time favorite of the beginning hiker, and the varied and good fishing for brook and rainbow makes it also an excellent angling choice.

DESCRIPTION (Leisurely trip)

1st Hiking Day (**Mosquito Flat** to **Gem Lakes**, 4 miles): The magnificent Sierra crest confronts the traveler at the very outset of this trip. From the trailhead at Mosquito Flat, the wide, rocky-sandy trail starts southwest toward the imposing skyline dominated by soaring Bear Creek Spire. In a few minutes we enter John Muir Wilderness and then reach a junction at which the Mono Pass Trail is the right fork and our trail, the Morgan Pass Trail, the left fork. Soon our route tops a low, rocky ridge just west of Mack Lake, and from this ridge one has good views of green-clad Little Lakes Valley. Gazing out, one cannot help but feel a sense of satisfaction that this beautiful valley enjoys protection as part of John Muir Wilderness. Aside from some early, abortive mining ventures, this subalpine valley remains relatively unspoiled.

From the ridgetop our trail descends to skirt a marsh that was the west arm of Marsh Lake before it filled in. Anglers may wish to try their luck for the good fishing for brown and brook trout in Marsh Lake and the nearby lagoon areas of Rock Creek. While fishing on the numerous lakes and streams of Little Lakes Valley, one has views into the long glacial trough to the south—a long-time favorite of lensmen. Flanked by Mt. Starr on the right and Mt. Morgan on the left, the valley terminates in the soaring heights of Mts. Mills, Abbot, and Dade, and Bear Creek Spire, all over 13,000 feet. Glaciers on the slopes of these great peaks are reminders of the enormous forces that shaped this valley eons ago.

From the meadowed fringes of Marsh and Heart lakes, the trail ascends gently past the west side of Box Lake, fords Rock Creek (wet in early season) and reaches aptly named Long Lake. For the angler with a yearning to try different waters, the unnamed lakes on the bench just to the east offer good fishing for brook and rainbow. Beyond Long Lake the trail ascends through a moderately dense forest cover of whitebark pines past a spur trail branching left to Chickenfoot Lake. Then we dip to cross a seasonal stream, climb slightly, and dip again, to the outlet stream of the Gem Lakes. Ahead on the left we see the last switchback on the trail up Morgan Pass, through which the abandoned road that has been our trail once reached the tungsten mines in the Pine Creek drainage.

Just after a rockhop ford of the Gem Lakes outlet, we take the trail that leads 150 yards up beside this stream to the lowest of the three main Gem Lakes. Many excellent campsites in clumps of whitebark pines are scattered around these emerald-green lakes, under the sheer north wall of Peak 11654. Fishing is fair-to-good for brook and rainbow trout (to 10″). The Treasure Lakes, located in barren cirques above here, are traditional basecamp locations for climbers bound for the high peaks to the west.

2nd Hiking Day: Retrace your steps, 4 miles.

Bear Creek Spire above tarn on Mono Pass Trail

11 Mosquito Flat to Fourth Recess

Trip	From Mosquito Flat to Fourth Recess
Distance	13 miles
Type	Out and back trip
Best season	Mid or late
Topo maps	**Mt. Abbot** 15′; Mt. Morgan, Mt. Abbot 7½′
Grade (hiking days/recommended layover days)	
Leisurely	4/2
Moderate	2/1
Strenuous	—
Trailhead	Mosquito Flat (1)

HIGHLIGHTS   This trip offers incomparable, varied scenery to the hiker who enjoys high elevations and doesn't mind company. Beginning at the highest trailhead in the Sierra, the 1800-foot ascent to Mono Pass over excellent trail affords views down into many exquisite lakes of the Little Lakes Basin. From the pass, a barren moonscape of mammoth boulders and sand, the hiker descends into the lush Mono Creek drainage and forest cover to reach superbly scenic Fourth Recess Lake. A layover day here offers tempting choices: exploration of the lake's 1000-foot waterfall or exploration of Hopkins Lakes or the lakes of Pioneer Basin.

DESCRIPTION (Moderate trip)

1st Hiking Day (**Mosquito Flat** to **Fourth Recess**, 6½ miles): From the trailhead at Mosquito Flat the wide, rocky-sandy trail starts southwest toward the imposing skyline dominated by Mts. Mills, Abbot and Dade and Bear Creek Spire. A short distance from the trailhead, we come to a signed junction with the Little Lakes Valley/ Morgan Pass trail. Here our route branches right (west) and ascends steeply on rocky switchbacks. In the course of this switchbacking ascent, the moderate-to-dense forest cover of whitebark and lodge- pole diminishes in density as we near timberline. Views during the climb include the glacier-fronted peaks named above and, midway up the ascent, imposing Mt. Morgan in the southeast. Immediately below to the east, the deep blue of Heart and Box lakes and some of the Hidden Lakes reflects the sky above, and the viewer looking at the panorama of the valley can envisage the glacial history that left these "puddles" behind.

The trail descends slightly and forks at the edge of a meadow densely inhabited by Belding ground squirrels. The right branch contours around the meadow's edge and then ascends nearly 1000 feet to Mono Pass. To visit Ruby Lake, you continue straight ahead ¼ mile on the left fork, into the meadow. To your left ripples the outlet stream from Ruby Lake, which is just a short climb ahead, but invisible from here. Ruby Lake (11,000′) completely fills the bottom of a towering cirque. Sheer granite composes the upper walls of the cirque, and the crown is topped by a series of spectacular pinnacles, particularly to the west. To the north, also on the crest, a notch indicates Mono Pass, and close scrutiny will reveal the switchbacking trail that ascends the south ridge of Mt. Starr. The lower walls of the cirque are made up mostly of talus and scree that curve outward to the lake's edge, and it is over this jumbled rock that ambitious anglers must scramble to sample the fair fishing for brook, rainbow and brown (to 12″). Good campsites can be found near the outlet of the lake.

After seeing Ruby Lake, retrace your steps to the Mono Pass Trail and turn left to continue your climb to the pass. Following a general east-to-west course, the trail climbs by long, steady switchbacks up the north wall of the cirque, and after a long traverse veers northward to ascend steeply—with a couple of minor dips—to the summit of Mono Pass (12,000′). The best views from the pass area are obtained by climbing the easy granite shoulder of Mt. Starr, to the east. Views from this shoulder include Mts. Stanford, Huntington, Crocker and Hopkins and Red and White Mountain to the north; and Mts. Abbot, Dade and Humphreys and Bear Creek Spire to the south.

The trail continues north from the pass, descending steadily on granite sand. It traverses the west side of shallow, rockbound Summit Lake, and then descends more steeply to the slopes above Trail Lakes. The westward descent past Trail Lakes turns north, and then the trail drops to ford Golden Creek. Here this route re-enters forest cover, and it continues to descend as it passes the lateral to Pioneer Basin to your right and the lateral to Fourth Recess Lake to your left.

Turn left on the Fourth Recess Lake lateral. A gentle ½-mile walk brings you to the meadowy pools of the outlet of Fourth Recess Lake (10,132′). The east and south sides of this lake are sheltered by vast granite walls. Piercing the south wall is a 1000-foot waterfall, which can be reached by climbing the gentler west side. In the early morning, when the lake is still, the reflections of these sheer walls make you wonder which way is up. Excellent but hardened campsites are located near the outlet on the east side. Fishing is good for brook (to 14″). Serious anglers may wish to alter their hiking plan with a rewarding excursion to the excellent brook (some rainbow and golden) fishing at the lower Pioneer lakes.

2nd Hiking Day: Retrace your steps, 6½ miles.

Fourth Recess Lake and its waterfall

Mosquito Flat to Second Recess 12

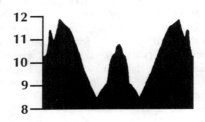

Trip	From Mosquito Flat to Second Recess via Mono Pass
Distance	32 miles
Type	Out and back trip
Best season	Mid or late
Topo maps	**Mt. Abbot** 15′; Mt. Morgan, Mt. Abbot 7½′

Grade (hiking days/recommended layover days)

Leisurely	—
Moderate	5/1
Strenuous	4/1
Trailhead	Mosquito Flat (1)

HIGHLIGHTS Mosquito Flat at 10,230′ is the highest trailhead in the Sierra, and the trail to Mono Pass is in excellent condition, so this route offers unusually quick and easy access to the high country and alpine terrain. The trail up toward Mono Pass gives you sweeping vistas of the many jewel-like lakes that stud Little Lakes Valley, lakes surrounded by snowclad peaks and cirques.

If you are not well acclimated to high altitude by the time you start, you will find this very high trailhead and pass extremely arduous.

DESCRIPTION (Moderate trip)

1st Hiking Day: Follow Trip 11 to **Fourth Recess**, 6½ miles.

2nd Hiking Day (**Fourth Recess** to **Fish Camp**, 5 miles). Reverse your steps to the Mono Creek Trail and turn west (left) onto it. The trail soon fords the outlet streams from Pioneer Basin. Mono Rock towers on the left as the route passes the Third Recess Trail lateral to your left and, about a mile farther, the lateral to Hopkins Lakes and Hopkins Pass to your right. Anglers who wish to sample the good fishing for brook, rainbow and occasional golden in Mono Creek will find many fine, deep holes along this stretch of trail.

There is camping the entire length of this trail, which never gets far from the creek. For the most part, Mono Creek rushes along briskly, but occasional potholes and level stretches in the stream bed contribute to the good spawning areas that any good Sierra trout stream requires. Anglers and hikers alike will appreciate the abundance of quaking aspens that line Mono Creek. For those with color film in their cameras, the best time to capture the aspen color is usually late September or early October. This route then passes the Grinnell Lakes lateral and descends to Fish Camp (8550'). The Second Recess Trail goes left here and descends through an overused camping area. Better campsites are found up- and downstream.

3rd Hiking Day (**Fish Camp** to **Lower Mills Creek Lake**, 4½ miles): Reverse the steps of the first two paragraphs of the 5th hiking day, Trip 9.

4th and 5th Hiking Days: Retrace your steps, 16 miles.

Mt. Morgan above Little Lakes Valley

Pine Creek Roadend to Honeymoon Lake   **13**

Trip	From Pine Creek Roadend to Honeymoon Lake
Distance	11 miles
Type	Out and back trip
Best season	Mid
Topo maps	**Mt. Abbot** 15′; Mount Tom 7½′.

Grade (hiking days/recommended layover days)

Leisurely	2/1
Moderate	2/0
Strenuous	Day
Trailhead	Pine Creek Roadend (2)

HIGHLIGHTS   The winding ascent to Honeymoon Lake offers breathtaking over-the-shoulder views across Owens Valley to the White Mountains, and the Honeymoon Lake campsite views of the Sierra Crest make this an outstanding choice for a base-camp location on the east side of the Sierra.

The start of this trip is very steep: 2000 feet in first 2½ miles, mostly on a rocky-dusty, dry 4WD road. The idle tungsten mill and its settling ponds at the bottom of Pine Creek's canyon are eyesores. But the wilderness pleasures that await you are worth the trouble.

DESCRIPTION (Moderate trip)

1st Hiking Day (**Pine Creek Roadend** to **Honeymoon Lake**, 5½ miles): The trailhead (7400′) is located at the pack station just south of Pine Creek. The dusty duff trail ascends steeply from the pack station through a dense, mixed forest cover of Jeffrey pine, juniper, red fir, quaking aspen and birch, and fords several branchlets of an unnamed creek that feeds Pine Creek. These fords are decorated by plentiful blossoms of wild rose, columbine, tiger lily and Queen Anne's lace. About ⅓ mile beyond these fords, the trail emerges from the forest cover, directly opposite the Union Carbide tungsten mill, and presently merges with the rocky remains of a 4WD road leading uphill to the now-closed Brownstone Mine.

Although the slope into the Pine Creek canyon is steep, the road's grade is, for the most part, moderate, and this route segment is simply a matter of slog-and-pant. Three welcome streams break the monotony of the climb, and the view (despite the ugly roadcut that scars Morgan Creek) is spectacular. Through the Pine Creek valley that slopes away to the northeast, one can look across the Owens River drainage to the volcanic tableland and White Mountain (14,242') on the skyline. Where the road zigs left to the now-quiet mine, our trail goes ahead toward the cascades of Pine Creek.

Activity at the tungsten mine is limited to maintenance now, but that could change whenever sources of cheaper foreign tungsten are threatened. When the mill is busy, one has only to watch the antlike scurrying there to fully appreciate the slow, peaceful pace of the wilderness traveler. It's a scene that could be re-created at any time. From the mine-road junction, the trail ascends over talus and scree by short, steep switchbacks. Along this ascent one sees juniper, limber pine and lodgepole pine, and the juniper have left beautiful, weathered snags of a dramatic golden hue.

With the steepest part of the ascent behind, the trail fords another unnamed tributary, switchbacks past a sign at the boundary of John Muir Wilderness, and veers north to join Pine Creek ⅓ mile below Pine Lake. Here, the creek alternates in cascades, falls and chutes in a riot of white water. The trail fords the stream via boulders or a flattened log, and amid a moderate forest cover of lodgepole pines arrives at the northeast end of Pine Lake. This medium-sized lake (16 acres) is a popular overnight camping place (campsites along the northeast shore), and anglers may wish to tarry here to sample the fair fishing for brook (to 12"), but fishing is generally better at Upper Pine Lake.

Our trail passes through a drift fence, skirts the rocky northwest side of Pine Lake and ascends through forest to the outlet stream from Birchim Lake, which we ford. After climbing over a small ridge, the trail parallels the outlet stream from Upper Pine Lake, and arrives at the north side of the lake (10,200'). Anglers will find that brook, rainbow and some golden (to 12") frequent these waters, and angling is good. After skirting the meadowy areas at the north side of the lake, the trail crosses the multibranched inlet stream via boulders. Then, after a moderate ½-mile ascent, we arrive at the Pine Creek Pass/Italy Pass junction. The sign, if still there, is inconspicuous and nearly illegible, so be alert for a junction with a dusty trail that veers off sharply to the left (east); it's the Pine Creek Pass Trail.

Our route turns right, away from the Pine Creek Pass Trail and onto the Italy Pass Trail, and soon turns right again on the unmarked short lateral to the outlet of Honeymoon Lake (10,400′). This moderate-sized lake (10 acres) has good campsites near the outlet stream and excellent sites above the head of the waterfall in the inlet stream, reached by following the trail up from the lake's south end. Fishing for brook and rainbow (to 10″) is good. This lovely lake makes an excellent base camp for side excursions to 40 surrounding lakes in 4 drainages, or for climbing five nearby peaks that exceed 13,000 feet in elevation.

2nd Hiking Day: Retrace your steps, 5½ miles.

Looking north from Pine Creek Pass

14   Pine Creek Roadend to Moon Lake

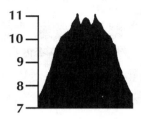

Trip	From Pine Creek Roadend to Moon Lake via Pine Creek Pass
Distance	20 miles
Type	Out and back trip
Best season	Mid
Topo maps	**Mt. Abbot** 15′; Mount Tom 7½′. Mt. Hilgard 7½′ needed for lakes north and west of French Canyon.

Grade (hiking days/recommended layover days)

Leisurely	4/1
Moderate	3/1
Strenuous	2/1
Trailhead	Pine Creek Roadend (2)

HIGHLIGHTS   The mining scars around the first part of this trail belie the primitive country that lies beyond the first climb. Pine Creek, from its lower aspen-clad banks to its tundra-meadow birthplace, is the kind of stream that can delight hiker, angler, photographer and naturalist alike. Moon Lake's "moon-scape" setting is a superb base for exploring beautiful French Canyon and the many alpine lakes on the benches above it.

As for Trip 13, the start of Trip 14 is demanding but worth it. Bouldering skills will be helpful in exploring the lakes high above French Canyon.

DESCRIPTION (Leisurely trip)

1st Hiking Day (**Pine Creek Roadend** to **Upper Pine Lake**, 5 miles): Follow most of the 1st hiking day, Trip 13, to Upper Pine Lake.

2nd Hiking Day (**Upper Pine Lake** to **Moon Lake**, 5 miles): Continue as for the 1st hiking day, Trip 13, to the Italy Pass-Pine

Creek Pass trail junction. From this poorly marked junction, our route bears left on a steady ascent toward Pine Creek Pass. Originally a Mono Indian trading route, this route and pass have been used by people for almost five hundred years. The moderate forest cover of lodgepole and then whitebark thins as the trail climbs, passing a small lake. Tiny, emerald-green, subalpine meadows break the long granite slabs, and wildflower fanciers will find clumps of color that include wallflower, shooting star, penstemon, lupine, primrose and columbine. The trail comes to a small creek that is the headwaters of Pine Creek and ascends a long swale between two granite walls before making the final steep, rocky climb through a drift fence to Pine Creek Pass (11,100′) on the Sierra Crest. From the vicinity of the pass, one has excellent views to the north of Bear Creek Spire. The trail remains fairly level as it passes a pair of tarns. As it begins to descend through a rocky meadow, views open up of Elba Lake to the south, of Pilot Knob (and behind it the Glacier Divide) to the southwest, and of Merriam and Royce peaks to the west. The trail then drops to French Canyon over lupine-dotted ledges. Soon our route meets the fisherman's trail branching left to Elba, Moon and L lakes.

Turn left onto this fisherman's trail, which ascends 300 feet up the steep south wall of French Canyon to the unmarked Moon-Elba junction. The left fork goes to Moon Lake, the right to Elba Lake (fair campsites at the northeast end). Turn right to visit Elba first. Typical of these high, montane lakes, Elba seems virtually devoid of life. First-time visitors to this country often refer to it as "moon country," but those who come to know and love it soon discover the beauty that hides close beneath the near-sterile veneer. Spots of green between the tumbled talus blocks indicate grassy tundra patches or clumps of willows, and occasionally the weathered landscape is broken by a dwarfed lodgepole or whitebark pine. Steady, silent scrutiny will usually discover movement that indicates animal life. A bird is usually the first to be detected, and most likely it will be either a rosy finch or a hummingbird. Four-footed movement among the rocks is most likely a cony or a marmot, or it just might be a wolverine or a bushy-tailed wood rat. Anglers will soon find life in the lake, for Elba Lake has a good population of golden and golden hybrids (to 12″).

From Elba, you ascend the inlet stream steadily to larger Moon Lake (10,998′). Fair campsites can be found along the southeast side of the lake. Fishing for golden (to 12″) is excellent, and, using Moon Lake as a base, anglers can explore eight more fishing lakes sharing this same bench system.

3rd and 4th Hiking Days: Retrace your steps, 10 miles.

15   Pine Creek Roadend to Lake Italy

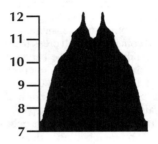

Trip	From Pine Creek Roadend to Lake Italy via Honey-moon Lake, Italy Pass.
Distance	23 miles
Type	Out and back trip
Best season	Mid or late
Topo maps	**Mt. Abbot** 15'; Mount Tom, Mt. Hilgard, Florence Lake, Mt. Givens 7½'

Grade (hiking days/recommended layover days)

Leisurely	—
Moderate	4/1
Strenuous	3/1
Trailhead	Pine Creek Roadend (2)

HIGHLIGHTS   This is a beautiful and adventurous route for an ambitious intermediate backpacker desiring to get the "feel" of a Sierra-crest crossing. The route embraces the steep eastern escarpment and crosses the barren, glaciated granite of the Sierra crest.

Some cross-country skills are needed near Italy Pass on both sides.

DESCRIPTION (Moderate trip)

1st Hiking Day: Follow Trip 13 to **Honeymoon Lake**, 5½ miles.
2nd Hiking Day (**Honeymoon Lake** to **Lake Italy**, 6 miles): The track to Lake Italy requires some route-finding skills, as it grows increasingly faint through Granite Park and vanishes altogether in upper Granite Park. To begin, return to the Italy Pass Trail and climb,

then descend, to the south end of Honeymoon Lake, where the track disappears in a jumble of boulders (there may be ducks). Climb steeply up the boulders, cross the first inlet in a willow thicket, and pick up the track again as it crosses the bench above the lake's southeast side. There are excellent campsites on this bench, particularly a little north of where the track crosses the next inlet. From here the trail winds up the jumbled valley, sometimes steeply, on the north side of the creek that drains Granite Park. The route passes many lovely little swales and crosses sparkling creeks four times as it ascends through thinning whitebark pines. If you lose the trail, look for it in places with soil, since it mostly avoids crossing bedrock or talus.

The trail arrives in Granite Park in a lovely meadow at treeline where the brook-trout-filled stream momentarily flows slowly. The trail fords the creek here and then doubles back to cross it again at the highest stand of whitebark pines. Then the route winds up the open, rocky expanses of upper Granite Park. The beaten track fades out abreast of the second-highest large lake, and we veer off into the boulders on the north side of the stream. Soon we come to the northeast shore of the highest lake, and the hiker can admire the views to the east before beginning the last climb to Italy Pass (12,400'). A faint trail-of-use to the top may be found directly below the pass. Views from the north side of this saddle are excellent, including—clockwise from the east—Mt. Tom, Mt. Humphreys, the Palisades, Seven Gables, Mt. Hilgard, Mt. Gabb, and, nearby in the north, Mt. Julius Caesar.

From the pass, we descend cross-country around the north side of a cirque and, after following a creek here for a short distance, drop down to the slopes above the north shore of Jumble Lake. The trail traverses the hillside far above the north side of the lake and then descends to skirt the moraine that dams Jumble Lake. Where the trail crosses the outlet below this moraine turn right and descend along this creek to the south shore of Lake Italy (11,154'). As this lake's shape resembles that of the European peninsula, you are now at the heel of the Italy boot, so to speak. There is plenty of room to camp here.

3rd and 4th Hiking Days: Retrace your steps, 11½ miles.

16   Pine Creek Roadend to Medley Lakes

Trip	From Pine Creek Roadend to Medley Lakes via Honeymoon Lake, Italy Pass, Selden Pass, Hutchinson Meadow, French Canyon, Pine Creek Pass
Distance	53½ miles
Type	Semiloop trip
Best season	Mid or late
Topo maps	**Mt. Abbot** 15′; Mount Tom, Mt. Hilgard, Florence Lake, Ward Mountain 7½′

Grade (hiking days/recommended layover days)

Leisurely	—
Moderate	—
Strenuous	6/2

Trailhead   Pine Creek Roadend (2)

HIGHLIGHTS   This long loop carries you through the densely forested lakes of the Pine Creek watershed to barren Granite Park, where you can explore snow-bound lakes and high alpine flora. Once you cross Italy Pass and pass Lake Italy, you return to forest cover. Then you reach the John Muir Trail, on which you cross Selden Pass and ascend the South Fork San Joaquin River watershed to Medley Lakes. A base camp here gives you a wide choice of lakes where you can fish, swim, photograph, or simply be. Leaving the Muir Trail at Piute Creek, your route loops back to rejoin the Pine Creek Trail via Pine Creek Pass.

This trip is recommended for the experienced backpacker who is comfortable walking bouldery terrain and is in excellent condition.

DESCRIPTION (Strenuous trip)

1st and 2nd Hiking Days: Follow Trip 15 to **Lake Italy**, 11½ miles.

3rd Hiking Day (**Lake Italy** to **Medley Lakes**, 11½ miles): First, follow the south shore west to the outlet. Then the trail descends along the east bank of the Hilgard Branch past the low ridge behind which lie Teddy Bear and Brown Bear lakes, and then it switchbacks down steeply to a ford of the creek. The trail levels out as it winds through a sparse forest cover of lodgepole. About a mile farther, it descends steeply once more, via rocky switchbacks, and after losing 500 feet it levels out. This loss of altitude brings an increase in density of the forest cover—mostly lodgepole—and the individual trees no longer appear gnarled and stunted. The route then fords the outlet stream from Hilgard Lake, and beyond Hilgard Meadow we make a final switchbacking drop into the main canyon of Bear Creek. Here we turn left on the Muir Trail and follow the 2nd hiking day, Trip 6, from this junction on.

4th Hiking Day (**Medley Lakes** to **lower Sallie Keyes Lake**, 5 miles): Follow the first part of the 3rd hiking day, Trip 7.

5th Hiking Day (**Lower Sallie Keyes Lake** to **Hutchinson Meadow**, 12½ miles): An early start for this hiking day is advisable in order to complete the long, sometimes steep, always dusty descent into the South Fork San Joaquin River drainage and the undulating ascent up Piute Canyon. From Sallie Keyes Lakes (10,200′), the duff trail descends through heavy stands of lodgepole interspersed with tiny meadows. Colorful wildflowers, often in patches, dot this stretch of trail: Indian paintbrush, Douglas phlox, shooting star, yellow and white cinquefoil, penstemon, lupine and western mountain aster. Now your route swings eastward and crosses two terminal moraine ridges.

The sometimes rocky trail then descends to ford Senger Creek in a lovely forested flat, where it leaves the heavy concentration of lodgepole behind. Alternately steep and moderate descents characterize the southeastward course of the trail, and the traveler soon enters a drier area of manzanita and fractured granite. Views are excellent to the south and west of the resistant granite slopes of Mt. Shinn and Ward Mountain. To the southeast, the skylined peaks of the LeConte Divide and Emerald Peak dominate the view until your Muir Trail passes the lateral to Blayney Meadows, and then makes the final descent to a junction with the main Florence Lake Trail. A prelunch swim in the nice holes of the South Fork San Joaquin River to the west of the junction is in order, and fishermen will find fair fishing for golden in the same vicinity. Several fair-to-good campsites are near the junction.

From this junction, our route continues east on a duff-and-granite-sand trail through a mixed forest cover of Jeffrey pine and juniper interspersed with occasional red and white fir. The trail crosses an easy series of ridges and descends past several good campsites to the Piute Canyon Trail junction, where our route branches left, away from the John Muir Trail. The rocky trail climbs and then descends briefly to the creek (last easy access to water late in a dry year until West Pinnacles Creek). From here, the trail keeps to the west side well above briskly flowing Piute Creek and fords multibranched Turret Creek (may be dry in a dry year). We climb and descend hot chaparral slopes on switchbacks affording poor footing, but we are rewarded by the excellent views of highly fractured Pavilion Dome and the surrounding, unnamed domes composing the west end of the Glacier Divide. The trail then swings east through a narrowing canyon, crosses a couple of gullies on log bridges, fords tiny West Pinnacles Creek, and pursues a steep, rocky course until it enters a moderate lodgepole forest cover before reaching the East Pinnacles Creek ford. Views of the cascading tributary streams are frequent along this trail section. From the ford, the trail ascends gently to beautiful Hutchinson Meadow (9438′), where travelers will find excellent campsites near the Pine Creek Pass Trail junction. Fishing for golden and brook is good-to-excellent (to 9″). The lovely meadow setting provides excellent campsite views of several granite peaks, including Pilot Knob, to the east and northwest.

6th Hiking Day (**Hutchinson Meadow** to **Pine Creek Trailhead**, 13 miles): This hiking day's route leaves the Piute Pass Trail and ascends moderately up French Canyon. Our rocky, dusty trail rolls up and down through the forested edge of the canyon. Fishing along these upper reaches of French Canyon creek is good to excellent, despite the diminishing size of the stream. The trail crosses several unnamed tributaries draining the east and west slopes of Royce and Merriam peaks, and soon climbs above the timberline. The spectacular, noisy waterfall on the outlet of the Royce Lakes captures our attention as the flower-spangled meadows of upper French Canyon open around us, and the character of the canyon walls reflects the increase in altitude: barren granite, mostly white and heavily fractured, scoops away to the east, making a broad-headed, typical cirque basin. The footing becomes very rocky as the trail passes the faint fisherman's trail to Elba, Moon and L Lakes and then veers north, climbs steeply, and crosses a long granite bench. From the bench, it is but a short, easy climb to the summit of Pine Creek Pass; along the way, there are excellent views of Bear Creek Spire, Royce and Merriam peaks, Pilot Knob, the Glacier Divide and Mt. Humphreys.

Directly ahead, the trail descends a long, talus-ridden swale. This descent soon enters a sparse forest cover of lodgepole, winding between large slabs of granite past a small lake. Tiny subalpine meadows fill the gaps in the rock, and the traveler is sure to see western wallflower, shooting star, penstemon, lupine, primrose and columbine. The trail veers away from the trickling Pine Creek headwaters, crosses a slight rise, and then drops to the hard-to-see junction with the Italy Pass Trail. Our route keeps to the right, fords the North Fork Pine Creek just above the cascading inlet to Upper Pine Lake, and arrives at the excellent campsites along the west side of the lake and below the outlet (10,200'). Good fishing for brook, rainbow, and some golden (to 12") can be had on Upper Pine Lake. From here, retrace most of the steps of the 1st hiking day, Trip 13 (5 miles).

Aerial view of Royce Lakes looking west

North Lake to Piute Lake

10 ⌐
9 ⌐

Trip   From North Lake to Piute Lake
Distance   7 miles
Type   Out and back trip
Best season   Mid or late
Topo maps   **Mt. Goddard** 15′, **Mt. Darwin** 7½′
Grade (hiking days/recommended layover days)
   Leisurely   2/0
   Moderate   —
   Strenuous   Day
Trailhead   North Lake (4)

HIGHLIGHTS   This trip offers an easy walk into the high country to a lake with large trout. It's an excellent choice for beginning backpackers who want to sample a near-alpine setting with only a modest effort. And for your effort, you're rewarded with fine scenery: the forested flower gardens along the North Fork Bishop Creek near the start; the rugged orangeish face of Piute Crags; the showy cascade where the creek leaps free of the lakes; and the chain of high, blue lakes leading to Piute Lake.

DESCRIPTION (Leisurely trip)

1st Hiking Day (**North Lake** to **Piute Lake**, 3½ miles): Shortly after leaving the trailhead (9360′), this route enters John Muir Wilderness and then ascends gently along slopes dotted with meadowy patches, aspen groves and stands of lodgepole pine. In season the traveler will find a wealth of wildflowers in these little meadows and in the sandy patches among the granite slabs, including paintbrush, columbine, tiger lily, spiraea and penstemon. After the trail fords and quickly refords the North Fork Bishop Creek, the ascent becomes moderate. Aspen is left behind, the lodgepole becomes sparse, and some limber pine is seen. This glaciated canyon is flanked by slab-topped Peak 12691 on the south and 13,118-foot Mt. Emerson on the north. The newcomer to the High Sierra will marvel at how the great granite slabs maintain their precarious perches atop Peak 12691, seeming to be almost vertically above him or her. But they all topple eventually, due to the action of frost wedging, and add to the piles of talus at the foot of the peak.

Approaching Loch Leven, the trail levels off, and the angler may wish to try the lake waters for brook, rainbow and brown trout (to 10"). There's a campsite north of the trail, near the lake's west end. The trail then ascends moderately again, through a cover of sparse lodgepole and whitebark, winds among large, rounded boulders, passes through a drift fence, and skirts a pair of small lakes before arriving at the next bench up the canyon, which contains this day's destination, Piute Lake (10,958'). The traveler may wish to consider the wind in selecting a campsite, as it often blows stiffly in this Piute Pass country. There are overused campsites on the north side close to the trail. Fishing for brook and rainbow is fair (to 18"). Those who would go out of their way to find seclusion may elect to scramble southeast up a fairly steep slope to granite-bound Emerson Lake.

2nd Hiking Day: Retrace your steps, 3½ miles.

Marmots live in rocky territory

18 North Lake to Humphreys Basin

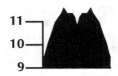

Trip	From North Lake to Humphreys Basin via Piute Lake, Piute Pass
Distance	14 miles
Type	Out and back trip
Best season	Mid or late
Topo maps	**Mt. Goddard** 15′; Mt. Darwin 7½′. Mount Tom 7½′ needed for Desolation lakes.

Grade (hiking days/recommended layover days)

Leisurely	4/1
Moderate	3/1
Strenuous	2/0
Trailhead	North Lake (4)

HIGHLIGHTS   Humphreys Basin offers excellent cross-country dayhiking to dozens of lakes, from huge, barren Desolation Lake to lightly forested, turquoise Packsaddle Lake. Many offer good fishing, too. The intricate, twisting beauty of the basin's many stream channels surpasses any human design. You can easily spend a day rambling up and down one. There are peaks to bag, ranging from difficult Mt. Humphreys—Class 4 by the easiest route—to gentle, unnamed knobs. A base camp here gives you access to countless high-country delights.

The trail is easy. Away from it, be ready for cross-country hiking that grades from easy off-trail to enjoyable but demanding boulder-scrambling.

DESCRIPTION (Leisurely trip)

1st Hiking Day: Follow Trip 17 to **Piute Lake**, 3½ miles.

2nd Hiking Day (**Piute Lake** to **Humphreys Basin**, 3½ miles): From Piute Lake, the trail ascends an open, rocky slope to treeline, overlooking alpine meadows threaded by streamlets and dotted with bright pools. Sooner than you might expect, it switchbacks up to the last traverse before Piute Pass. Here in midsummer you'll probably pass through a "road cut" in a snowbank, created by packers using

sand and shovels. At the pass (11,423') there are grand views west
to Pilot Knob and the canyon of the South Fork San Joaquin river,
south to Glacier Divide—the north boundary of Kings Canyon
National Park—and north over barren blue lakes to the unnamed
ridge separating Humphreys Basin from French Canyon and to Mt.
Humphreys, highest peak this far north in the Sierra. If it could
acquire 14 feet from somewhere, Bishop residents would have their
own 14,000-foot Sierra peak.

The rocky-dusty main trail descends briefly toward pale blue
Summit Lake and then curves northwest high above the lake, along
the treeless edge of the great cirque that is Humphreys Basin. (The
old trail that followed the creek down to the bottom of the cirque has
been abandoned.) Below you to the south, the headwaters of Piute
Creek spill ribbonlike down the basin, forming a lake here, a pond
there. Unseen above you to the north lie the Marmot and Humphrey
lakes, whose outlets you splash across where they nourish trailside
patches of willows, shooting stars and sneezeweed. A few small,
high campsites with panoramic views cling to the open slopes
between the trail and these remote lakes.

At a point where the main trail is above and north of a small lake
with a green island, you meet the unmarked use trail north to the
Desolation lakes. Those intrigued by the Desolation lakes' reputa-
tion for fishing and fond of treeless, open camps will find a campsite
or two east of the use trail above Lower Desolation Lake, and some
wind-raked flats among the great white boulders surrounding aptly
named Desolation Lake (good fishing for golden trout to 20").

The main trail continues to descend to the cascading outlet of the
Desolation lakes—the last reliable water before Hutchinson Meadow
in a dry year. If you missed the use trail to the Desolation lakes, you
can follow the outlet northward from here. Below, the Golden Trout
lakes gleam down in the cirque bottom. Those heading for the
campsites on the knolls around Upper Golden Trout Lake, about ½
mile south depending on your route, will spy some use trails or find
a cross-country route down the shrubby slopes to the lake. On the
knolls, small whitebark pines shelter little flats overlooking the
water, which mirrors the Glacier Divide. There are fine views
northeast to Mt. Humphreys and west to Pilot Knob. Lower Golden
Trout Lake (fair fishing for golden to 10") is closed to camping
within 500 feet of its shoreline.

These sites and many others in Humphreys Basin make fine base
camps for exploring the basin's wonders. Use stoves; downed wood
is very scarce to nonexistent here.

3rd and 4th Hiking Days: Retrace your steps, 7 miles.

19 North Lake to Hutchinson Meadow

Trip	From North Lake to Hutchinson Meadow via Piute Lake, Piute Pass, Humphreys Basin
Distance	24 miles
Type	Out and back trip
Best season	Mid or late
Topo maps	**Mt. Goddard** 15′; Mt. Darwin, Mt. Hilgard 7½′. Mount Tom (7½′) needed for Desolation lakes.

Grade (hiking days/recommended layover days)

Leisurely	5/2
Moderate	3/1
Strenuous	2/0
Trailhead	North Lake (4)

HIGHLIGHTS   Hutchinson Meadow is one of the finest meadows in the High Sierra, and the trail to it beside Piute Creek takes the traveler through several miles of wild mountain "lawns" and gardens, where Sierra wildflowers are at their best. Add the views of dominating Mt. Humphreys and the spectacular Glacier Divide, and this trip becomes one of the most scenic in all the Sierra. Plan a layover day in Humphreys Basin, famous for its golden trout, to fish and dayhike.

The trail part is easy. Away from it, be ready for cross-country hiking that grades from easy off-trail to enjoyable but demanding boulder-scrambling.

DESCRIPTION (Leisurely trip)

1st and 2nd Hiking Days: Follow Trip 18 to **Humphreys Basin**, 7 miles.

3rd Hiking Day (**Humphreys Basin** to **Hutchinson Meadow**, 5 miles): Return to the main trail near the crossing of the outlet of Desolation lakes. Turn west and descend the gentle, dusty trail, which soon enters a sparse lodgepole forest. The trail becomes rockier as the descent steepens to moderate and the forest cover thickens.

About 4 miles from Piute Pass the display of flower-studded green "lawn" begins—in a year of normal precipitation. From here to Hutchinson Meadow, the traveler is seldom out of sight of these subalpine gardens. The amateur botanist will discern paintbrush, shooting star, fleabane, swamp onion, red mountain heather, butter-cup, cinquefoil, penstemon, buckwheat, yarrow, milfoil, senecio and Douglas phlox, along with Labrador tea, lemon willow and alpine willow. Rollicking Piute Creek is often close at hand, lending its music to complete this scene of mountain beauty.

Beyond a drift fence, the trail levels out and fords the distribu-taries of French Canyon Creek, arriving at the good campsites at forested Hutchinson Meadow (9438'). Here beneath Pilot Knob and Peak 12402, anglers will find the riffles of Piute Creek good-to-excellent fishing for brook and some golden (to 9"), or they may cautiously approach the little pools on the distributaries of French Canyon Creek, which spread out through the east side of the meadow and offer equally good fishing.

4th and 5th Hiking Days: Retrace your steps, 12 miles.

Mt. Humphreys above Humphreys Basin

20 North Lake to Lamarck Lakes

Trip   From North Lake to Lower Lamarck Lake
Distance   6 miles
Type   Out and back trip
Best season Mid
Topo maps   **Mt. Goddard** 15', Mt. Darwin 7½'
Grade (hiking days/recommended layover days)
   Leisurely   2/0
   Moderate   Day
   Strenuous   —
Trailhead   North Lake (4)

HIGHLIGHTS   Using Lower Lamarck Lake as a campsite, you can choose among wilderness experiences. Wander cross-country a gentle half a mile northwestward to reach the first of the string of seldom-visited Wonder Lakes, each more magical and private as you climb. Or explore stark Upper Lamarck Lake, less than a mile upward on a good trail. Or follow the trail toward Upper Lamarck Lake, head south on a distinct trail just before the lake's outlet, and ascend 1860 strenuous feet to Lamarck Col (12,880'), from which you can look into Darwin Canyon and Evolution Valley 4000 feet below.

The trail to Lower Lamarck Lake is steep in some sections, with occasional rough footing.

DESCRIPTION (Leisurely trip)

1st Hiking Day (**North Lake** to **Lower Lamarck Lake**, 3 miles): From the west side of the North Lake campground (9360'), the signed trail heads south. You cross Bishop Creek on a comfortably constructed log bridge, and enter moist woods that abound with wildflowers even in a dry year. Soon you undertake a long set of moderate switchbacks through aspen and lodgepole pines, which are joined by limber pines as you approach a saddle at about 9900 feet. You then pass a signed trail to your left that leads to Grass Lake. Shortly, your trail becomes exposed, steep and rough as it switchbacks upward. On several of the north tips of the switchbacks, you can look back into Bishop Creek and down at your North Lake starting point.

You also have many views down to marshy Grass Lake. The trail passes a small lake to the right (several campsites), and within a few hundred feet you arrive abruptly at Lower Lamarck Lake (10,662′). There are attractive but heavily used campsites along the east side of the lake; excellent campsites can also be found above the lake on the northeast shore. No wood fires are permitted.

2nd Hiking Day: Retrace your steps, 3 miles.

Duck on glacial erratic

21 Lake Sabrina to Emerald Lakes

Trip	From Lake Sabrina to Emerald Lakes via Blue Lake
Distance	8 miles
Type	Out and back trip
Best season	Mid or late
Topo maps	**Mt. Goddard** 15′; Mt. Thompson, Mt. Darwin 7½′

Grade (hiking days/recommended layover days)

Leisurely	2/0
Moderate	—
Strenuous	½ day
Trailhead	Lake Sabrina (3)

HIGHLIGHTS   The sparkling blue lakes near the head of the Middle Fork Bishop Creek, nestled close under 13,000-foot peaks, are among the loveliest on the Sierra Nevada's east slope. Most of the lakes have dramatic, granite settings, but the little Emerald Lakes sit cupped in wooded bowls, their tranquil waters rippling gradually away into emerald-green meadows—an unexpectedly intimate setting for this altitude.

DESCRIPTION (Leisurely trip)

1st Hiking Day (**Lake Sabrina** to **Emerald Lakes**, 4 miles): From the designated backpackers' parking area below Lake Sabrina, your route follows the Lake Sabrina road ½ mile to the trailhead, on the left about 100 yards below the Sabrina Dam. The well-used trail, signed SABRINA BASIN TRAIL and BLUE LAKE TRAIL, climbs above Sabrina Dam (9180′) and begins a long traverse of the slope above the blue expanses of Lake Sabrina. The route is initially through lush greenery and over small streams but it soon strikes out across the dry, sunny hillside above the lake, where there is a sparse cover of aspen, Jeffrey pine, juniper, lodgepole pine, western white pine and mountain mahogany. Where the dusty trail crosses talus, you encounter many aspen, indicating a plentiful underground water supply. Views from here are excellent, extending all the way to the Sierra Crest.

The trail undulates gently until about halfway along the lake, and then it ascends steadily to pass a junction with the George Lake Trail, branching left. Soon beyond, the trail descends to ford the cascading outlet from George Lake, where we find our first water and shade since the north end of Lake Sabrina.

From here the trail switchbacks steeply through a moderate cover of lodgepole pine, crosses a small stream, climbs onto the ridge north of Blue Lake and swings south. The remaining ascent to Blue Lake is up a quiet ravine that heads just above the lake's north shore. A short descent through overused campsites brings you to the outlet of picturesque Blue Lake (10,388'; no camping within 300 feet). This spot is a photographer's delight, with weatherbeaten lodgepoles along the uneven shoreline and rugged Thompson Ridge towering above the clear waters of the lake.

From the rockhop ford of the outlet, the trail winds through granite outcrops on the west side of the lake. About midway along this side is a trail junction, where going straight would head to Donkey Lake. Our route turns right toward Dingleberry Lake. The winding trail passes over a low saddle, down across a rocky slope and back up granite ledges into a grassy valley spotted with lodgepole pines. Soon you reach the shaded outlet of the lowest of the Emerald Lakes. Although these lakes are closer in size to ponds, they are indeed little gems. The trail then curves toward the Sierra Crest, and we soon reach the use trail to Emerald Lakes—right to Dingleberry, left to Emerald. We turn left, striking out south across a wet meadow. It is a short distance to the next larger of these lakes, where there are good campsites. More secluded camping can be found at the largest and westernmost Emerald Lake, reached by ascending southwest from the second lake for ¼ mile over broken granite. The fishing in these lakes is fair-to-good for brook (to 8").

2nd Hiking Day: Retrace your steps, 4 miles.

Thompson Ridge towers over Blue Lake

22 Lake Sabrina to Midnight Lake

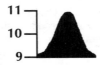

Trip	From Lake Sabrina to Midnight Lake
Distance	13 miles
Type	Out and back trip
Best season	Early
Topo maps	**Mt. Goddard** 15′; Mt. Thompson, Mt. Darwin 7½′

Grade (hiking days/recommended layover days)

Leisurely	3/0
Moderate	2/0
Strenuous	Day
Trailhead	Lake Sabrina (3)

HIGHLIGHTS   This leisurely, gentle trip lets you explore a large number of lovely lakes in unsurpassed surroundings. Their backdrop is the Sierra Crest, some 2500 feet above. From a Midnight Lake campsite, you can follow the almost level trail to stark Hungry Packer Lake. As you return, detour to Moonlight Lake—you will pass by waterfalls and pools to play in. A further, relatively easy 550-foot ascent cross-country brings you above treeline to Echo Lake. Or, if you prefer a more challenging ascent cross-country, Blue Heaven Lake and Hell Diver Lakes can be reached by a clamber up the west side of Midnight Lake's bowl.

DESCRIPTION (Leisurely trip)

1st Hiking Day: Follow Trip 19 to **Emerald Lakes**, 4 miles.

2nd Hiking Day (**Emerald Lakes** to **Midnight Lake**, 2½ miles): Retrace your steps to the main trail and continue west. The trail ascends gently to a saddle, where you can look down on lovely Dingleberry Lake, to which the trail shortly descends. The south side of Dingleberry Lake is swampy and beloved by mosquitoes, but apart from the mosquitoes, you'll find excellent camping there.

Your route to Midnight Lake continues southwest on the main trail. Soon you pass an unsigned spur trail to the left that leads to Pee Wee and Topsy Turvy lakes. A few moderate switchbacks carry you up past the signed trail to Hungry Packer Lake. Almost immediately you cross the outflow creek from Hell Diver Lakes, which are nestled about 650 feet above you to the west. Soon you come to a tarn; from here you climb easily over granite shelves and quickly reach Midnight Lake (10988′). The lake lies at treeline in a granite bowl with sheer sides stretching upward to the Sierra Crest. A 300-foot waterfall courses down to its western shore. Excellent camping begins at the tarn and continues among the lodgepole pines that end at the lake's outlet.

3rd Hiking Day: Retrace your steps, 6½ miles.

Puppet Lake and Pilot Knob

23 Lake Sabrina to George Lake

Trip	From Lake Sabrina to George Lake
Distance	6.4 miles
Type	Out and back trip
Best season	Mid and late
Topo maps	**Mt. Goddard** 15′; **Mt. Thompson** 7½′

Grade (hiking days/recommended layover days)

Leisurely	2/0
Moderate	Day
Strenuous	½ day
Trailhead	Lake Sabrina (3)

HIGHLIGHTS   Few lakes reachable by trail and so close to a road offer as much solitude as George Lake. After the day-hiking anglers leave, you may have the lake to yourself.

DESCRIPTION (Leisurely trip)

1st Hiking Day (**Lake Sabrina** to **George Lake**, 3.2 miles): Follow Trip 21 to the George Lake Trail junction and turn left, uphill, onto that trail. This steep path switchbacks up an open, exposed hillside for more than ½ mile before it reaches the first clumps of welcome whitebark pines. When you come to the first stream, cross it and almost immediately recross it to continue on switchbacks up the steep hillside. As the forest cover grows thicker, the steep grade abates, becoming mild and then, very soon, you reach the level foot of a valley. At the head of a meadow, cross the stream to the right side and continue up the valley. Then the trail veers left to cross a sloping, willowed meadow. Beyond this meadow, the sandy trail rises steeply for about 100 vertical feet, and then suddenly you are at George Lake (10,700′). There are good campsites near the trail on the east side of the lake, and fishing is good for brook and rainbow (to 12″).

2nd Hiking Day: Retrace your steps, 3.2 miles.

Lake Sabrina to Tyee Lakes **24**

Trip	From Lake Sabrina to South Lake road via George Lake and Tyee Lakes
Distance	7.7 miles
Type	Shuttle
Best season	Mid or late
Topo maps	**Mt. Goddard** 15′; Mt. Thompson 7½′

Grade (hiking days/recommended layover days)

Leisurely	2/0
Moderate	—
Strenuous	Day
Trailhead	Start at Lake Sabrina (3), end at South Lake Road (26)

HIGHLIGHTS   The views from the plateau atop Table Mountain give you an ineffable feeling of grandeur that is not soon forgotten. Beyond and below, the numerous Tyee Lakes offer hundreds of bays and bowers to swim and picnic in.

DESCRIPTION (Leisurely trip)

1st Hiking Day: Follow Trip 23 to **George Lake**, 3.2 miles.

2nd Hiking Day (**George Lake** to **South Lake Road**, 4½ miles): Before reaching the far end of George Lake (10,716′), the trail turns left (northeast) up slopes of granite sand dotted with whitebark pines. Although the tread is not always distinct on this slope, the route is not hard to follow. Switchbacking some 500 feet up the increasingly steep trail, you have increasingly good views of George Lake and the Sierra Crest beyond. Near the summit is a small stream and a multitude of arnica in bloom in midsummer. The trail becomes nearly level before reaching its high point (11,400′), and on this barren-seeming, rocky plateau grow many clumps of white phlox and lavender whorled penstemon.

Beyond the summit we head down the trailless east side of a tributary of Tyee Lakes creek and enter corn-lily country. This tall flowering plant looks like a cornstalk and grows profusely in dozens of soggy hillside gardens here until late season. Where the little valley narrows and steepens, a trail becomes obvious on the right side of the creek. Just before this creek drops into a gorge there is a beautiful lunch spot beside the stream with a commanding view of the fifth and largest Tyee Lake. Then the trail winds down to that lake, which has fair campsites on its north side in groves of whitebark pines. After we cross the outlet stream, the trail becomes more distinct, and it remains so to the end of this trip. We circle the fourth lake, keeping some distance from its shore until we near the outlet. Beside the outlet are some much-used but otherwise good campsites near a very picturesque, rock-dotted pond.

Beyond these campsites the trail again crosses Tyee Lakes creek and then winds down-canyon far from the third lake, seen in the east, to the shores of small, partly reed-filled lake #2, whose campsites are poor. Lake #1 has practically no campsites, and we skirt its swampy west edge, then veer away from its outlet to begin a moderate descent through increasingly dense forest. In ½ mile the trail crosses Tyee Lakes creek, and then it switchbacks in a generally eastward direction, crossing another refreshing stream soon after. The descent continues on dusty switchbacks down an often steep hillside, finally ending at a bridge across the South Fork Bishop Creek just downstream from a parking area on the South Lake road 5.0 miles up that road from the Lake Sabrina road.

The Inconsolable Range

Lake Sabrina to Baboon Lakes **25**

Trip	From Lake Sabrina to Baboon Lakes
Distance	9 miles
Type	Out and back trip
Best season	Mid or late
Topo maps	**Mt. Goddard** 15′; Mt. Thompson, Mt. Darwin 7½′

Grade (hiking days/recommended layover days)

Leisurely	2/0
Moderate	—
Strenuous	Day
Trailhead	Lake Sabrina (3)

HIGHLIGHTS   Sooner or later, everyone who returns to the High Sierra will want to try a little cross-country hiking. This fairly short trip is a fine choice for travelers who have reached that point in their careers.

DESCRIPTION (Leisurely trip)

1st Hiking Day (**Lake Sabrina** to **Baboon Lakes**, part cross country, 4½ miles): Follow the 1st hiking day, Trip 21, to the trail junction on the west shore of Blue Lake. Here we go straight and walk through granite-slab terrain under a forest of lodgepole pine, passing the south end of Blue Lake (not visible) and crossing a seasonal tributary. From where the trail meets the main stream we stay on its west side, avoid the turnoff (left) to Donkey Lake, and climb over slabs for 250 yards. Then the route climbs a steep, 20-foot-high slab at the top of which we turn right, uphill. We then climb over more slabs and through a fissure before we cross the creek in a meadow. Beyond, head south up a ravine, descend briefly and turn right to climb a steep slope that heads to a narrow ravine and lower Baboon Lake (10,976′). Baboon Lakes support brook trout.

2nd Hiking Day: Retrace your steps, 4½ miles.

26   Florence Lake to Lost Lake

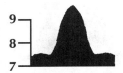

Trip   From Florence Lake to Lost Lake
Distance   18 miles
Type   Out and back trip
Best season   Early or mid
Topo maps   **Mt. Abbot** 15′; Florence Lake, Ward Mountain 7½′
Grade (hiking days/recommended layover days)
   Leisurely   —
   Moderate   2/0
   Strenuous   —
Trailhead   Florence Lake (7)

HIGHLIGHTS   Almost every "Lost Lake" in the Sierra Nevada
                  is somewhat lost in the sense that there is no
regular, maintained trail to it, and the Lost Lake of Florence Lake
country is no exception. This trail situation always makes for
seclusion and solitude, which are becoming ever more valuable.

DESCRIPTION (Moderate trip)

1st Hiking Day (**Florence Lake** to **Lost Lake**, 9 miles): From the
foot of Florence Lake, the hiker has a choice of walking the trail
around the west side of the lake or taking the ferry to the lakehead.
(Write Muir Trail Ranch, Box 176, Lakeshore, CA 93634 for details.
Please enclose a SASE.) The description in this book covers the trail
route from the parking area at the foot of the lake.

Leaving the parking area, the route follows a maintenance road
(closed to public vehicles) for ⅛ mile as it skirts the west side of the lake,
before giving way to a trail which veers off to the right and undulates
over granite ridges that form a series of spines down to the lake. This
trail rolls through a mixed forest of Jeffrey pine, juniper, aspen, white
fir and lodgepole pine. Previews of the kind of country to come are
provided by views southward of Ward Mountain and Mt. Shinn and
northward of the granite walls across the lake, and glimpses of the San
Joaquin drainage to the east. Now in John Muir Wilderness, about
halfway to the head of the lake this route passes a junction with a
Thomson Lake/Hot Springs Pass Trail (not maintained).

Just before the ford of Boulder Creek, a second, unsigned lateral to Thomson Lake takes off to the right (south), and it is our trail. From the west side of the log-bridge crossing of Boulder Creek this trail climbs steeply up a hot, manzanita-covered hillside under a sparse-to-moderate forest cover of Jeffrey pine, mountain juniper and a few firs and lodgepoles. The trail comes momentarily alongside the welcome creek and then swings away and climbs moderately to steeply through thinning forest. As the trail tops the canyon wall, you obtain good views of Mts. Hooper, Senger and Shinn, and the valley of the South Fork San Joaquin River. Just beyond, we ford small, brook-trout-inhabited Boulder Creek and then climb moderately as the forest cover slowly increases with the additions of western white pine and mountain hemlock. Soon the trail rounds a shallow ridge and then climbs steadily to the Lost Lake Trail, which branches left to that lake and then leads west to Thomson Lake. Our route crosses the outlet stream from Thomson Lake and then parallels the outlet of Lost Lake (9600') to the campsites on the lake's northern edge.

2nd Hiking Day: Retrace your steps, 9 miles.

Florence Lake

27 Florence Lake to Courtright Reservoir

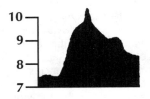

Trip	From Florence Lake to Courtright Reservoir
Distance	21 miles
Type	Shuttle
Best season	Early or mid
Topo maps	**Mt. Abbot** 15′; Florence Lake, Ward Mountain, Courtright Reservoir 7½′

Grade (hiking days/recommended layover days)

Leisurely	—
Moderate	—
Strenuous	2/0

Trailhead   Start at Florence Lake (7), end at Courtright Reservoir (14)

HIGHLIGHTS   Appealing to the forest lover, this shady route spends most of its tranquil miles among magnificent trees. From dense lodgepole-pine thickets to stately groves of giant red fir, you may feel at times that the word for the world is forest, though you will also find a few panoramic vistas.

DESCRIPTION (Strenuous trip)

1st Hiking Day: Follow Trip 26 to **Lost Lake**, 9 miles.

2nd Hiking Day (**Lost Lake** to **Courtright Reservoir**, 12 miles): We begin this hiking day by contouring at 9600′ from Lost Lake west to the outlet of Thomson Lake. A campsite is at the outlet, and the meadows around the lake show signs of grazing cattle. Angling southeast, our trail climbs steeply toward Thomson Pass under a moderate-to-dense forest cover of lodgepole and western white pines. At the top of this climb, views of the Silver Divide and the Ritter Range improve as we pass a few small springs which may offer a usable draught. At Thomson Pass views are poor, and it's worth walking north a few hundred yards to the top of a small ridge, where you get magnificent views to the north. From this pass our trail descends moderately through dense lodgepole forest to a meadow crossing of the West Fork Burnt Corral Creek. Then the trail makes a long, gentle descent through thick lodgepole forest where the forest floor is a lovely carpet of grass. This descent can be very pleasant and quiet unless summer-grazing cattle are mooing somewhere nearby.

About 35 yards northeast of where the trail fords the West Fork Burnt Corral Creek for the second time, several very cold springs provide a refreshing reason for the thirsty hiker to pause before continuing down to the Long Meadow/Chamberlain's Camp junction. Taking the right fork at this junction, we make a gentle-to-moderate ascent to serene Hobler Lake, where good campsites can be found among the giant red firs and the lodgepole pines. Ascending gently, the trail then leaves John Muir Wilderness, crosses the outlet of a tiny lake to the west, and meets the Courtright/Blackcap Basin Trail on a ridge above Chamberlain's Camp. From here we retrace part of the 1st hiking day, Trip 28.

Glacier Divide to Bubbs Creek

This area is bounded by Glacier Divide on the north, Owens Valley on the east, Courtright and Wishon reservoirs on the west, and Bubbs Creek on the south, and it contains the greatest single block of unbroken wilderness in the southern Sierra. Still untainted by roads, its core enjoys the protection of National Park status, and the adjacent peripheral zones to the west, north and east are declared Wilderness areas. Spread out over roughly 1200 square miles, this country boasts some of the most remote and scenic sections of the Sierra, and it is replete with scores of peaks that soar above 13,000 feet, hundreds of lakes and thousands of miles of sparkling streams. Were you able to take every trip suggested in this section, you would have a solid sampling of four life zones ranging in altitude from 5000 feet to well over 12,000 feet. Further, you would have crossed ten major divides, visited three major watersheds, and enjoyed a wilderness experience perhaps unequaled anywhere else in the world.

Topographically, the country divides neatly into three disparate types: the west slopes, Kings Canyon National Park, and the eastern escarpment. The Park, the heart of the high country, was established in 1940 when Congress recognized the obvious need to protect this fragile wilderness from the increasing encroachment of stockmen and local, shortsighted business interests. The Park "heartland" is the rugged, comparatively barren, mostly alpine zone that lies between the Sierra Crest and the LeConte/White Divide. Here are the headwaters of the South Fork of the San Joaquin and the Middle and South Forks of the Kings River. The latitudinal watershed divides, within the Park, are the Goddard Divide (separating the South Fork San Joaquin River from the Middle Fork Kings River), and the Monarch/Cirque Crest divide (splitting the watersheds of the Middle Fork and the South Fork Kings River). Several longitudinal divides serrate the topography into a complex ridge-chasm conformation. Most outstanding among these secondary divides are the White Divide, Ragged Spur, the Black Divide and King Spur.

In contrast to the gentle slope of the west side, the eastern escarpment rises steeply to the crest. From Rock Creek all the way to Horseshoe Meadow, the escarpment is severe and forbidding. The stretch between Big Pine Creek and Onion Valley is particularly lacking in heavily used roadheads and trails. Most of the many eastside streams flow into the Los Angeles Aqueduct, and they are separated by towering spur ridges that protrude from the backbone of the crest. Peculiar also to the east side is the lower juniper woodland belt, replete with the scattered grasses, piñon pine, Utah juniper and brush plants associated with the Great Basin. Fortunately for those who enjoy and would preserve the east escarpment's native primitive appeal, the higher elevations of it are protected by a long, narrow belt of wilderness designation.

Similarly, the western slopes (west of the Park boundary) enjoy this protection. The terrain of these western slopes is remarkable for its absence of outstanding peaks. In general it is a gradual, steady ascent to the LeConte/White Divide and the timbered rise of Kettle Ridge. The pleasant, rolling landscape of Woodchuck Country and the several alpine basins nestled at the foot of the LeConte Divide make up the headwaters of the North Fork Kings River.

Looking at topo maps of this section one can readily ascertain the comparatively heavy forestation of the region west of the LeConte Divide. Travelers working their way up any one of the various dendritic tributaries of the North Fork Kings River will discover for themselves the magnificent spectrum of Sierra flora that attends these westside entries to the high country. Beginning in the lower elevations around 6500 feet are the stately mixed conifers such as sugar pine, ponderosa pine and incense-cedar. Ponderosa pine, with its distinctive bark plates and its long needles, is frequently mistaken for its close cousin Jeffrey pine, which is usually of a higher elevation but sometimes found in the same locale. There are many distinguishing characteristics, but the surest is the difference in their cones. The naturalist's rule of thumb is, "If you can comfortably catch a tossed cone, it is a cone of Jeffrey pine." This differentiation arises from the fact that the prickle found on the end of each scale of the Jeffrey cone turns inward, whereas the prickle on the ponderosa cone turns outward. But the most distinctive cone of all belongs to the sugar pine. Sometimes as long as a person's arm, it is an impressive fruit whether found on the ground or seen hanging in clusters at the ends of massive branches.

Climbing a little higher, one enters the fir belt. First comes the white fir, along with occasional groves of Jeffrey pine, and finally the noble stands of red fir. Being rather brittle, red firs are frequently associated with a heavily littered forest floor that is noticeably devoid of ground-cover species. Standing in a cathedral-like grove

of red firs, it is the easiest thing in the world to empathize with John
Muir's bitterness when he wrote:

> Any fool can destroy trees. They cannot run away; and if they
> could, they would still be destroyed—chased and hunted down as
> long as fun or a dollar could be got out of their bark hides,
> branching horns, or magnificent bole backbones. Few that fell
> trees plant them; nor would planting avail much toward getting
> back anything like the noble primeval forests. During a man's life
> only saplings can be grown, in the place of the old trees—tens of
> centuries old—that have been destroyed. It took more than three
> thousand years to make some of the trees in these Western
> woods—trees that are still standing in perfect strength and beauty,
> waving and singing in the mighty forests of the Sierra. Through
> all the wonderful, eventful centuries since Christ's time—and
> long before that—God has cared for these trees, saved them from
> drought, disease, avalanches, and a thousand straining, leveling
> tempests and floods; but he cannot save them from fools—only
> Uncle Sam can do that.[*]

The "gentle country" of the trees continues as the trails wind
upward through dense groves of the two-needled lodgepole pine.
Near treeline the slim lodgepole pine no longer appears in tall, dense
stands—now its trunk is bent to the unchecked winds of alpine
country. Occasional clumps of whitebark pine and mountain hemlock dot those spaces among the granite that are not already filled
with the tender-yet-tough grasses of an alpine meadow.

This, then, is the land and the forests of the west slopes—an
environment that has nurtured and awed people since their first
acquaintance with it. It is an often-ignored fact that the first visitors
to these slopes were Native Americans, and there is adequate
evidence to show that they were leaching ground acorn meal at the
sites of Simpson and Zumwalt meadows long before Europeans had
settled the eastern shores of America. While Englishmen and Spaniards fought sea battles for supremacy of the ocean trade routes, the
Indians of the Mono and Monache groups were peacefully plying
their primitive trade routes over Piute, Bishop and Kearsarge passes.
Using laurel-wood bows and cane arrows that were dipped in a
poison concoction of crushed, rattlesnake-venomed deer liver, Indian hunting parties ranged the upper watershed of the Kings and San
Joaquin rivers while Europeans were establishing the first Presidio-
Mission complexes in Alta California. In Philadelphia, civilized
men of 1776 used a bird feather and decomposed animal fat to paint
their names on a piece of wood pulp that historians now call a historic
document. At almost the same time, in Tehipite Valley, an unknown

[*]*Our National Parks,* by John Muir.

Indian artisan using a similar stain produced a series of amebalike figures—and today's archeologist-historian refers to them as primitive graffiti.

The first meetings of these original inhabitants and exploring white men had the seeds of disaster. Gabriel Moraga, among the first white men to penetrate this country, was called the greatest pathfinder and Indian fighter of his day. Subsequent incursions by trappers, pioneer settlers and gold seekers brought the inevitable confrontation and, to the Europeans' discredit, the inevitable eradication of Native Americans. Like grizzly bears, they were judged nuisances, and were considered "fair game." Today, both species are extinct in this region.

Early exploratory ventures from west to east into the heartland of this region were so arduous as to render their continuation impractical. This is quite understandable, as any examination of the topography will show. Numerous divides, nearly all exceeding 12,000 feet, cross-hatch the landscape, making passage even to this day lengthy and arduous. John C. Frémont, in December 1845, endeavoring to carry out a rendezvous with Theodore Talbot and Joseph Walker on the westside river they called Lake Fork, led an unsuccessful sally into the reaches of the North Fork Kings River. He was turned back by snow and "impossible" going. Jedediah Smith's party, in an earlier attempt during spring, had suffered the same travails, and the subsequent annals of the Brewer Survey parties of 1864 and 1870 tell a similar story.

The actual trail-blazers of currently used trails were, however, not the Spaniards or the trappers. Most of the earliest trails were those of the sheepherders who grazed their flocks in the backcountry during the last half of the 19th century. Among the better known of these sheepherders were Bill Helm and Frank Dusy, whose early exploratory efforts on the west slopes culminated in the discovery of Tehipite Valley and in the building of the Tunemah Trail. W. Bird, operating in the same vicinity, established what is now known as the Hell-for-Sure Pass Trail, and although the 1864 Brewer Survey party was the first to visit the area, it is assumed that Portuguese sheepmen were the first to establish the current western access route to the Evolution region.

Wood fires are *prohibited* above 10,000′ in Kings Canyon National Park and from the Onion Valley roadend to the Park boundary. *Use a gas stove.*

urtright Reservoir to Post Corral Meadows

Trip	From Courtright Reservoir to Post Corral Meadows via Chamberlain's Camp
Distance	15 miles
Type	Out and back trip
Best season	Early to mid
Topo maps	Courtright Reservoir, Ward Mountain 7½'

Grade (hiking days/recommended layover days)

Leisurely	2/0
Moderate	—
Strenuous	Day
Trailhead	Courtright Reservoir (14)

HIGHLIGHTS A fine weekend selection, this two-day trip visits enchanting Long and Post Corral meadows. The dense forests of fir and lodgepole that line the route are a pleasant habitat for a variety of wildlife. This trip is an excellent selection for the beginner.

DESCRIPTION (Leisurely trip)

1st Hiking Day (**Courtright Reservoir** to **Post Corral Meadows**, 7½ miles): From the Maxson trailhead your trail leaves the west side of the paved lot, descends north next to the Dusy Jeep Trail for 300 yards, and then joins it. Now on a dirt road, you make a short descent and then ascend gently under moderate lodgepole-pine forest. After 1 mile the dirt road veers left and your trail goes right at a sign declaring NO MOTOR VEHICLES. Across a meadow the trail passes a sign: WILDERNESS PERMIT REQUIRED AHEAD. The shaded trail now ascends moderately on the west side of a flower-lined creek and then levels off to ford it at the foot of Maxson Meadows. Staying east of the meadows, you pass Chamberlain's Camp and climb 500 feet to a junction with a trail to Burnt Corral Meadows. Here, your trail veers right, crosses a seasonal creek and then descends to the head of aptly named Long Meadow. For ¾ mile the sandy trail winds along the margins of the nearly level meadow, which is drained by a small stream. You then boulder-hop the stream and swing away from the meadow, passing through dense stands of ubiquitous lodgepole pine. Soon a gentle descent leads to the grassy environs of Post Corral Meadows and you pass a faint trail leading to a privately owned cabin on Forest Service land leased to people who graze cattle. Most of Sierra National Forest, including parts of John Muir Wilderness, is grazed by cattle, as Forest Service multiple-use land policy provides for cattle grazing.

It's another mile to the ford of Post Corral Creek (8201′) (wet in early season) but you can avoid the often crowded camping there by finding good, more private campsites nearby between the trail and the creek. Post Corral Meadows support a variety of plants and animals. Wildflowers found here include paintbrush, Fendler's meadow rue and streamside marsh marigolds. Bird life makes itself readily known: groups of small, black-and-white dark-eyed juncos flit from branch to branch in search of insects. Robins are common, but you might also see a great horned owl or a Cooper's hawk. Post Corral Creek has a subaqueous ecosystem ruled by the brook trout, which isn't a true trout but a charr—imported from the eastern United States. Fishing is fair-to-good (to 7″).

2nd Hiking Day: Retrace your steps, 7½ miles.

Along Post Corral Creek

29   Courtright Reservoir to North Fork Kings

Trip	From Courtright Reservoir to North Fork Kings River via Post Corral Meadows
Distance	23 miles
Type	Out and back trip
Best season	Early to mid
Topo maps	Courtright Reservoir, Ward Mountain, Blackcap Mtn. 7½′

Grade (hiking days/recommended layover days)

Leisurely	4/1
Moderate	3/1
Strenuous	2/0
Trailhead	Courtright Reservoir (14)

HIGHLIGHTS   Beautiful forested meadows and easy terrain make this a good trip for the beginner. During early season runoff, the North Fork Kings River can be powerfully impressive as it surges down over granite slabs. During these times you may need to wade across the ford of Post Corral Creek.

DESCRIPTION (Leisurely trip)

1st Hiking Day: Follow Trip 28 to **Post Corral Meadows**, 7½ miles.

2nd Hiking Day (**Post Corral Meadows** to **North Fork Kings River**, 4 miles): On the east side of the ford of Post Corral Creek (wet in early season) you pass the Hell-for-Sure Pass Trail branching left, but your trail heads south through dense stands of lodgepole pine. After crossing an unnamed creek, the sandy, almost level trail winds through forest and small meadows for 2 miles before climbing over a ridge. From the ridgetop you have a good view of the granitic North Fork Kings River canyon. The entire valley was covered with glacial ice many times during the past million years, and the most recent glacier retreated up-canyon only about 11,000 years ago. Many more glacial advances are likely, as our earth seems to be in the midst of a series of ice ages.

At this point it is interesting to speculate on the route followed by Capt. John C. Frémont, the "Pathfinder." Historians are unsure of the exact route, but they do agree that Frémont's party got lost high in this drainage. They were caught in an early winter storm, were forced to eat their saddle stock, and finally retreated.

After descending an open hillside to slabs near the river, the trail turns east and climbs gently to a forested flat. Just before you cross Fleming Creek, you can turn right and find good campsites near the river (8028′) a short distance away. Fishing along the river is good for brook, brown and rainbow trout (to 8″).

3rd and 4th Hiking Days: Retrace your steps, 11½ miles.

30   Courtright Reservoir to Rae Lake

Trip	From Courtright Reservoir to Rae Lake via Post Corral Meadows
Distance	26 miles
Type	Out and back trip
Best season	Mid to late
Topo maps	Courtright Reservoir, Ward Mountain, Blackcap Mtn., Mt. Henry 7½′

Grade (hiking days/recommended layover days)

Leisurely	4/2
Moderate	3/1
Strenuous	2/1
Trailhead	Courtright Reservoir (14)

HIGHLIGHTS   Situated beneath Fleming Mountain, Rae Lake's innate beauty and its proximity to 25 other lakes and the intervening streams make it a choice base camp for exploration of Red Mountain Basin.

DESCRIPTION (Leisurely trip)

1st Hiking Day: Follow Trip 28 to **Post Corral Meadows**, 7½ miles.

2nd Hiking Day (**Post Corral Meadows** to **Rae Lake**, 5½ miles): Just east of the ford of Post Corral Creek (8201′) (wet in early season) your route leaves the Blackcap Basin Trail and takes the Hell-for-Sure Pass Trail up the ridge separating Post Corral Creek and Fleming Creek. At first the ascent is moderate under shady lodgepole pines, but in less than a mile the grade steepens and the trail crosses several unsightly sections of dynamited slabs. To dynamite these granite slabs is a policy decision—an unfortunate and unrepresentative policy under which the Forest Service maintains many backcountry trails for horses and pack animals when the overwhelming use of those trails is by hikers on foot.

As you near the top of the ridge, the trail crosses a small, forested flat, and then switchbacks the last few hundred feet to the ridgetop.

Turning northeast, you soon begin a gently rolling ascent up the forested north side of Fleming Creek canyon. After 1½ miles you swing north and ascend steep, rocky switchbacks to the meadows surrounding small Fleming Lake. Now the country takes on a definite subalpine character: the lodgepole pines are fewer and more stunted, and one may see bright mountain bluebirds perched on top of small trees.

The trail crosses the outlet at Fleming Lake and soon meets a junction with the Hell-for-Sure Pass Trail at the foot of a long, flower-dotted meadow. Here you turn left and then climb to a shaded hillside junction with the spur trail to Rae Lake (9889'). There are excellent campsites under trees on the north side of this meadow-fringed lake. Fishing is good for brook trout (to 9"). Rae was originally named Wolverine Lake, but it is unlikely that there are any wolverines left in the area. Several nearby lake basins offer a variety of good day-hiking options.

3rd and 4th Hiking Days: Retrace your steps, 13 miles.

Spotted sandpiper's nest with egg

Jeff Schaffer

31   Courtright Reservoir to Devils Punchbowl

Trip	From Courtright Reservoir to Devils Punchbowl; return via Meadow Brook and North Fork Kings River
Distance	35 miles
Type	Semiloop trip
Best season	Mid to late
Topo maps	Courtright Reservoir, Ward Mountain, Blackcap Mtn., Mt. Henry 7½′

Grade (hiking days/recommended layover days)

Leisurely	6/2
Moderate	5/2
Strenuous	4/1

Trailhead   Courtright Reservoir (14)

HIGHLIGHTS   Traveling along what was originally known as the Baird Trail (a sheepherders' route), this trip takes you down aptly named Meadow Brook. There you will find one of the Sierra's most beautiful subalpine meadows, even if cattle are there.

DESCRIPTION (Leisurely trip)

1st and 2nd Hiking Days: Follow Trip 30 to **Rae Lake**, 13 miles.
3rd Hiking Day (**Rae Lake** to **Devils Punchbowl**, 4 miles): Descending from Rae Lake (9889′), your trail meets and joins the trail from Lower Indian Lake, and a few hundred yards farther (in the meadow) meets the Hell-for-Sure Pass Trail. Here your route turns left, then fords Fleming Creek and ascends a tree-covered slope. At first you cross meadowy sections that often boast paintbrush, daisies and fireweed, but soon the soil becomes dry and sandy. Near the top of this 500-foot ascent you can look back on much of the country surrounding the Fleming Creek drainage. The extensive forests you see have grown on a thin layer of soil that formed in the 10,000 years since the last glaciers covered this basin. From the ridgetop the trail crosses open meadows and several seasonal creeks and then, next to a tall, gray stump, meets a junction with the trail to Devils Punchbowl.

Turning right at this junction, your route descends gently past a small, meadow-fringed lake and then drops 300 feet to the grassy environs of the East Fork Fleming Creek. Beyond a rock ford (wet in early season) you make a moderate 300-foot ascent to the low ridge on the north side of large, deep Devils Punchbowl (10,098'). Good campsites can be found to the left on the east side of the lake. This lake is heavily used, so please try to make a minimal impact. Fishing is good for brook trout (to 13"). Anglers spending layover days may wish to explore Red Mountain Basin, all of whose main lakes have been planted. For anyone who loves rugged, alpine country, the basin merits investigation.

4th Hiking Day (**Devils Punchbowl** to **North Fork Kings River**, 6½ miles): On the north side of the lake you join the trail and head south along the granitic ribs that dam the lake. Midway along the lake you get a bird's-eye view, from the edge of the escarpment, of two lakes to the west. At the southwest corner of Devils Punchbowl the trail makes several short switchbacks up to a low saddle. The following 2000-foot descent to the North Fork Kings River starts with a sandy 200-foot slope to the lush meadows at the head of Meadow Brook.

For the next mile the trail skirts the forest-meadow margin where dry, sandy soil borders the wet, organic-rich soil of the meadow. With these meadows in the foreground you get beautiful vistas of the far side of the North Fork Kings River drainage. The pond in the upper meadow is often the summer home for a family of mallards, and the flowers that bloom here include lavender shooting star, purple Sierra gentian and several species of monkey flower. Cattle may or may not be run in this drainage in a given year, but if present they definitely detract from the appeal of meadows like these. Sierran meadows evolved in the absence of cattle; their grazing and sharp hooves damage turf and their by-products pollute both trails and streams.

For over a mile your trail follows the lush meadows along Meadow Brook. Then the grade steepens and the trail swings away from the creek, angling down a forested moraine. When the trail levels off temporarily, it crosses a seasonal stream and again nears Meadow Brook. Soon the trail begins to switchback, and the last 1000 feet to the canyon floor are marked by the appearance of red fir, Jeffrey pine, Sierra juniper and quaking aspen. At the bottom of the grade you cross slabs to a junction with the Blackcap Basin Trail. Turning right, you soon reach a California Cooperative Snow Survey cabin next to a waterfall and a large pool in the river. For ½ mile you stay close to rock outcrops on the right before descending to ford multi-branched Fleming Creek on logs. Beyond the ford you can turn left to the good campsites along the North Fork Kings River. Fishing is good for brook, brown and rainbow trout (to 8").

5th and 6th Hiking Days: Reverse the steps of Trip 29, 11½ miles.

32   Courtright Reservoir to Guest Lake

Trip	From Courtright Reservoir to Guest Lake via Post Corral Meadows and North Fork Kings River
Distance	36 miles
Type	Out and back
Best season	Mid to late
Topo maps	Courtright Reservoir, Ward Mountain, Blackcap Mtn., Mt. Goddard 7½′

Grade (hiking days/recommended layover days)

Leisurely	6/1
Moderate	5/1
Strenuous	4/0
Trailhead	Courtright Reservoir (14)

HIGHLIGHTS   Of the three lake basins lying close under towering LeConte Divide, Bench Valley is the least known and least visited. This is surprising in view of the excellent angling at McGuire Lakes and Guest Lake. The other lakes of this basin are among the most picturesque in the Sierra, and you journey through stirring subalpine scenery en route.

DESCRIPTION (Leisurely trip)

1st and 2nd Hiking Days: Follow Trip 29 to **North Fork Kings River**, 11½ miles.

3rd Hiking Day (**North Fork Kings River** to **Guest Lake**, 6½ miles): First, hike the easy mile south in the canyon to the junction with the trail up Meadow Brook. Heading upstream beside the North Fork from the junction, you first cross multi-branched Meadow Brook and then swing near a large pool in the river. The trail ascends gently for about a mile and then makes four switchbacks to gain the top of a bench. The grade is again easy to the rock-and-log ford of the several channels of Fall Creek (wet in early season). About 350 yards beyond the last channel of Fall Creek is a junction with a trail climbing left to Bench Valley. We take this faint trail (not on the topo map), which climbs steeply up the rocky hillside on the south side of cascading Fall Creek.

After gradually leveling off into dense lodgepole forest, the trail meets a trail ascending from the North Fork Kings River above Big Maxson Meadow. Your route then winds along the luxuriantly foliaged banks of Fall Creek, where blossoms of shooting star, penstemon, larkspur, monkshood, monkey flower, columbine, wall-flower and paintbrush nearly fill the valley floor in season.

After traveling a small distance beside the creek, our trail climbs steeply for a short time and then moderately for a while, to reach the outlet from McGuire and Guest lakes. Here the trail begins a 300-foot series of short switchbacks which soon become rocky and steep, but suddenly we arrive at the outlet of meadow-fringed lower McGuire Lake. The lake's waters appear suddenly only a few feet from the precipitous drop-off, and from this point one can indeed ascertain the true meaning of the term "hanging valley."

Our route passes several campsites as it rounds the north side of lower and upper McGuire Lakes. Both of these lakes afford excellent fishing for brook (to 15″). Through moderate-to-sparse timber, the trail crosses an easy ridge to the fisherman's lateral that turns off the main trail and leads to Guest Lake (10,160′). Good campsites with unobstructed views of Blackcap Mountain line the north shore of this lovely granite-lined lake, and it is a fine choice as a base camp for excursions to 20 nearby lakes in this basin. At Guest Lake fishing for brook trout (to 12″) is good. Fishing in the lakes of the upper Bench Valley Basin varies from good to excellent, and offers the eager angler a creel of both brook and rainbow trout.

4th, 5th, and 6th Hiking Days: Retrace your steps, 18 miles.

Devils Punchbowl

33   Courtright Reservoir to Devils Punchbowl

Trip	From Courtright Reservoir to Devils Punchbowl via Post Corral Meadows, North Fork Kings River, Guest Lake, cross country to Devils Punchbowl, then by trail to North Fork Kings, Post Corral Meadows
Distance	42½ miles
Type	Semiloop trip
Best season	Mid to late
Topo maps	Courtright Reservoir, Ward Mountain, Blackcap Mtn., Mt. Henry 7½'

Grade (hiking days/recommended layover days)

Leisurely	—
Moderate	7/1
Strenuous	4/1
Trailhead	Courtright Reservoir (14)

HIGHLIGHTS   This loop trip will provide a good feel for the gentle wilderness west of the LeConte Divide. The rugged cross-country segment between two basins makes it a trip for experienced hiker-climbers only, but the grand vistas encountered along this route more than compensate for the demands on scrambling skill and energy.

DESCRIPTION (Moderate trip)

1st, 2nd and 3rd Hiking Days: Follow Trip 32 to **Guest Lake**, 18 miles.

4th Hiking Day (**Guest Lake** to **Devils Punchbowl** via cross country, 6½ miles): From Guest Lake follow the fisherman's trail that joins the main Bench Valley Basin Trail ascending to Horsehead Lake. This ascent winds north through a moderate cover of whitebark pines, passes Colt Lake and then it descends to the southeast shore of Horsehead Lake, where there is a campsite. After the trail arrives at the grassy fringes of Horsehead Lake, the traveler has excellent views to the east and northwest of the barren crest of the LeConte Divide. From this lake's open shores we can readily see that we have surmounted a series of hanging valleys, and that this hanging-valley chain continues in the tiny cirques carved out of the granite divide to the east and northeast.

Beyond the marshy inlet to Horsehead Lake, this route rounds the east side of the lake, fords the east inlet (from Filly Lake), and then climbs along the north inlet stream. Faint anglers' routes crisscross this drainage, and any ducks placed by well-meaning visitors should be taken with a grain of salt. Anglers passing through this country will be able to sample the brook and rainbow (to 10″) at Horsehead Lake; brook (to 8″) at Roman Four Lake; rainbow (to 11″) at West Twin Buck Lake (East Twin Buck Lake is barren); and rainbow (to 7″) at Schoolmarm Lake.

From the west side of Twin Buck Lakes we ascend northward to the outlet of Schoolmarm Lake. From there our trail climbs north-west and emerges above treeline in a high, rolling valley. After crossing two small creeks, our route ascends steeply to the saddle just north of Peak 11404. From this point, the route contours around to the notch just to the northwest and makes a steep descent into the cirque east of Devils Punchbowl. This descent should be undertaken only by experienced hikers with rudimentary climbing skills. Our route passes a small, golden-trout-filled lakelet and then makes another, less steep descent down to the first of the two little lakes above Devils Punchbowl, called Big Shot and Little Shot. After descending past Little Shot Lake, our route arrives at the moderate-to-dense forest cover at the east side of Devils Punchbowl (10,098′). There are several good campsites here, and fishing for brook (to 13″) is good. This lake is a perennial choice among anglers as a base camp for side trips into Red Mountain Basin.

5th Hiking Day (**Devils Punchbowl** to **North Fork Kings River**, 6½ miles): Follow the 4th hiking day, Trip 31.

6th and 7th Hiking Days: Reverse the 1st 2 hiking days, Trip 29, 11½ miles.

34 Courtright Reservoir to Portal Lake

Trip	From Courtright Reservoir to Portal Lake (Blackcap Basin) via Post Corral Meadows, North Fork Kings River
Distance	44 miles
Type	Out and back
Best season	Mid to late
Topo maps	Courtright Reservoir, Ward Mountain, Blackcap Mtn. 7½'

Grade (hiking days/recommended layover days)

Leisurely	6/1
Moderate	5/1
Strenuous	4/1
Trailhead	Courtright Reservoir (14)

HIGHLIGHTS   Portal Lake lives up to its name. It is indeed the door to Blackcap Basin, a beautiful, austere, granite basin forming the headwaters of the North Fork Kings River. This trip offers an encompassing look at west-slope ecology over a 2500-foot elevation span.

DESCRIPTION (Leisurely trip)

1st Hiking Day: Follow Trip 28 to **Post Corral Meadows**, 7½ miles.

2nd Hiking Day (**Post Corral Meadows** to **Big Maxson Meadow**, 8 miles): Follow the 2nd hiking day, Trip 29, to the North Fork Kings River. Then proceed to the junction of the trail to Bench Valley as described in the 3rd hiking day, Trip 32. From this junction, your Blackcap Basin Trail continues south along the North Fork Kings River. Fishing along the river continues to be good for brook and rainbow (to 12"), and occasional pools, usually located at the foot of a chute or a fall, make for fine late-season swimming. The narrowing canyon walls open briefly as the trail reaches wide Big Maxson Meadow (8480'). Formerly a sheepherders' camp, and more recently grazed by cattle, this meadow offers fair-to-good campsites at its northwest end. If used as a base-camp location, these meadow campsites are central for side trips to subalpine Halfmoon Lake and to the alpine lakes of upper Bench Valley. The trail to Halfmoon Lake leaves the meadow right across the river from the cabins in the meadow.

3rd Hiking Day (**Big Maxson Meadow** to **Portal Lake**, 6½ miles): As the trail leaves the open flats of the meadow, the traveler has excellent views east-southeast to the glacially smoothed, narrowing walls of the canyon. Bearing in the direction of these canyon narrows, our duff trail passes the main Bench Valley Trail. The louder river sounds on the right are due to the steepening slopes as our trail returns to riverside near some fine campsites under lodge-pole pines with views of beautiful pools in the North Fork. Very soon, the trail veers away from the stream again, then leads southeast for about ⅓ mile before once more approaching the river across some expansive granite slabs. Beyond these boulder-dotted slabs we traverse a bog for about 100 yards to a ford of the North Fork (difficult in early season). Immediately beyond the ford is a junction with the Blackcap Basin Trail, coming over from Halfmoon Lake.

Beyond this junction the route swings east, following the North Fork, and passes a campsite with a table and a label "Snowslide Camp." This gentle-to-steady ascent through moderate-to-dense lodgepole forest traverses some areas that have been swept by avalanches where the lodgepoles have been replaced by willows. The North Fork on our left, sometimes near and sometimes far, sometimes meandering slowly through meadows and sometimes tumbling down large slabs, contains an adequate population of golden, brook and brown trout.

About 1½ miles beyond Snowslide Camp the trail steepens, veers south toward Portal Lake, and joins its outlet stream. You climb to a meadowy area where there is a campsite on the right beside the junction with the Crown Basin Trail. Just beyond this campsite is the easy-to-miss rock ford (difficult in high water) of the outlet from Portal Lake. Beyond the ford, our trail climbs via short switchbacks to the poor-to-fair campsites on the north shore of jewellike Portal Lake. Other campsites may be found by following the trail ¼ mile to the unnamed lake northeast of Portal Lake.

4th, 5th, and 6th Hiking Days: Retrace your steps, 22 miles.

35 Courtright Reservoir to Florence Lake

Trip	From Courtright Reservoir to Florence Lake via Post Corral Meadows, Hell for Sure Pass, John Muir Trail and Blayney Meadows
Distance	42½ miles
Type	Shuttle trip
Best season	Mid to late
Topo maps	Courtright Reservoir, Blackcap Mtn., Ward Mountain, Florence Lake, Mt. Henry 7½'

Grade (hiking days/recommended layover days)

Leisurely	6/2
Moderate	5/2
Strenuous	4/1
Trailhead	Start at Courtright Reservoir (14), end at Florence Lake (7)

HIGHLIGHTS Crossing the LeConte Divide at Hell for Sure Pass, this fine shuttle trip tours the headwaters of two major Sierra drainages—North Fork Kings River and South Fork San Joaquin. This route is a tour in geological diversity, taking in some unusual and colorful nongranitic landscapes as well as a hot spring.

DESCRIPTION (Moderate trip)

1st and 2nd Hiking Days: Follow Trip 30 to **Rae Lake**, 13 miles.
3rd Hiking Day (**Rae Lake** to **Lower Goddard Canyon**, 11 miles): This is a very long day on sometimes-poor trails, with considerable elevation gain and loss and with great scenery to enjoy, so an early start is in order. Proceed to the Devils Punchbowl Trail junction as described in the 3rd hiking day, Trip 31, and go left (east). From this junction our trail ascends steadily above the meadowed

basin to the sparsely wooded bench north of Disappointment Lake. Far from being a disappointment, anglers will find the brook-trout fishing in this lake to be good to excellent (to 15″).

The trail then fords the outlet of Chagrin Lake (10,450′—just northeast of Disappointment Lake) and ascends gently, then moderately, to the north end of barren Hell for Sure Lake (10,800′). This large (58-acre) lake with its narrow northern meadow fringe occupies a large part of the upper cirque of Red Mountain Basin. Smoothed and polished slab granite rises from the lake's waters, broken only by an occasional glacial erratic or a small patch of green. The lake is a fine fishing spot for rainbow trout (to 10″).

Just beyond the slab granite, the broken slopes of talus and scree lead up to abrupt, metavolcanic-topped LeConte Divide. The notch to the northeast of Hell for Sure Lake marks Hell for Sure Pass, and the 500-foot climb to this saddle is a loose, steep, switchbacking, rocky slog. However, it is not as bad as the name would suggest, and one soon arrives at the windswept saddle of Hell for Sure Pass (11,297′). From the pass, barren Hell for Sure Lake and the bold north face of Mt. Hutton make up most of the scenery to the south, but one can see a good part of the way down the forested Fleming Creek drainage. The most impressive view, however, is of Emerald Peak, Peter Peak, Mt. McGee and Goddard Canyon to the east and northeast. Made of the dark gray volcanic rock characteristic of the Goddard area, the steep canyon walls plunge uninterrupted nearly 2500 feet to the valley floor below (not visible yet).

This breathtaking view lasts most of the steep, loose, rocky way down—a couple of long zigzags through a steep meadow, a crossing of a small bench, and a switchbacking dive down the canyon wall to the ford of the first unnamed tributary feeding the South Fork San Joaquin River. From this ford (about halfway down the 2100-foot vertical distance) the trail traverses the west canyon wall on a long, up-and-down descent that crosses two more tributaries, and meets the Goddard Canyon Trail at a junction where, in 1989, the signs sat in a pile of rocks. On the Goddard Canyon Trail we then double back northwest along the South Fork. The subsequent steady-to-moderate descent stays on the west side of the river and refords the tributaries cited above. The trail crosses over mostly rock, some talus and scree, and occasional meadowy sections. Willow clumps along the river always ensure the presence of birdlife, and the passerby is likely to encounter Brewer blackbirds, hummingbirds, fly catchers, fox sparrows, Lincoln sparrows, nuthatches, robins and an occasional finch.

We continue the gentle descent through long, lodgepole-dotted Franklin Meadow, separated from the river by a low ridge. At the meadow's north end we pass through a stock drift fence. The trail passes another drift fence a short way upstream from the John Muir Trail junction, and arrives at the fair-to-good campsites south of the wooden bridge (8470′) for the John Muir Trail near the river's confluence with Evolution Creek. Fishing for brook and some rainbow in the river remains fair-to-good despite heavy angling pressure.

4th Hiking Day (**Lower Goddard Canyon** to **Blayney Hot Springs**, 8½ miles): Quickly stepping onto the John Muir Trail, we pass but do not cross the wooden bridge and make a gentle descent on dusty underfooting through stands of quaking aspen, lodgepole and some juniper. Gardens of wildflowers line the trail, including sneezeweed, penstemon, yellow cinquefoil, pennyroyal, Mariposa lily and lupine. As the trail approaches a wood-and-steel bridge crossing of the South Fork San Joaquin River, the canyon walls narrow and rise V-shaped from the canyon floor. On the north wall one can make out the unmistakable striations carved there by ice-driven rocks in the latest glacial stage.

Our route passes several more campsites on the right, and then, just before we cross the bridge, a short spur trail leads west to some campsites on the south side of the river. Beyond the bridge, we descend a short, rocky stretch over morainal debris. This steady descent levels out through a densely forested flat ("Aspen Meadow") that is made up of postglacial alluvial deposits. An occasional Jeffrey and juniper add variety to the forest cover as the route leaves the flat and descends steeply on a rocky, dusty trail. Looking back, one has a last look at Emerald Peak, V'd by the steep canyon walls. Our route passes a sign indicating our exit from Kings Canyon National Park and entry into John Muir Wilderness and then crosses Piute Creek on a wood-and-steel bridge, where the trail to Piute and Pine Creek passes branches right (possible campsite).

From this junction our route undulates via rocky trail down the South Fork San Joaquin River canyon. The mostly sparse forest cover has changed from a predominance of lodgepole to Jeffrey, juniper, some red and white fir, and the seepage-loving quaking aspen. The trail junction where our Florence Lake route leaves the Muir Trail makes an excellent lunch or swimming stop. Now in heavy forest cover, you continue along a series of moderate ups and downs to a junction with a trail climbing north to meet the Muir Trail on the canyonside. From here you follow the last part of the 3rd hiking day, Trip 7 ("Shortly you meet the lateral . . .").

5th Hiking Day (**Blayney Hot Springs** to **Florence Lake**, 10 miles, or 5 miles using the ferry). Follow the 4th hiking day, Trip 7.

Courtright Reservoir to Crown Valley Trailhead **36**

Trip	From Courtright Reservoir to Crown Valley Trailhead via Post Corral Meadows, North Fork Kings River, Blackcap Basin, cross country to Blue Canyon, then by trail to Cabin Creek
Distance	47½ miles
Type	Shuttle trip
Best season	Mid to late
Topo maps	**Mt. Goddard** 15′; Courtright Reservoir, Ward Mountain, Blackcap Mtn., Mt. Goddard, Slide Bluffs, Tehipite Dome, Rough Spur 7½′

Grade (hiking days/recommended layover days)

Leisurely	—
Moderate	8/2
Strenuous	6/1
Trailhead	Start at Courtright Reservoir (14), end at Crown Valley Trailhead (16)

HIGHLIGHTS   This challenging, part cross-country route covers a wide range of terrain, from mighty mid-elevation forests to high, fractured granite ridges. The crossing of the White Divide requires a bit of rock climbing, though it needs no special equipment and is easy for an experienced peak scrambler.

DESCRIPTION (Strenuous trip)

1st, 2nd and 3rd Hiking Days: Follow Trip 34 to **Portal Lake**, 22 miles.

4th Hiking Day (**Portal Lake** to **Blue Canyon**, 7 miles cross country): Staying on the north side of the outlet stream from Midway Lake, our route ascends the steep, fractured granite slope above Portal Lake. One may be able to follow ducks and other signs of use up the short headwall to arrive at Midway Lake. After skirting the north shore of this lake, our route follows its inlet stream past several rocky tarns to medium-sized (32 acres) Cathedral Lake. Fair fishing for rainbow and some brook trout (to 10″) is available here. This high, alpine lake is typical of the lakes of Blackcap Basin: situated in a granite pocket, ringed by cirque walls on three sides, characterized by deep, cold waters, and relieved only by an occasional clump of willow, heather or stunted lodgepole. Our route rounds the north side of the lake, then turns southeast and climbs talus and steep granite slabs to a jagged notch at the top of a scree slope on the White Divide north of Finger Peak.

From the notch, walk right a few yards down a narrow ledge and descend into the talus-strewn cirque on the north side of Finger Peak. The traverse to Blue Canyon Pass requires little elevation loss but a large amount of boulder-hopping, which should be done with much caution. After a good mile of rugged cross-country walking, we arrive at Blue Canyon Pass, the first saddle east of Finger Peak. Views from this saddle are superlative of the White Divide, Goddard Divide and Ragged Spur, and into southern Kings Canyon National Park.

Thence our route descends by chutes to the northernmost, unnamed lakes of the Blue Canyon Creek drainage, and follows the southwestward course of this drainage over slab granite. The route veers left and drops down to the west side of granite-bound Lake 10364. From the outlet of this lake, our route crosses the stream and descends into lodgepole forest at about the 10,000-foot level, and soon we pick up a trail on the south side of the creek. From the slopes on the left, we are very apt to hear the piping of a marmot as we round the turn in the canyon that gives a view of the lovely, open meadows below. On this trail, scramble down to the head of these meadows, skirt the eastern fringe, and arrive at the log ford leading to the good campsites up and downstream from the landmark cabinsite (8430′). Fishing for brook (to 10″) in Blue Canyon Creek is good.

5th and 6th Hiking Days: Reverse the steps of Trip 42, 18½ miles.

Wishon Reservoir to Halfmoon Lake   **37**

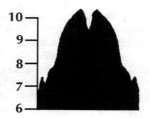

Trip	From Wishon Reservoir to Halfmoon Lake
Distance	24 miles
Type	Out and back
Best season	Early or mid
Topo maps	Rough Spur, Courtright Reservoir, Blackcap Mtn. 7½′

Grade (hiking days/recommended layover days)

Leisurely	4/1
Moderate	3/0
Strenuous	2/0

Trailhead   Wishon Reservoir (15)

HIGHLIGHTS   Halfmoon Lake is unusual. For one thing, it's at a lower elevation than most Sierra lakes, and as a result it's had more time to mature since the glaciers finished creating it. Its age gives Halfmoon Lake a gentle, timeless feel, with large trees and smooth, lichen-covered cliffs. The 3700-foot elevation gain en route traverses a wide range of intriguing landscapes.

DESCRIPTION (Leisurely trip)

1st Hiking Day (**Wishon Reservoir** to **Moore Boys Camp**, 6 miles): From the Woodchuck trailhead parking lot your trail heads south up granite benches, gaining several hundred feet. Then you turn east and climb steeply, crossing a dirt road. Soon in shade, your trail passes a spur coming in from a packer's trailhead on the left and then another coming in on the right. After 500 feet of climbing, the trail swings north and begins a traverse high on the forested ridge east of Wishon Reservoir. The trail undulates under lush forest with tall white firs, and as you pass many flower-lined creeks, you can see but probably won't hear the activity at the Pacific Gas and Electric base on the west side of the reservoir. After nearly 2 miles the trail turns east around a ridge into the canyon of Woodchuck Creek. Looking north, you can see granitic Lost Peak and other domes. Much of what you can see was under glaciers at times during the past 1 million years, and as you walk east you are on top of a moraine put here by a glacier. At this point you may hear the Helms Project Powerhouse, far across the North Fork Kings River canyon to the north.

Beyond an aspen-dotted meadow the trail turns left and descends to cross Woodchuck Creek on boulders (wet in early season). From this ford the wide, dusty trail, just downstream from a little gully, ascends gently north under tall conifers and then turns east to switchback 500 feet up a shaded slope. Beyond these switchbacks the grade is easy for over a mile past a ford of the North Fork Woodchuck Creek. A little beyond some campsites along Wood-chuck Creek is a short section of new, overconstructed switchbacks and then another gentle ascent.

About when you begin to see lodgepole pine you pass a trail to Chuck Pass branching right at an unnamed creek, which you cross via several bridges that were built from living trees in order to accommodate stock. Turning north, your trail makes a short but steep ascent over a moraine to the south end of sloping Moore Boys Camp (8710′). There is a California Cooperative Snow Survey course here where measurements of snow depth and water content are periodi-cally taken. Crossing these lush meadows in spring can be wet, but you can skirt the meadow on the east. At the far side of the meadow, beyond two collapsing cabins, is a well-used campsite near the creek. Fishing is poor for brook trout (to 6″).

2nd Hiking Day (**Moore Boys Camp** to **Halfmoon Lake**, 6 miles): Just beyond Moore Boys Camp is a junction with a trail up-canyon to Woodchuck Lake. Here, you turn east and ascend steeply to a small meadow supporting rangers button, tall mountain helenium and Bigelow's sneezeweed. You are now in Woodchuck Country, named for the many marmots in the area. (Resembling the wood-chuck of the eastern United States, marmots were misidentified by people from the East.) After further steep climbing under red fir and western white pine, you pass a second trail to Woodchuck Lake in another meadow. Continuing the climb past outcrops of ancient volcanic mudflows, you cross abrupt boundaries between wet and dry ground; one moment you're walking on dry sand, the next moment you're on mud.

Near a grove of aspen you pass a pond, and then you pass a third trail to Woodchuck Lake branching north. Beyond a second pond the trail levels off on a sandy flat. Here you pass an unmarked trail of use branching left before climbing up slabs. Ascending a gentle-sided dome, your faint, ducked trail winds between sand and slab, generally heading northeast to cross the shoulder of the 10,400-foot dome ¼ mile southeast of its summit. Only a hiker totally dedicated to pushing on up the trail could pass up the exhilarating panorama from the top of this rock island: an east-west spectrum from the LeConte Divide and Kettle Ridge down to the forested slopes west of Wishon Reservoir, and a north-south range from the Minarets near Mammoth to the high peaks of the Great Western Divide and the Kings-Kern Divide. Seen through a notch in the latter divide, Mt. Whitney doesn't seem to be the highest peak in California, but it is.

From the top of the climb you descend northeast to a junction signed CROWN PASS (10,188'), where you meet a trail going south to Crown Lake, and shortly a rough, unmaintained trail going north down Nichols Canyon. Heading east toward Blackcap Basin you wind down a granitic ridge to an overlook of Halfmoon Lake (9430'). The trail then switchbacks down an open slope to the timbered north shore of this lovely lake. Good but heavily used campsites can be found near the trail and on the peninsula bulging into the north side of the lake. Firewood is nonexistent, so please use a stove. Brook trout are plentiful in the lake (to 10").

3rd and 4th Hiking Days: Retrace your steps, 12 miles

Chimney Lake

38 Wishon Reservoir to Portal Lake

Trip	From Wishon Reservoir to Portal Lake via Halfmoon Lake and the North Fork of the Kings
Distance	37 miles
Type	Out and back
Best season	Mid
Topo maps	Rough Spur, Courtright Reservoir, Blackcap Mtn. 7½′

Grade (hiking days/recommended layover days)

Leisurely	6/1
Moderate	4/1
Strenuous	3/0
Trailhead	Wishon Reservoir (15)

HIGHLIGHTS Of the two trails to the headwaters of the North Fork Kings, this is the one less traveled. The views around Crown Pass are exceptional for the elevation—10,400 feet— and there are many side-trip opportunities, both on and off trail.

DESCRIPTION (Leisurely trip)

1st and 2nd Hiking Days: Follow Trip 37 to **Halfmoon Lake**, 12 miles.

3rd Hiking Day (**Halfmoon Lake** to **Portal Lake**, 6½ miles): On the north side of the lake, our route passes a TRAIL sign by the outlet, the trail north (left) to Big Maxson Meadow. We take the right fork, cross the creek and head east through lodgepole-pine forest. Soon we climb around a rocky ridge and then turn southeast, winding gently along a forested bench. The trail skirts a number of meadowy areas, and conies and marmots can be heard in the talus at the base of the wall on the right. After a short descent and a ford of the outlet of Maxson Lake, this trail meets the North Fork Kings River Trail coming up on the left. From this signed junction you follow the latter part of the 3rd hiking day, Trip 34 to Portal Lake.

4th, 5th and 6th Hiking Days: Retrace your steps, 18½ miles.

Wishon Reservoir to Crown Lake 39

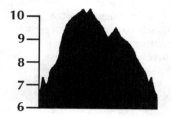

Trip	From Wishon Reservoir to Crown Lake
Distance	24½ miles
Type	Semiloop trip
Best season	Early or mid
Topo maps	Rough Spur, Courtright Reservoir, Blackcap Mtn., Tehipite Dome 7½′

Grade (hiking days/recommended layover days)

Leisurely	4/1
Moderate	3/1
Strenuous	2/0
Trailhead	Wishon Reservoir (15)

HIGHLIGHTS Everyone wants to get off the beaten path, but if everybody goes to the same unused place, it will be beaten. This guidebook attempts to offer a number of selections for solitude, so that your chances of being alone when you go to one of them will be pretty good. This excursion touches a number of such places.

DESCRIPTION (Leisurely trip)

1st Hiking Day: Follow Trip 37 to **Moore Boys Camp**, 6 miles.

2nd Hiking Day (**Moore Boys Camp** to **Crown Lake**, 5 miles): Follow the 2nd hiking day of Trip 37 to the junction of the Crown Lake Trail at Crown Pass and turn right (south) on it.

From the junction, the trail descends steeply south 400 feet to the large, lodgepole-ringed meadow of Crown Lake (9713′). Viewed from the pass, the lake does have a crownlike shape, but its west side, containing several small pools, can be quite marshy at times, and campsites are best on the east side of the lake, where the trail skirts it.

3rd Hiking Day (**Crown Lake** to **Indian Springs**, 6 miles): The trail becomes somewhat indistinct as it crosses the marshy south end below Crown Lake, but it can easily be located as it follows along the east side of the outlet creek. Here we descend easily in moderate forest, at first lodgepole, but later mixed with western white pine. Intermittent marshy patches interrupt the duff trail as it descends gently south on the east side of this creek. You pass a junction with the Scepter Lake Trail and then cross the creek. Then the trail swings west of Scepter Creek, so that it is out of sight and sound, but returns to creekside at another meadow.

Beyond this lovely meadow we cross another and then continue south up to a junction with the Chuck Pass Trail. After turning west on this level trail, we soon ford the sandy-bottomed, unnamed stream that drains Chuck Pass and then climb moderately up the southwest side of the little creek. The string of forest-bordered meadows along the creek's headwaters are, in the mountain springtime, narrow emerald ribbons interspersed with lush gardens—one of the finest series of meadows in the Sierra.

After topping out at Chuck Pass (9540'), our rocky trail leads down through heavy, parklike pine forest on a set of steep, dusty switchbacks. Soon the route passes above a rocky, snag-strewn meadow and then it descends to pass a series of sweeping green meadows, where the wildflower population boasts dozens of species. Descending gently, the trail crosses a creek and skirts a large meadow. Soon you arrive at the good campsites at the west end of the meadow beside Indian Springs, between the trail and Woodchuck Creek.

4th Hiking Day: (**Indian Springs** to **Wishon Reservoir**, 7½ miles): The trail down the valley of Woodchuck Creek, often soft and muddy from the seepage of springs, penetrates a dense forest of lodgepole pine and reaches a junction with the Hoffman Mountain Trail. Here it veers north and immediately passes the ruins of an old cabin. This sandy forest path then dips west to meet the Wishon/Halfmoon Trail at a junction passed on the first hiking day. From here we retrace our steps to the trailhead.

Crown Valley Trailhead to   **40**
Cabin Creek

Trip	From Crown Valley Trailhead to Cabin Creek
Distance	9 miles
Type	Out and back trip
Best season	Early
Topo maps	Rough Spur, Tehipite Dome 7½
Grade (hiking days/recommended layover days)	
Leisurely	2/1
Moderate	2/0
Strenuous	Day
Trailhead	Crown Valley (16)

HIGHLIGHTS   When the high country is still under snow, you can sample the Sierra springtime, with its millions of wildflowers, on this trip to a small but extremely attractive stream. This trip takes you through some of the justly famous mid-elevation forest on the west slope of the Sierra. Part of this route witnesses government-sponsored destruction of ancient forest.

DESCRIPTION (Leisurely trip)

1st Hiking Day (**Crown Valley Trailhead** to **Cabin Creek**, 4½ miles): We begin under stately sugar and Jeffrey pine and white fir. Just beyond a low rise we temporarily join a jeep road, and then cross a small Jeffrey pine plantation. Then we cross Little Rancheria Creek and begin the 1500-foot climb to Cabin Creek.

Gentle at first, our ascent passes a trail to Spanish Lake. Soon the trail becomes steep, dusty and sunny, and an early start avoids the hottest part of a summer's day. By the time we reach Three Springs, we look forward to a shady rest. In late season, however, there isn't a lot of water, due to the timber sale above. This cut has damaged, among other things, the water table and we feel the heat as we hike through it, reminded that our Forest Service always intends to cut all the way to designated wilderness boundaries. Soon, though, we pass the Finger Rock Trail and enter John Muir Wilderness.

Our trail is gentle and shady now, and we can marvel at the mighty fir forest. During autumn, you can hear the high-pitched call of the chickaree, or Douglas squirrel. Periodically, you may hear the thud of fir cones hitting the ground, telling us that it's harvest time for the chickarees. John Muir was enchanted by this dynamic "furry lightning bolt." Indeed, chickarees will race up a huge tree, cut off some cones at the top and run down with dazzling speed, energy and assertion. Equally fast at dismantling cones, the chickaree harvests the seed pods and leaves the rest in the messy piles we see scattered about the bases of trees. Here, in this sacred ancient forest, we experience a living ecosystem while in some far-off city bureaucrats and corporate executives are calculating board feet, dollars, and shiploads of woodchips sold to Japan.

Our climb tops out at 8330 feet and soon we cross an unnamed creek. Beyond a low ridge we arrive at delightful Cabin Creek (8280'). This small, flower-lined creek is quite lively and it even supports a few brook trout. Level areas can be found in the campsites just upstream.

2nd Hiking Day. Retrace your steps, 4½ miles.

Crown Valley Trailhead to Crown Creek **41**

Trip	From Crown Valley Trailhead to Crown Creek via Cabin Creek
Distance	21 miles
Type	Out and back trip
Best season	Early to mid
Topo maps	Rough Spur, Tehipite Dome 7½′

Grade (hiking days/recommended layover days)

Leisurely	4/1
Moderate	3/0
Strenuous	2/0
Trailhead	Crown Valley Trailhead (16)

HIGHLIGHTS   Few trips offer so much time among such magnificent trees, giving a lasting impression of mid-elevation forests of the western Sierra. Crown Creek, near the boundary of Kings Canyon National Park, may be difficult to cross in early season.

DESCRIPTION (Leisurely trip)

1st Hiking Day: Follow Trip 40 to **Cabin Creek**, 4½ miles.

2nd Hiking Day (**Cabin Creek** to **Crown Creek**, 6 miles): Leaving Cabin Creek, the trail climbs steeply and then crosses two easy saddles and descends past the jeep road to a little meadow where there is a junction with a trail to Chain Lakes and Hoffman Mountain. Our route then joins a jeep road and climbs over another easy ridge, then traverses the slope above Cow Meadow, leaves the jeep road, and soon comes to a junction with the Statham Meadow Trail branching right. The red-fir-and-lodgepole forest is dense as we pass Summit Meadow (incorrectly labeled "Wet Meadow" on the topo map). Just beyond a sandy flat we come to a junction with the trail to Fin Dome and Geraldine Lakes, branching right.

Our duff-and-sand trail winds through dense timber and passes a lateral on the right leading to Spanish Lakes before it arrives at the uniquely constructed Crown Valley Guard Station, where emergency services are perhaps available. Turning somewhat north, the trail descends to the lupine-infested and ghost-snagged west end of Crown Valley meadows, where we cross a small creek. The trail then winds around the fenced southern edge of the grassland, crossing several corduroy log bridges to arrive at a junction with the Tehipite Valley Trail. Just north of this junction are the half dozen or so buildings of the Crown Valley Ranch. About ⅓ mile beyond the ranch, the trail to Mountain Meadow branches left.

From here the trail descends moderately, then steeply, into the drainage of Crown Creek. Occasional tree-shrouded views of Kettle Dome, Monarch Divide and Tombstone Ridge can be had on the upper part of this descent. About 1½ miles from the ranch our trail fords little Deer Creek and then Willow Creek. Then the trail climbs an easy ridge under a dense forest cover and drops down to the campsiteless ford of Bob Creek. Ahead, on the last, steep, sandy slope above Crown Creek is a junction signed CAMPSITE, from where a lateral trail goes left, up-canyon, ¾ mile and fords Crown Creek (difficult in high water) to arrive at a campground (7040′). This site becomes overused by deer season, in late September.

3rd and 4th Hiking Days: Retrace your steps, 10½ miles.

On Mt. Hooper

Crown Valley Trailhead to Blue Canyon **42**

Trip	From Crown Valley Trailhead to Blue Canyon via Cabin Creek and Crown Creek
Distance	37 miles
Type	Out and back trip
Best season	Mid or late
Topo maps	**Mt. Goddard** 15'; Rough Spur, Tehipite Dome, Slide Bluffs 7½'

Grade (hiking days/recommended layover days)

Leisurely	7/2
Moderate	6/1
Strenuous	4/1
Trailhead	Crown Valley Trailhead (16)

HIGHLIGHTS   This trip winds through magnificent stands of fir and lodgepole before crossing lofty Kettle Ridge to Blue Canyon. The headwaters basin of Blue Canyon Creek is far off the beaten path, offering opportunities to find solitude.

DESCRIPTION (Leisurely trip)

1st 2 Hiking Days: Follow Trip 41 to **Crown Creek**, 10½ miles.
3rd Hiking Day (**Crown Creek** to **Randle Corral**, 4½ miles): Retrace your steps to the main trail, and turn left toward Crown Creek. After descending a few yards from this junction, the trail fords Crown Creek (difficult in early season) and continues eastward in fairly level fashion. As the trail nears the foot of Kettle Ridge, Kettle Dome comes into view as a granite finger. The trail crosses several small run-off streams (not all are indicated on the topo; fill your water bottle at the third stream), and at the Kings Canyon National Park boundary begins a steady climb.

For those who are interested, the 7600-foot contour marks the best place to begin a side excursion to ascend Tehipite Dome. As a historical sidelight, Frank Dusy, a local sheepherder around the turn of the century pursued a wounded grizzly bear approximately along this route. Further exploration by Dusy for grazing areas resulted in the blazing of this crossing of Kettle Ridge and the old Tunemah Trail (leading to Simpson Meadow).

The trail soon becomes very steep, with exceptionally few switchbacks, and this poor trail construction results in the trail's being heavily washed—a condition not helped by the heavy stock traffic it suffers. As the trail ascends, the forest cover thins somewhat, but still includes sugar pine, red fir, lodgepole and Jeffrey. The underbrush, for the most part, is manzanita and snowbrush.

Eventually you reach the top of the ridge; it is time well spent to detour off to the right of the trail for the unsurpassed views of the Monarch Divide, Cirque Crest, the Middle Fork Kings River watershed, and a large part of eastern Kings Canyon National Park. The panorama of the Monarch Divide encompasses Goat Crest, Slide Peak, Kennedy Mountain and Hogback Peak. Slide Peak, with its clearly defined avalanche chutes, is particularly arresting, and above the canyon's blue haze one can trace the glacial paths on the far side that left the remarkable, unnamed, finlike ridge to the east-southeast.

The trail then descends steeply from the top of the ridge, and this descent offers a different set of views, including Burnt Mountain, a little bit of Blue Canyon, Marion Peak, parts of Cirque Crest, Goat Crest and some of the Monarch Divide. The descent levels off in a meadowed bench, Randle Corral, containing a small tributary stream (unnamed), where there are several good campsites around the meadow above the ford (8200'). These campsites are due east of Kettle Dome, and about 1000 feet above the Blue Canyon floor. The creek here, though small and isolated, has a fairly large population of rainbow trout.

4th Hiking Day (**Randle Corral** to **Blue Canyon Cabinsite**, 3½ miles): The dusty, rocky trail descends by steady, steep switchbacks the remaining 1000 feet to the canyon floor. This descent meets the tributary on which the campsites for the previous hiking day were situated and then swings up-canyon as it nears Blue Canyon Creek. Ascending the rocky slopes of Blue Canyon, the trail alternates between steady and steep climbing through a moderate forest cover that includes white fir and Jeffrey pine, with manzanita and deerbrush underneath. Some cottonwoods appear along the creek, and as we climb higher some aspens, junipers and lodgepole pines join the forest's ranks. Looking back down Blue Canyon, one has **V**'d views across the Middle Fork Kings River to the "turrets" surrounding the Gorge of Despair.

Along this ascent you can enjoy the blossoms of Indian paintbrush, pennyroyal, Mariposa lily, pussy paws, scarlet gilia and larkspur. Just north of a large campsite, the trail crosses to the east side of the creek via a shallow wade-across ford, and then continues its steady climb. Above this ford, Blue Canyon Creek exhibits some inviting granite-bottomed chutes: the water slides down these chutes, which are up to several hundred feet long, and are marked at either end by cascades or waterfalls. At the head of one of these sections, the trail emerges at Blue Canyon meadows. Here, in contrast to the white-water maelstrom below, Blue Canyon Creek winds docilely in typical meadow-meandering fashion, and immediately on the left one can see the old notched-log sheepherder cabin across the creek. Good campsites lie near the cabin, and angling for brook and rainbow (to 10″) in Blue Canyon Creek is good. These campsites make a good base camp for angling and discovery side trips to the head of Blue Canyon basin.

5th, 6th, and 7th Hiking Days: Retrace your steps, 18½ miles.

Alpine gold grows high above treeline

43 South Lake to Treasure Lakes

Trip	From South Lake to Treasure Lakes
Distance	5 miles
Type	Out and back trip
Best season	Mid or late
Topo maps	**Mt. Goddard** 15′; Mt. Thompson 7½′

Grade (hiking days/recommended layover days)

Leisurely	2/0
Moderate	Day
Strenuous	½ day
Trailhead	South Lake (8)

HIGHLIGHTS   This short trip is a fine "weekender." Touching the upper reaches of a tributary of the South Fork Bishop Creek, it exposes the traveler to three life zones with a very limited expenditure of energy and time. As a bonus, the Treasure Lakes don't get the high use found just over the ridge along the Bishop Pass Trail.

DESCRIPTION (Leisurely trip)

1st Hiking Day (**South Lake** to **lower Treasure Lake**, 2½ miles): From the roadend (9760′) the trail climbs steadily along the east side of South Lake. A moderate-to-dense forest cover of lodgepole pine lines the rocky route as it meets and turns onto the Treasure Lakes Trail. Mostly over duff and sand, the trail descends to ford a stream, ascends briefly, and then descends again to a bridge over Bishop Creek's South Fork. This stretch affords good views of Hurd Peak and the backgrounding, glacially topped peaks to the north. The trail then meanders over to the outlet from the Treasure Lakes, parallels it briefly downstream, and crosses it on a log. Beyond this ford we begin a moderate-to-steep ascent on a duff-and-sand trail.

As the elevation increases, the forest cover shows increasing whitebark pine mixed with the lodgepoles, and there is an abundance of wildflowers lining the trail and clustered in the grassy patches that seam the granite. Although this trail does see some stock traffic, it is, for the most part, a hiker's trail. The ascent steepens, crosses an area of smoother granite slabs dotted with glacial erratic boulders, and fords the outlet stream from lower Treasure Lake 10668 (difficult in early season). Then, in an easy ½ mile, we arrive at the good campsites on the northeast side of that lake, directly under dramatic, pointed Peak 12047. This lake, the largest in the Treasure Lakes basin (12 acres), affords fair-to-good fishing for golden (to 12″). Anglers who wish to spend a layover day here will find that the fishing gets better in the lakes of the upper basin.

2nd Hiking Day: Retrace your steps, 2½ miles.

Highest Treasure Lake above, second and third highest below

44 South Lake to Treasure Lakes

Trip	From South Lake to Treasure Lakes, return via cross-country route to Long Lake
Distance	8 miles
Type	Semiloop trip
Best season	Mid or late
Topo maps	**Mt. Goddard** 15'; Mt. Thompson 7½'

Grade (hiking days/recommended layover days)

Leisurely	—
Moderate	2/0
Strenuous	Day
Trailhead	South Lake (8)

HIGHLIGHTS   The ascent to lower Treasure Lake carries you through wet forest densely populated with flowers, birds, and insects, up past granite ledges with expanding views of South Lake, into the subalpine zone. The upper Treasure Lakes offer alpine scenery at its best and spectacular camping among dense, wind-sheared whitebark pines. Views from the Hurd Peak saddle are well worth the steep climb, and you return via the Bishop Pass Trail past a string of lovely, forested lakes.

The cross-country segment of this trip requires route-finding skills. The terrain is steep, and taking the wrong route could be exhausting!

DESCRIPTION (Moderate trip)

1st Hiking Day: Follow Trip 43 to **lower Treasure Lake**, 2½ miles.

2nd Hiking Day (**Lower Treasure Lake** to **South Lake**, 5½ miles, part cross country): Cross the creek connecting the two lower Treasure Lakes, then follow the faint trail up along the outflow from the upper Treasure Lakes. Your route here stays near the water, though several offshoots up to your right from the trail lead to lovely overviews of the two lower Treasure Lakes. Then the trail disappears among rockfall. When you have ascended about 500 feet and are about level with the cirque holding the three upper Treasure Lakes, cross the creek and travel east (left) over a low ridge. Like the lower Treasure Lakes, these three lakes contain good populations of golden trout (to 15"). Trout were originally backpacked in by A. Parcher, son of the pioneer resort owner W. C. Parcher, and the spawn of that initial plant provide good fishing for today's anglers. There is excellent camping among the whitebarks at the northwest end of the first upper Treasure Lake (11,200').

There is no trail around these lakes. The west side of the first two is slightly easier going; then cross to the east side at the outflow of the highest lake. Continue around the lake until you are just beneath the obvious saddle 500 feet above, then aim directly for it. This ascent crosses ledges and some loose rock south of the gray, fractured slopes of the southern outlier of Hurd Peak. Grand views from this saddle include Mts. Gilbert, Johnson and Goode to the west, and the spectacular comb ridge of the Inconsolable Range rimming the South Fork Bishop Creek drainage to the east.

From the saddle, the best route descends gently north-northeast about 100 yards, then veers over beside the little stream here, paralleling it momentarily beside a short waterfall. From there you scramble and stroll almost directly to Margaret Lake, visible down the valley. On the northwest side of this lovely lake you'll find a use trail that leads northeast to the southernmost point of Long Lake. A few steps up the inlet of this lake are places to ford the inlet, which is the South Fork Bishop Creek. Then walk quickly past some incredibly overused campsites to find the Bishop Pass Trail, and turn left (north) on it.

After fording the willow-infested outlet of Ruwau Lake, your trail passes a lateral trail to that lake and then closely skirts the east shore of Long Lake. At the lake's north end you ford another inlet stream and pass the Chocolate Lakes Trail as you begin the long descent to the trailhead. The trail is dusty and overused, but it passes a number of charming pocket meadows and crosses dozens of runoff rills. Not far beyond the Mary Louise Lakes Trail we cross the outlet of those lakes on a small log bridge, and then reach the start of the Treasure Lakes Trail. Now we retrace the first mile of the first hiking day.

45   South Lake to Dusy Basin

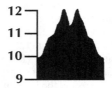

Trip	From South Lake to Dusy Basin via Bishop Pass
Distance	14 miles
Type	Out and back trip
Best season	Mid or late
Topo maps	**Mt. Goddard** 15'; Mt. Thompson, North Palisade 7½'

Grade (hiking days/recommended layover days)

Leisurely	—
Moderate	2/0
Strenuous	Day
Trailhead	South Lake (8)

HIGHLIGHTS   A popular route, the Bishop Pass Trail climbs the scenic course of the South Fork Bishop Creek to enter Kings Canyon National Park and the high, barren granitoid country of Dusy Basin. A campsite here allows you to visit the nearby lakes or you can climb over Knapsack Pass and explore beautiful Palisade Basin.

DESCRIPTION (Moderate trip)

1st Hiking Day (**South Lake** to **Dusy Basin**, 7 miles): Starting from the roadend (9760')—about ¼ mile above the South Lake dam—the somewhat rocky trail ascends through a moderate-to-dense forest cover of lodgepole, fir and aspen. This ascent traverses the morainal slope on the east side of South Lake, bearing toward Hurd Peak, and then passes a trail to the Treasure Lakes. After turning southeast, your trail soon crosses the Mary Louise Lakes outlet on a log bridge and then passes the trail to these lakes. Frequent patches of lupine, forget-me-nots, wallflowers and swamp onions delight travelers as they ford streamlets and cross swampy sections.

The trail then switchbacks up to a junction with the Bull/Chocolate Lakes Trail and levels off to reach the islet-dotted north end of Long Lake. After crossing this popular lake's outlet, it undulates along the east side of the lake (rainbow, brook and brown, to 17"). Near the lake's south end another trail goes east to Ruwau Lake, and then we cross the sparkling outlet stream from that lake to arrive in "tent city," the overused knolls above the south end of Long Lake.

The memorable vistas of the wooded and meadowed shores of Long Lake stay with visitors as they ascend through sporadic subalpine tarn-dotted meadows. Sometimes steep, this trail climbs steadily past spectacular Saddlerock Lake (rainbow to 10") and the unmarked fisherman's spur trail to Bishop Lake (brook to 14").

Beyond Saddlerock Lake, the trail passes treeline and begins a series of steep switchbacks at the head of a spectacular cirque basin. Excellent views of Mt. Goode appear on the right, and the incredible comb spires of the Inconsolable Range on the left accompany the panting climber, making breather stops unforgettable occasions. Glacially smoothed ledge granite and quarried blocks on every hand line this well-maintained trail. Occasional pockets of snow sometimes blanket the approach to Bishop Pass (11,972') late into the season, and care should be exercised in the final steep part of the ascent to the summit. Views from the pass are excellent of the Inconsolable Range to the north; Mt. Agassiz to the southeast; Dusy Basin immediately to the south, flanked by Columbine and Giraud peaks; and the Black Divide on the distant western skyline.

From the pass our route, the main trail, descends on a sometimes switchbacking southwestward traverse. (There are a couple of use trails diverging from the main trail here, but the westbound main trail is the most heavily used and generally shows the hoofprints and dung of pack animals, too.) This sandy descent contours over rock-bench systems some distance north of the basin's northernmost large lake (11,350') (not the small lake just west of Mt. Agassiz). Where the trail comes near the lake's inlet, our route branches left, leaving the trail and crossing smooth granite and tundra to the fair campsites at the west end of this lake. Other fair campsites can be found a few yards to the southwest, along the outlet stream. Fishing for golden and brook trout on this northernmost lake is fair, but anglers should try the good-to-excellent golden and brook angling (to 22") at Lake 11393 and the lake just west of it, along with the connecting stream.

Alpine scenery from the above campsites is breathtaking in its vastness. One can see the Inconsolable Range as it rises behind Bishop Pass, and the climber's Mecca, the Palisades, fills the eastern skyline. Also to the east towers symmetrical Isosceles Peak. A very sparse forest cover of gnarled whitebark pines dots the granite landscape on all sides, and the fractures in the granite are filled with grassy, heather-lined pockets.

2nd Hiking Day: Retrace your steps, 7 miles.

46   South Lake to Chocolate Lakes

```
11 ─┐
10 ─┤ ▲
 9 ─┘
```

Trip	From South Lake to Chocolate Lakes
Distance	6 miles
Type	Out and back trip
Best season	Mid
Topo maps	**Mt. Goddard** 15′; Mt. Thompson 7½′

Grade (hiking days/recommended layover days)

Leisurely	2/0
Moderate	Day
Strenuous	½ day
Trailhead	South Lake (8)

HIGHLIGHTS   The Chocolate Lakes get their name from the white-and-rich-brown peaks that form their immediate backdrop. Mirrored in the lakes, the higher peaks of the Inconsolable Range are colorful and stark. Fishing is good, and the trail well-maintained: this trip makes a grand weekend vacation for the beginning hiker or a warmup for more strenuous hikes.

DESCRIPTION (Leisurely trip)

1st Hiking Day (**South Lake** to **Chocolate Lakes**, 3 miles): Follow Trip 45 to the Bull/Chocolate Lakes Trail junction. Here our route turns left, away from the Bishop Pass Trail. Ascending moderately, the trail fords a tributary of the South Fork Bishop Creek, and arrives at sparsely timbered, moderate-sized (10-acre) Bull Lake. Rock-encircled clumps of willows alternate with grassy sections as the trail skirts the north side of the lake. Anglers may wish to sample this lake's fair brook trout fishing (to 9″) before continuing up the lake's inlet stream to lower Chocolate Lake (11,000′).

This ascent crosses rocky talus stretches as it fords and refords the stream. Breather stops offer sweeping views back across the South Fork Bishop Creek drainage to Mts. Goode, Johnson, Gilbert and Thompson. Dominating all views to the east are the barren, pinnacle-comb formations of the somber Inconsolable Range. The granitic Chocolate Lakes chain consists of three lakes that are progressively larger as one ascends the basin. Necklaced together, they hang like sapphire jewels around the northeast side of red-rocked Chocolate Peak. The trail passes several good campsites at lower Chocolate Lake. All these lakes have a fair fishery of brook (to 10″), and the upper, larger lake (11,100′) affords good campsites.

2nd Hiking Day: Retrace your steps, 3 miles.

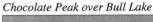

Chocolate Peak over Bull Lake

47 South Lake to Palisade Basin

Trip	From South Lake to Dusy Basin, then cross-country to Palisade Lakes, down the John Muir Trail to the Middle Fork Kings River, up to Dusy Basin, return via Bishop Pass.
Distance	37½ miles
Type	Semiloop trip
Best season	Mid or late
Topo maps	**Mt. Goddard** 15′; Mt. Thompson, North Palisade, Split Mtn. 7½′

Grade (hiking days/recommended layover days)

Leisurely	—
Moderate	—
Strenuous	6/2
Trailhead	South Lake (8)

HIGHLIGHTS   Those who yearn to go "high and light" will find this rugged route to their liking if they are qualified to tackle it. Along the way, the charming lakes of the South Fork Bishop Creek are succeeded by the splendid lakes of Dusy Basin. The incomparable Palisade crest dominates the high-altitude parts of the route, while the woodsy coziness of Palisade Creek and LeConte Canyon dominates the low-altitude parts. The ascent of Dusy Branch along cascades splashing over white granite is a scenic delight.

The cross-country segment, involving three Class 2–3 climbers' passes, requires experience and skill in navigation with map and compass, and in Class 2–3 travel with a full pack. If you have trouble finding the first climbers' pass, we recommend you not continue on the cross-country segment. Stoves are a must on this treeless route.

DESCRIPTION (Strenuous trip)

1st Hiking Day: Follow Trip 45 to **Dusy Basin**, 7 miles.
2nd Hiking Day: (**Dusy Basin** to **Lake 11672**, 6 miles cross-

country). You can contemplate crossing to Palisade Basin via any one of three climbers' passes: 1) Knapsack Pass; 2) the unnamed pass between Columbine Peak and Isosceles Peak; and 3) what has come to be known as "Thunderbolt Pass," just southwest of Thunderbolt Peak. The route described here uses Knapsack Pass (11,673'), the prominent saddle just south of Columbine Peak. Whichever route you choose, don't expect to find ducks.

Leaving your campsite at the northernmost large lake in Dusy Basin, you cross the low ridge to the east and obtain a view of Lake 11393, then wander generally southward down this upper chain of lakes. You pass one beautiful lake or pond after another, skirt pocket meadows bright with wildflowers in season, and are awed by the sheer walls of Isosceles and Columbine peaks. This route crosses the outlet of the lowest large lake in the upper basin and then bends south-southeast toward the lower end of a boulder avalanche on the southwest slope of Columbine Peak. Cross-country routes to Knapsack Pass converge here at a well-beaten path through the boulder field.

The path soon gives way to a steady, trackless ascent over heavily fractured rock. It requires a little route-finding and becomes steeper on the final climb to the pass. Impossible as it may seem, there are recorded visits to Palisade Basin via this pass with stock! Views from the pass include Black Giant, Mt. Powell and Mt. Thompson to the northwest, and the Palisade Basin and crest to the east. These peaks look as one climber expressed it, "like mountain peaks are supposed to look." Precipitous faces composed of relatively unfractured rock, couloirs, buttresses and glaciers combine to make this crest one of the finer climbing areas in the Sierra Nevada. From this vantage point, the vast, convoluted expanses of Palisade Basin appear totally barren of life except for an isolated whitebark pine or a spiring snag.

From Knapsack Pass, you keep to the left at first, ascending a little before descending moderately to steeply over talus and then a ledge system to the westernmost large lake in the Barrett chain (Lake 11468). After passing around the south end of this rockbound lake, this boulder-hopping route crosses the rocky saddle east of the lake to the largest lake of the chain (Lake 11523) and follows a fisherman's track around the north end. From this lake the sheer cliffs of the west face of North Palisade dominate the skyline, and our route continues east, climbing past several tiny, rockbound lakelets. Those preferring a less strenuous trip will enjoy an overnight in Palisade Basin.

You climb the ridge east of Lake 11523 to the saddle just northeast of point 12005. Keeping to the left, you descend a little into the shallow bowl west of Potluck Pass and pass a lakelet west of which there's a possible campsite. Continuing, you ascend the easier west side of Potluck Pass, the definite saddle between Point 12698 and Polemonium Peak. Along with the continuing views of the Palisades, this vantage point also looks across the Palisade Creek watershed to Amphitheater Lake. To the southwest the terrain seems swirled into peaks like meringue topping on a pie.

The descent from Potluck Pass is a scramble over a steep, smoothed granite ledge system, keeping to the right. This downgrade continues over scree and then levels out near an unnamed small lake. Now you scramble over a slabby ridge separating that lake from rockbround Lake 11672 (3559 metric). At this lake, there are good campsites on the west shore and just below the lake around the outlet, which becomes Glacier Creek. Fishing at this lake is poor-to-fair for golden (to 8″). Grassy sections around the sandy-bottomed lake provide a foothold for colorful alpine wildflowers, including yellow columbine, sturdy white heather and blue sky pilot.

3rd Hiking Day (**Lake 11672** to **Deer Meadow**, 5 miles, part cross-country): An early start is in order, for your cross-country ascent is followed by a 3200-foot descent whose first 1300 feet are trailless and challenging. After fording the outlet—Glacier Creek— you ascend steep granite ledges up the slope east of the creek to the saddle, called Cirque Pass (12,440′). Cirque Pass is the most difficult of the three climbers' passes on this route. The ascent is relatively short, however, and views from this saddle are good of Devils Crags and Mt. McDuffie to the west, North Palisade to the north, and Middle Palisade to the east.

Sometimes over snow, the long, steep descent on talus and ledges passes several tiny tarns in the fractured granite. Partway down, Palisade Lakes and the glacially smoothed bowl-like cirque surrounding the lakes come into view. The route levels out briefly as it crosses a bench and veers westward past a pair of lakelets. Beyond the bench, the descent becomes steeper and more exposed as it nears the little lake west of Palisade Lakes. Class 3 slabs separated by steep, wet, grassy sections are found if descending directly toward the little lake; reportedly, a Class 2–3 route can be worked out by staying more to the west as you approach the lake, where there's a possible campsite. From the little lake, the descent becomes much easier as you curve east for the final 200 feet, meeting the John Muir Trail just west of the Palisade Lakes (possible campsites; no wood fires). Those in search of a less strenuous day will enjoy an overnight stay in this area.

Westward on the Muir Trail, the route descends by seemingly endless, zigzagging switchbacks along the north side of Palisade Creek. The top of these switchbacks is an excellent vantage point from which to see the crest of Middle Palisade peak to the northeast, and in the west beyond Deer Meadow, lying immediately below,

Devils Crags, Wheel Mountain and Mt. McDuffie. Slopes on both sides of this steep descent are dramatically glacially smoothed. As the trail reaches the head of the flats above Deer Meadow, it enters a moderate stand of lodgepole and western white pine. Abundant wildflowers, including western mountain aster, Douglas phlox, pennyroyal, red columbine and tiger lily, appear as the trail comes close to the creek, and red fir, juniper and aspen occasionally mingle with the predominantly lodgepole forest cover. The trail then passes several possible campsites before fording Glacier Creek via several step-across branchlets.

The trail soon reaches Deer Meadow—not really a meadow since it is overgrown with lodgepole pines. You are now two days' walk from any trailhead, and even though you are on the Muir Trail you may find considerable privacy. In September of 1991, one of us saw grass growing in the tread of the John Muir Trail along Palisade Creek! There are several campsites here (8870'), and fishing for golden and brook trout is excellent (to 12").

4th Hiking Day (**Deer Meadow** to **Grouse Meadows**, 5 miles): About 100 yards below these campsites the trail fords the unnamed, multibranched outlet of Palisade Basin, and it then descends moderately through a moderate-to-dense forest cover. You pass a campsite about 1½ miles farther on, and then more campsites a short distance beyond that. Concentrations of wildflowers here include Indian paintbrush, penstemon, white cinquefoil, Mariposa lily and goldenrod. The underfooting is mostly duff and sand, through alternating forest and meadow, where camping and fishing are good. Then the trail veers away from Palisade Creek, only to return, passes through a drift fence, and, keeping to the north side of the creek, descends steadily over morainal debris to the confluence of Palisade Creek and the Middle Fork Kings River. A bridge used to connect the Middle Fork Kings River Trail with the John Muir Trail here, but high water destroyed it in the early 1980s, and there are no plans to replace it.

You, however, don't need the absent bridge, as your route turns right, up LeConte Canyon along the Middle Fork Kings River, and proceeds for a moderate uphill mile over an easy ridge to the overused campsites at the east side of scenic, peaceful Grouse Meadows. Sites on the meadows' edges are probably no longer legal, but there are a few hard sites to the east a little uphill of the trail. If these are full, backtrack about ¼ mile.

5th Hiking Day (**Grouse Meadows** to **Dusy Basin**, 7½ miles): Follow the 5th hiking day, Trip 59.

6th Hiking Day (**Dusy Basin** to **South Lake**, 7 miles): Reverse the 1st hiking day of Trip 45.

48   South Lake to North Lake

Trip	From South Lake to North Lake via Dusy Basin, LeConte Canyon, Muir Pass, Evolution Valley, Blayney Hot Springs, Piute Canyon and Piute Pass
Distance	60½ miles
Type	Shuttle trip
Best season	Mid or late
Topo maps	**Mt. Goddard, Mt. Abbot** 15′; Mt. Thompson, North Palisade, Mt. Goddard, Mt. Darwin, Mt. Hilgard, Mount Tom 7½′

Grade (hiking days/recommended layover days)

Leisurely	—
Moderate	7/1
Strenuous	5/0
Trailhead	Start at South Lake (8), end at North Lake (4)

HIGHLIGHTS   This trip is the quintessential High Sierra hike. In between two crossings of the Sierra backbone, it visits beautiful and famous Evolution Valley, and spends a night at a campground by a hot-spring pool which beats any hot tub. As a bonus, the nearness of the two trailheads to each other makes the shuttle almost short enough to walk.

DESCRIPTION (Moderate trip)

1st Hiking Day: Follow Trip 45 to **Dusy Basin**, 7 miles.

2nd Hiking Day (**Dusy Basin** to **Big Pete Meadow**, 6 miles): The trail from the northernmost large lake of Dusy Basin descends over smooth granite ledges and tundra sections. Occasional clumps of the flaky-barked, five-needled whitebark pine dot the glacially scoured basin, and impressive Mts. Agassiz and Winchell and Thunderbolt Peak continue to make up the eastern skyline. To the south the heavily fractured and less well defined summits of Columbine and

Mt. Goode over Long Lake

Giraud peaks occupy the skyline. This moderate descent swings westward above the lowest lakes of the Dusy Basin, and begins a series of steady switchbacks along the north side of Dusy Branch creek. Colorful wildflowers along this descent include Indian paintbrush, pennyroyal, lupine, white cinquefoil, penstemon, shooting star and some yellow columbine. Just below a waterfall, a wooden bridge crosses to the creek's east side. Views of the U-shaped Middle Fork Kings River canyon are seen constantly during the zigzagging downgrade, and on the far side of the valley one can see the major peaks of the Black Divide, foregrounded by The Citadel and Langille Peak.

As the trail descends, the very sparse forest cover of stunted whitebark seen in most of Dusy Basin gives way to the trees of lower altitudes, including western white pine, juniper, lodgepole, aspen, and some red fir near the foot of the switchbacks. The trail recrosses Dusy Branch creek at the head of a stepladdering bench, and then makes the final 1½-mile switchbacking descent, passing through a drift fence, to a junction with the John Muir Trail in LeConte Canyon. Emergency services are perhaps available from the ranger station just a few yards northwest of the junction.

Our route turns right, onto the famous Muir Trail, and ascends moderately over duff through moderate-to-dense stands of lodgepole. Langille Peak dominates the views to the left, and its striking white, fractured granite face is a constant reminder of the massive forces exerted by the river of ice that once filled this canyon. Abundant fields of wildflowers color the trailside, including corn lily, tiger lily, fireweed, larkspur, red heather, shooting star, monkey flower, pennyroyal, penstemon, goldenrod and wallflower. As the trail approaches the south end of Little Pete Meadow, occasional hemlock is found mixed with the lodgepole, and the view north at the edge of the meadow includes Mts. Powell and Thompson. There are good but heavily used campsites at Little Pete Meadow, and fishing for rainbow, golden and brook is good (to 13").

The trail from Little Pete to Big Pete Meadow makes a moderate ascent on rock and sand through a sparse-to-moderate forest cover of lodgepole and occasional hemlock. Looking back over one's shoulder rewards one with fine views of LeConte Canyon, while ahead the granite walls where the canyon veers west show glacially smoothed, unfractured faces. Some quaking aspen can be seen as the trail passes through a drift fence, ascends through Big Pete Meadow (more forest than meadow) and reaches a large area of campsites (9200').

3rd Hiking Day (**Big Pete Meadow** to **Wanda Lake**, 8½ miles): As the trail turns westward, one has excellent views of the darker rock of Black Giant, and a few yards beyond the turn the trail fords the stream draining the slopes of Mts. Johnson and Gilbert. Passing more campsites, the trail continues west on an easy-to-moderate ascent through grassy extensions of Big Pete Meadow. Most of the rock underfooting encountered to this point has been of the rounded morainal variety, but as soon as the trail leaves the westernmost fringes of Big Pete Meadow, the rock exhibits sharp, fractured edges. Over this talus, the trail ascends more steeply through a partial forest cover of western white, lodgepole and whitebark pine and some hemlock. Loose rock and sand make poor footing, while the dashing cascades of the Middle Fork offer visual relief on this steep, rugged ascent. The meadowed flat where the trail jogs north toward the tiny, unnamed lake east of Helen Lake supports a sparse forest fringe.

The ascent to Muir Pass starts with a steady climb over sand and rock through a sparse timber cover of whitebark pine. That timber cover soon disappears, giving way to low-lying heather. At the talus-bound, round, unnamed lake east of Helen Lake, the trail veers west, crossing and recrossing the trickling headwaters of the Middle Fork Kings River. Excellent views to the southeast of the Palisades and Langille, Giraud and Columbine peaks make the breather stops welcome occasions. The trail becomes rocky and the slope more

E.P. Pister

Wanda Lake and Mt. Goddard—aerial view

moderate as it passes the next unnamed lake and winds up the terminal shoulder of the Black Divide to Helen Lake. Rocks in the colorful reds, yellows, blacks and whites that characterize this metamorphic divide are on every hand. The trail rounds the loose-rocked south end of this barren lake, and ascends steadily over a rocky slope that is often covered with snow throughout the summer. Looking back, one can see the striking meeting of the black metamorphic rock of the Black Divide and the white granite just east of Helen Lake.

Muir Pass (11,955′) is marked by a sign and a unique stone shelter. This hut, erected by the Sierra Club in memoriam to John Muir, the Sierra's best-known and most-loved mountaineer, stands as a shelter for stormbound travelers. In a sense, it is a wilderness monument, and should be treated as such—leave nothing but your boot tracks. (Even human waste has become a problem in the vicinity.) From this pass the views are magnificent. In the morning light, the somber crags to the north and south relieve the intense whites of the lighter granite to the east. Situated in a gigantic rock bowl to the west, Wanda Lake's emerald-blue waters contrast sharply with its lower white edges, which, on the south side, merge into the darker rock of the Goddard Divide.

The descent from the pass is moderate and then gentle over fragmented rock, and then it levels out, passing the southeast end of Lake McDermand. Skirting the east side of Wanda Lake (11,426′), the trail affords excellent views of snow-and-ice-necklaced Mt. Goddard, and then arrives at the fair if barren campsites near the lake's outlet. The expansive views from these campsites include Mt.

Goddard and the Goddard Divide to the south, and Mts. Huxley, Spencer, Darwin and Mendel to the north.

4th Hiking Day (**Wanda Lake** to **Colby Meadow**, 6½ miles): Soon occasional wildflowers, including heather, wallflower and penstemon, can be seen as the trail descends over rock and sand. Below Wanda Lake the trail crosses Evolution Creek and stays on the west bank on a moderate descent that becomes switchbacks above Sapphire Lake. Fine views of the Sierra Crest to the east make watching one's footing a difficult task. Sapphire Lake is indeed a high-country gem, fringed with green, marshy grass, and situated on a large glacial step, with some very large trout. (In 1991, CCC crews were working on a 10-year project to reroute the trail out of the deep ruts on the meadowed edges of these lakes and onto the harder soils above them.) Our route traverses its steeper west side and, after a steady descent, refords Evolution Creek just above Evolution Lake (difficult ford in early or mid season). The trail crosses a meadowy section before winding the length of the lake's east shore. Glacial smoothing and some polish can be seen in the granite surrounding the lake, and on the abrupt walls on either side of the lake.

After passing several campsites just below the lake, the trail makes a brief northward swing before switchbacking down to Evolution Valley. This northward swing passes the trail ascending to Darwin Canyon and the route to the Darwin Glacier. The zigzagging

Evolution Lake

downgrade over morainal debris re-enters forest cover and passes clumps of seasonal wildflowers that include penstemon, paintbrush, swamp onion, lupine, forget-me-not, cinquefoil, buckwheat and tiger lily. At the foot of the grade, where the trail fords the stream emptying Darwin Canyon, our route passes more campsites, and then continues down a series of small benches through moderate stands of lodgepole to the good campsites at Colby Meadow (9840'). Fishing for golden is fair (to 9") in nearby Evolution Creek.

5th Hiking Day (**Colby Meadow** to **Blayney Hot Springs**, 12½ miles): This is a very long day, but it's almost all downhill. From Colby Meadow the route continues westward, passing McClure and Evolution meadows. The trail joining these meadows is a pathway that winds through moderate and dense stands of lodgepole and, midway down McClure Meadow, passes a ranger station (emergency services perhaps available here). The friendly intimacy of the meadows has, over the past ninety years, made this valley a favorite camping site for backcountry travelers, and one which, with the subsequent establishment of the John Muir Trail, has subjected these delicate wild pastures to serious overuse.

As our route winds past the campsites in McClure Meadow, the largest of the Evolution group, the traveler can see for himself the toll taken by the heavy traffic, both human and stock. Before controls were exerted upon grazing stock of large pack-train parties, the foraging animals trampled tender, young spring shoots of grass in such quantities as to change the meadow almost to a patchwork of barren hillocks. In the absence of grasses to hold back the water, serious erosion became a matter of concern, and today, to preserve these meadows, stock forage is limited, and the trail has been rerouted to skirt the meadows on the north side.

Our duff trail passes the drift fence below McClure Meadow on a moderate-to-steady descent that fords several tributaries draining the Glacier Divide. These fords are usually accomplished via footlogs or easy rock-hopping. Below Evolution Meadow the trail fords Evolution Creek (difficult at high water) for the last time, passes through a drift fence, and then continues west to the head of the switchbacks that drop down to the South Fork San Joaquin River. Views before the dropoff are excellent of the cascades of the stream draining Emerald Peak, the falls and cascades of Evolution Creek below the ford, and the South Fork San Joaquin River drainage.

Midway down the switchbacks, one has impressive views of Goddard Canyon. The forest cover along the zigzags is sparse-to-moderate lodgepole, juniper and some aspen, and mountain flowers seen along the trail include pennyroyal, larkspur, penstemon, cinquefoil, currant, monkey flower, buckwheat and paintbrush. The switchbacking trail crosses glacial polish exhibiting some striations, and, at the bottom, passes several good campsites as it leads through a heavy stand of lodgepoles. Just beyond these campsites, our trail crosses a footbridge, and meets the Goddard Canyon/Hell-for-Sure Pass Trail branching left. From this junction, follow the 4th hiking day, Trip 35, to Blayney Hot Springs.

6th Hiking Day: First, retrace your steps to the Muir Trail. Then follow the last paragraph of the 5th hiking day, Trip 16, from this junction to **Hutchinson Meadow**, 8 miles.

7th Hiking Day: Reverse Trip 19 to **North Lake**, 11 miles.

Looking down LeConte Canyon from near timberline

Big Pine Creek to North Fork Big Pine Creek

49

Trip	From Big Pine Creek Trailhead to North Fork Big Pine Creek
Distance	8 miles
Type	Semiloop trip
Best season	Early or late
Topo maps	**Mt. Goddard** 15'; Coyote Flat 7½'

Grade (hiking days/recommended layover days)

Leisurely	2/0
Moderate	Day
Strenuous	½ day

HIGHLIGHTS   Here's a weekend trip that gives you quick access to some big mountains. This justly popular trail leads to the Palisades, California's most ruggedly alpine area. Even though this trail is busy with both climbers and dayhikers, your campsite doesn't get much traffic. That's because your campsite is conveniently located between the climbers' camps and the trailhead campgrounds.

DESCRIPTION (Leisurely trip)

1st Hiking Day (**Big Pine Creek Trailhead** to **North Fork Big Pine Creek**, 4 miles): From the upper end of the parking lot the trail climbs an open slope, where sagebrush dominates the desert-like landscape. Very soon you pass the pack station and get a little shade before beginning a long, steady ascent along the north side of the canyon. The views warrant frequent pauses and you can well imagine how avalanches have helped shape the massive north slope of Kid Mountain, across the valley. Glacier Lodge stands at the base of this slope and is definitely in a high-risk avalanche zone. In fact, the original lodge was destroyed by an avalanche during the heavy winter of 1969. Apparently the owners couldn't take a hint.

Looking up the glacial canyon of the South Fork you can see the Palisade Crest, including Norman Clyde Peak. Norman Clyde was the premier peak climber of the Sierra and sometimes winter caretaker of Glacier Lodge. During the 1920s and 1930s he made first ascents of hundreds of major Sierra summits. Often climbing alone, he pioneered many routes that are still very challenging even by today's standards.

At the end of this stretch you turn right into the canyon of the North Fork. Just below now is Trail Camp, a walk-in campground at the top of First Falls. Passing beyond this area you soon meet a short lateral that leads down to the road by a bridge. Go down to the road and turn right, following the now-closed road to the old trailhead. In 1982 a flood washed out the road below, and this segment was never reopened, an all-too-rare case of the Forest Service making a road shorter rather than longer. The sandy roadbed reverts to regular-sized trail as you approach Second Falls, and you turn right to climb to a junction. Coming up on your right is the trail you left ¾ mile back, while dead ahead is the trail to Baker Lake. Turning left, you pass the wilderness ranger's message board. The dark, shrub-like tree you see here is mountain mahogany. There are a few blue-gray pinyon pine here, too, and together they make a sparse forest common in the eastern Sierra where the desert meets the mountains.

Climbing past Second Falls, you briefly join the shady creek and enter the John Muir Wilderness. The grade soon eases as your trail winds through Cienega Mirth, where aspen and lodgepole flourish among giant glacial erratic boulders. You pass the wilderness ranger's headquarters, the large stone house built in the 1920s by actor Lon Chaney. Catching glimpses of the peaks ahead, you climb some more as the trail swings near the creek again, only to veer away from it amid verdant, spring-fed gardens. The trail does this three times and passes a sign NO WOOD FIRES BEYOND HERE. A little beyond is a short section of rapids where the creek is close below the trail. At the top of this section, turn left down to a log bridge across the creek. On the south side of the creek are the telltale orange markers of the California Cooperative Snow Survey. This snowcourse runs through a large, open area where there are several good campsites. For better views of the mighty Palisades, you can take a short hike toward First Lake. Walking even a few hundred yards up the trail improves the views dramatically. The North Fork flows milky gray due to its load of fine glacial silt, so you may not see the many brook trout that live in it.

2nd Hiking Day (**North Fork Big Pine Creek** to **Big Pine Creek Trailhead**, 4 miles): Retrace your steps to the junction with the trail to Baker Lake. From here you can make a variation on the route you took coming up the first day; the Wilderness Press *Mt. Goddard* topo shows this variation well. From the junction, take the high trail—straight ahead—for ¾ mile to a junction with a short connector that descends to the old road by the bridge you passed on the first day. Cross this bridge and follow the road a short distance to a junction with a trail that veers left, toward First Falls. You now switchback down the shady slope just south of First Falls, passing a trail that leads up the South Fork Big Pine Creek.

At the base of the falls, which is really a series of cataracts, you recross the North Fork on a bridge. Just beyond, the trail joins a private road, and you pass several summer homes here on the north side of the North Fork. Beyond a locked gate, you meet the main public road and follow it ½ mile to the trailhead. Note that you don't return all the way to the turnoff to the trailhead but rather leave the main road and climb up the road embankment to the trailhead parking loop, which you will see when you get close to it.

Aerial view of the Palisades looking west   E.P. Pister

50 Big Pine Creek to Sixth Lake

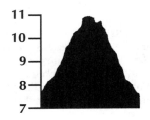

Trip	From Big Pine Creek to Sixth Lake via the North Fork Trail; return via Black Lake
Distance	16 miles
Type	Semiloop trip
Best season	Mid to late
Topo maps	**Mt Goddard** 15'; Coyote Flat, Mt Thompson, North Palisade, Split Mountain 7½'

Grade (hiking days/recommended layover days)

Leisurely	4/1
Moderate	3/0
Strenuous	Day
Trailhead	Big Pine Creek (9)

HIGHLIGHTS This spectacular trip retraces the path of ancient glaciers all the way to the top of the Big Pine Creek drainage at Sixth Lake. Here you will be in the throne room of the mountain gods, close up to the Palisades—one of the highest and most jagged crests in the contiguous 48 states. These colorful 13,000–14,000-foot peaks also hold the largest glacier in the Sierra, which you will be able to see from the trail. Even with these attractions, Sixth Lake is off the beaten path since it's away from the climbing routes and beyond the range of most hikers.

DESCRIPTION (Leisurely trip)

1st Hiking Day: Follow Trip 49 to the **North Fork of Big Pine Creek**, 4 miles.

2nd Hiking Day (**North Fork of Big Pine Creek** to **Sixth Lake**, 4 miles): Rejoin the trail and head upstream, crossing the tiny, meadowy north fork of the North Fork. Climbing moderately, the trail switchbacks through open aspen where a multitude of flowers beckon the eyes and nose, including the large globular flowers of swamp whiteheads. At the junction with the trail to Black Lake you turn left and wind over a low, glacially polished ridge, staying far above First Lake. Coming closer to Second Lake, you may start to crane your neck to see Temple Crag. Third Lake offers you the most awe-inspiring view of the massive cathedral of Temple Crag, fluted with a multitude of colorful pillars carved in stone. It's no wonder that climbers come here from around the world to attempt climbs with names like The Moon-Goddess Arete, The Sun-Ribbon Arete and Dark Star. First, Second and Third lakes are milky turquoise due to the fine glacial sediment suspended in the water. This fine sediment is produced as the glaciers grind away at the rocks under them.

Turning northwest from Third Lake you climb to a signed junction with the Sam Mack Trail, which heads southwest toward Palisade Glacier. Continuing northwest, you soon arrive at a four-way junction. Fifth Lake is ⅓ mile to the left and Black Lake is 1 mile to the right. You go forward around the west side of Fourth Lake and climb to a streamside trail junction. A brief detour to the right puts you at a breathtaking ridgetop camping area. The diverted stream channel here once fed water to Fourth Lake Lodge, a wilderness hotel that was built in the 1920s. The lodge had one stone house and 8 wooden cabins, and could be reached only by trail. After this area was included in the 1964 Wilderness Act, the Forest Service dynamited the stone house and removed the other cabins. You can still see pieces of the stone house. It's tragic that the stone house, at least, wasn't left as a public shelter.

From the junction the trail follows the creek for ¼ mile and then climbs steeply over a low ridge. Before your faint trail descends very far toward Fifth Lake, you turn right at an unsigned junction. The trail hugs the base of a cliff and then crosses a talus field (large boulders). Stay at about the same elevation as you cross the talus in order to find the trail on the other side. Now it's a short, gentle ascent to the meadowy outlet of Sixth Lake (11,100'). Cross the outlet and veer right a few hundred feet to one of the excellent campsites on the low rise near the lake. Seventh Lake is an easy hike from here (closed to camping), and you will find incredible landscapes in every direction. Fishing is good for brook trout (to 10").

3rd Hiking Day (**Sixth Lake** to **North Fork Big Pine Creek**, 4 miles): Retrace your steps to the four-way junction on the south side of Fourth Lake. Turn left onto the Black Lake Trail and head east, crossing the outlet of Fourth Lake. Soon you climb over a low ridge, where you catch glimpses of jagged, spiring peaks through the trees. A short descent brings you to the south shore of Black Lake. Continuing your descent, you cross the outlet and leave forest cover.

Here the plant community changes abruptly into an open, desert-like environment, complete with the spicy aroma of sagebrush. As you descend steadily, you have wide-open views of Temple Crag, Mt Sill and North Palisade. This is a good place from which to picture the ancient streams of ice that poured down this canyon, scooping out the basin of Second Lake, rising over the subsequent bedrock ridge and falling again to scoop out the basin of First Lake. Several long switchbacks return you to the trail junction that you passed on the way up. From here you know the way back to the campsite below.

4th Hiking Day. Retrace the steps of the 1st hiking day, 4 miles.

Amphibians are sensitive environmental indicators

Calvin Lee

Sawmill Creek Roadend to Sawmill Lake **51**

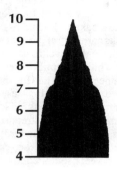

Trip	From Sawmill Creek Roadend to Sawmill Lake
Distance	16 miles
Type	Out and back trip
Best season	Early
Topo maps	Aberdeen 7½′

Grade (hiking days/recommended layover days)

Leisurely	—
Moderate	—
Strenuous	2/0

Trailhead   Sawmill Creek Roadend (11)

HIGHLIGHTS   This extremely strenuous trip starts up from hot Owens Valley at 4700 feet and ends at a lovely, cool lake at 10,000 feet. The long, steep, exposed climb may give you the satisfaction of getting high on your own sweat.

Only experienced hikers in top condition should undertake this long, steep, hot grunt.

DESCRIPTION (Strenuous trip)

1st Hiking Day (**Sawmill Creek Roadend** to **Sawmill Lake**, 8 miles): The route up from the trailhead climbs a hot, dry, sage-covered slope. In early summer, this desert slope is splashed with flowering shrubs and blossoms of bright blue woolly gilia and yellow and white buckwheat. From the trail you look down on the Big Pine volcanic field, spotted with reddish cinder cones and black lava flows that erupted from the west side of Owens Valley. At the top of the sage climb you see a line of trees on the crest. At this crest you suddenly enter different terrain. Molded rocks rise toward you and Sawmill Canyon opens up, with the waters of Sawmill Creek visible as a white ribbon 1000 feet below. The path descends slightly, then contours and finally climbs along the precipitous north wall of Sawmill Creek canyon. As we near the sloping ridge called The Hogsback, Jeffrey pines, oaks and white firs make a most welcome appearance. If one looks carefully at the lower end of The Hogsback, one can spot the remains of the Blackrock sawmill and flume, dating from the 1860s, after which Sawmill Creek and Sawmill Pass are named. For some distance above The Hogsback, one can occasionally see stumps, felled trees, and logs used as "gliders" in this century-old operation to supply Owens Valley miners with lumber.

The trail climbs to meet a tributary stream north of The Hogsback, the first water on this hot climb. You ford this creek three times before crossing The Hogsback. Once over the top of this long, rounded ridge, the path veers south, contouring and climbing on a moderate grade back into the main canyon, and reaches Sawmill Meadow, boggy and lush green in early summer, but drying considerably as the months progress. Beyond, the trail follows the creek, then zigzags steeply upward through Jeffrey pine and red fir to Mule Lake, perched on a small bench high up the canyon. Then you climb through a jumbled mass of metamorphic rocks that are home for a large colony of grass-harvesting conies. After crossing a creek you finally arrive at the northeast shore of beautiful Sawmill Lake (10,023'). Good campsites under clumps of foxtail pine are located here, and fishing for rainbow trout is fair to good.

2nd Hiking Day: Retrace your steps, 8 miles.

Sawmill Creek Roadend to Twin Lakes **52**

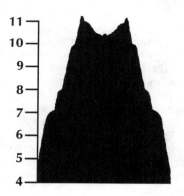

Trip	From Sawmill Creek Roadend to Twin Lakes via Sawmill Pass
Distance	28 miles
Type	Out and back trip
Best season	Mid or late
Topo maps	Aberdeen, Mt. Pinchot 7½′
Grade (hiking days/recommended layover days)	
Leisurely	—
Moderate	—
Strenuous	4/0
Trailhead	Sawmill Creek Roadend (11)

HIGHLIGHTS This trip begins with a horrendous 6700-foot ascent to Sawmill Pass. Enroute you have a chance to admire the improbable century-old sawmill hanging on a cliffside over the creek, built so that the logs could drop 2000 feet in a flume to the valley floor where you began. After reaching the pass, you go through the headwaters of Woods Creek into a high basin clothed with whitebark pine, textured meadows, and multihued alpine flowers.

Only if you are in top condition and acclimated to high altitude should you attempt this trip.

DESCRIPTION (Strenuous trip)

1st Hiking Day: Follow Trip 51 to **Sawmill Lake**, 8 miles.

2nd Hiking Day (**Sawmill Lake** to **Twin Lakes**, 6 miles). Above Sawmill Lake the trail winds up through a thinning forest of foxtail and whitebark pine, passes a lakelet, crosses a small treeline basin, and climbs steeply upward to Sawmill Pass (11,347'), on the border of Kings Canyon National Park. From the pass you walk northwest across nearly level talus and sand, then drop into a resplendent lake-dotted alpine basin, the headwaters of Woods Creek. The trail winds westward, gradually descending as it passes just north of two small, nameless lakes. The largest body of water in the basin—Woods Lake—is a short cross-country jaunt south of the trail. Excellent, secluded campsites abound here and at each of the many lakes nearby. Our route descends to the lower end of the basin, then turns abruptly north to climb and contour along the lower slopes of Mt. Cedric Wright. Spectacular views unfold southward down Woods Creek canyon. Here, very rough trail alternates with places showing recent trailwork. Finally, the trail drops to the North Fork Woods Creek, meets the John Muir Trail 100 feet west of the creek at an unsigned junction, and turns right on it. The trail then veers away from the creek into an avalanche area. A short half mile up, you turn off onto the Twin Lakes Trail. Follow it northeast to the good campsites on the west shore of Lower Twin Lake (10,565').

3rd and 4th Hiking Days: Retrace your steps, 14 miles. When returning, shortly beyond the avalanche area on the Muir Trail, look for the unmarked but obvious trail on the left as you near Woods Creek.

Woods Lake basin

Sawmill Creek Roadend to   **53**
Taboose Creek Roadend

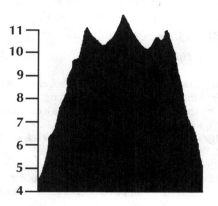

Trip	From Sawmill Creek Roadend to Taboose Creek Roadend via Sawmill Pass, Twin Lakes, Bench Lake and Taboose Pass
Distance	35½ miles
Type	Shuttle trip
Best season	Mid or late
Topo maps	Aberdeen, Mt. Pinchot, Fish Springs 7½′

Grade (hiking days/recommended layover days)

Leisurely	—
Moderate	—
Strenuous	4/1
Trailhead	Start at Sawmill Creek Roadend (11), end at Taboose Creek Roadend (10)

HIGHLIGHTS   So taxing is this trip that you will often have the trail and campsites to yourself. Just beyond Sawmill Pass you could spend days exploring the many unnamed lakes nestled among glaciated boulders and wind-shaped whitebark-pine trees, fishing, photographing or experiencing the wilderness quiet. The trail from Sawmill Pass to Taboose Pass brings you through highly varied and endlessly beautiful terrain, with expansive views into vast cirques and vivid peaks. There is water nearby, with wildflowers and wildlife, over much of your route.

This trip begins with a brutal 6700-foot climb, the first part exposed and waterless, much of it on very sandy trail. The Taboose Canyon descent, while spectacular, is a bruising 6000-foot, steep, unending knee strain over unmaintained trail often impeded and sometimes obliterated by rockslides. Only experienced hikers in the peak of condition at high altitude should venture here.

DESCRIPTION (Strenuous trip)

1st and 2nd Hiking Days: Follow Trip 52 to **Twin Lakes**, 14 miles.

3rd Hiking Day (**Twin Lakes** to **Bench Lake**, 9 miles). Retrace the half mile to the John Muir Trail and turn right. In about a mile the trail angles left toward Pinchot Pass. It leaves expansive meadows to switchback up over granite to the pass (12,110′). At the pass Mt. Wynne nudges your elbow on the east; you can see Mt. Pinchot itself north of Mt. Wynne, and to the northeast a valley of lakes shimmers below. You follow the switchbacks down to cross an icy rivulet; then you descend over granite benches, through boulder fields, toward magnificent Lake Marjorie, passing two stark lakelets. Soon you encounter stunted whitebarks, and the trail passes along the east shore of the lake. The setting is as richly colorful as any in the Sierra: to the left, ramparts of steel-gray granite rise abruptly from the lake. South, above the lake's head, are slopes of black and ruddy brown. Just visible if you look back at the skyline is the dark notch of Pinchot Pass. Excellent camping is found near the outflow of Lake Marjorie.

The trail descends gently, passing near several lakes. There is idyllic camping at each one. (One of us spent three days camped at one of these small unnamed lakes; a pair of ducks lived in a willow at the lake's edge and patrolled the lake early and late in the day.) Whitebarks give way to clumps of lodgepole pine where you pass through rocky meadows. As you walk past a fairly large lake below to your right, you may see a large tent: a ranger camps there at intervals during the summer months. Shortly beyond this lake, the unmarked but clearly visible trail to Bench Lake leaves to the left. You can recognize this intersection in two ways. There have been no trees for a bit, but there are two lodgepoles to the left at the trail junction. Also, if you have veered right and crossed a stream on the John Muir Trail, you have missed the Bench Lake turnoff: it's about 30 feet behind you. The easy trail leads west across a flower-bedecked meadow, descends a short distance, and then contours southwest along a granite bench under a canopy of lodgepole pines. You ford a shallow stream, pass two small tarns, and in 1½ miles from the John Muir Trail reach the northeast shore of Bench Lake

(3218 meters). In the clarity of its waters and in its splendid setting amid granite peaks and spurs, this sparkling jewel has few peers in the High Sierra. The distinctive pyramid of Arrow Peak reflects starkly in the lake's waters. Many fine campsites are located among the lodgepoles along the north shore.

4th Hiking Day (**Bench Lake** to **Taboose Creek Roadend**, 12½ miles): Rise early. This will be a long, arduous day. Retrace your steps to the John Muir Trail and turn left onto it. Immediately you ford a stream and shortly meet a junction with a trail to Taboose Pass, which forks to the right. Follow the Taboose Pass Trail as it makes its erratic way upward and the footing deteriorates. In compensation, increasingly splendid views of the Upper Basin of Kings Canyon open to your left. You leave forest cover and enter a vast meadow, continuing steadily northeast and upward toward Taboose Pass. The pass itself (11,418'), marked by a large sign, is a moonscape of boulders. You begin your arduous descent switchbacking down through very rocky, very steep terrain. Occasional rockslides obliterate the trail though they do not worsen the already miserable footing. In a little over a mile from the pass you reach Taboose Creek and the first whitebarks. There is sparse but good camping here. You cross the creek and continue your descent, hemmed in by rust-colored cliffs. Next you reach a choice point: you can recross the stream or continue downward on the north side. Both routes work. You descend steadily eastward through thickets of chinquapin, willow and other greenery. When you next ford the creek, at about 9240 feet (2800 meters, near the "C" in "Creek" on the *Mt. Pinchot* topo map), you again find camping. Then the footing eases somewhat as the trail changes to sand. You pass through white firs and Jeffrey pines and come to beautiful but waterless camping. The trail reverts to gravel and rock as you continue steeply down canyon, and the views in front change as the canyon twists; Owens Valley lies below you, far, far away. Finally, the trail crosses the creek for the fourth time. At last you exit the canyon walls and traverse a sage-covered moraine to the Taboose Creek roadend.

54   Sawmill Creek Roadend to Oak Creek

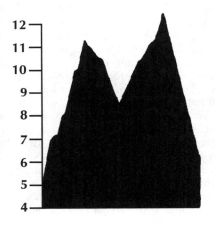

Trip	From Sawmill Creek Roadend to Oak Creek Roadend
Distance	33½ miles
Type	Shuttle trip
Best season	Mid
Topo maps	Aberdeen, Mt. Pinchot, Mt. Clarence King, Kearsarge Peak 7½′

Grade (hiking days/recommended layover days)

Leisurely	—
Moderate	—
Strenuous	4/1
Trailhead	Start at Sawmill Creek Roadend (11), end at Oak Creek Roadend (12)

HIGHLIGHTS   Another trip for those in top condition, this strenuous jaunt uses a small piece of the John Muir Trail to furnish passage between two out-of-the-way, lake-dotted alpine basins—the headwaters of Woods Creek and the Baxter Lakes basin.

DESCRIPTION (Strenuous trip)

1st Hiking Day: Follow Trip 51 to **Sawmill Lake**, 8 miles.

2nd Hiking Day (**Sawmill Lake** to **Woods Creek Crossing**, 8½ miles): Follow the 2nd hiking day, Trip 52, to the John Muir Trail and turn left (south) on it.

Your path veers southwest, ever dropping, following the U-shaped canyon left by the glacier that flowed down Woods Creek. You pass a fine campsite on the left, and when you abruptly emerge from the forest, the great trough of Woods Creek opens in full grandeur ahead. For the next 3 miles, the trail descends through the gorge, sometimes alongside the joyous creek but more often well above it, through tangled thickets of dwarf aspen, willow and other greenery. Wildflowers add an abundant splash of color, and you may see paintbrush, larkspur, purple aster, mountain violet, Bigelow's sneezeweed, Labrador tea and yarrow.

A ribbon of white water plunges from the dark cliffs high on the left. We cross several benches shaded by isolated clusters of lodgepoles, then ford the White Fork of Woods Creek (sometimes difficult in early season). Ahead is the great bend of Woods Creek, with the stupendous ramparts of King Spur as a backdrop. A descent over rocky terrain brings us back into the forest, now consisting of Jeffrey pines and gnarled junipers. The trail fords another side stream and drops alongside Woods Creek, its white froth spilling wildly over huge, inclined granite slabs. On the final descent to the canyon floor, manzanita provides a thick and thorny ground cover, with scattered Jeffrey pines for shade. At a major trail junction, the fork to the right is the Woods Creek Trail down to Paradise Valley; the Muir Trail goes left, and so do we. Where we re-reach Woods Creek (8493'), it is swollen to river proportions by the addition of its South Fork's waters, but a bridge may be there. Fair campsites, shaded by tall aspens and verdant white alders, are on both sides of the creek. Fishing for brook and rainbow trout (to 10") is fair to good.

3rd Hiking Day (**Woods Creek Crossing** to **Baxter Lakes**, 7 miles): After crossing the creek (difficult in early season if no bridge), we turn southeast and begin the long climb up the South Fork. Juniper and red fir provide forest cover as we pass several adequate campsites on the left, along the creek. Also to the left, half-hidden by foliage, is one of Shorty Lovelace's pigmy log cabins. Shorty ran a trap line through this country during the years before Kings Canyon National Park was established. Remains of his other miniature cabins are located in Gardiner Basin and along Bubbs Creek.

Presently the trail rounds the base of King Spur and climbs well above the stream, through alternating stretches of lush greenery and patches of wildflowers, and sparse forest of aspen, red fir and lodgepole pine. We jump the rivulet that hurries down from Lake

10296 and enter an open, rocky area. Beyond, a wooden span provides an easy crossing of a boggy meadow.

From the meadow, the trail climbs over a rocky ridge and fords the major creek descending from Sixty Lake Basin, passing through a gate in a drift fence. There are several small campsites here, under scattered pines. Across the canyon, Baxter Creek stitches a ribbon of white down the rock-ribbed slope. The trail climbs through rocky terrain, then approaches the main creek, passing a lodgepole-sheltered campsite on the left before again breaking into the open and ascending bouldery terrain. Ahead looms the peaked monolith of Fin Dome, heralding your approach to the beautiful Rae Lakes. To your right are the impressive steel-gray ramparts of King Spur. In contrast, the massive, sloping Sierra Crest in the east is made up of dark metamorphic rocks. The long black striations that cross the face of Diamond Peak and the ridge north of it are metamorphosed lava, visual evidence of ancient volcanic activity.

Finally this long ascent climbs over a low, rounded spur and abruptly reaches the northernmost of the Rae Lakes chain, jewel-like Dollar Lake. The setting here is magnificent; lodgepoles crowd the shore amid granite outcroppings, and Fin Dome, along with some blackish spires beyond, provides a jagged backdrop for the mirroring blue waters of the lake. (It is illegal to camp at Dollar Lake.) Look north across this lake's outlet for a little ridge that trends northeast-southwest. Cross the outlet to get to that ridge, and pick up the unsigned, faint Baxter Pass "Trail" on it.

Our route crosses the valley and then diagonals north up the valley's east wall, sometimes very steeply, over scree. From it we have fine views down the canyon of the South Fork. On the far side, a very evident line is the John Muir Trail, and most likely we will see a number of hikers on this wilderness boulevard. After a mile of ascent, the trail descends down into the Baxter Creek drainage, into a handsome grove of foxtail pines that give welcome shade. Then it swings east to continue the steep ascent to Baxter Lakes. The route here may be ducked but is sometimes hard to see as it follows the course shown on the topo map. The sparse forest cover thins as the route fords Baxter Creek and passes several tiny lakelets. Fair campsites may be found in a grove of whitebark pines below the highest lake (11,150′), where fishing for brook trout (to 12″) is good.

4th Hiking Day (**Baxter Lakes** to **Oak Creek Roadend**, 10 miles): After rounding the north side of the highest and largest lake in the basin (last reliable water until you are below timberline on the other side of the pass), the trail turns south as it ascends the steep scree slope above the lake. Excellent views of Mt. Baxter and

Acrodectes Peak to the north accompany the climb, and the coloring of the scree is extraordinary. Our mostly rocky footpath ascends southwest, mostly on a steep grade, and then descends momentarily across a snowfield. Even in this high, mineral world the vegetable kingdom stays alive, in the form of small specimens of alpine sorrel, Davidson's penstemon and Sierra primrose. Finally the trail twists steeply up to scree-laden Baxter Pass (12,320'), where one has fine views of the Sierra Crest, including multistriped Diamond Peak to the southwest, the North Fork Oak Creek canyon to the south, looking like a vertical-sided, giant gash, and even the town of Independence, far below in Owens Valley.

The east side of Baxter Pass involves a descent of 6300 feet in 9 miles on an irregularly maintained trail through a narrow canyon of rotten rock. This descent calls for patience and care. The upper 1300 feet are scree, and the route is subject to washouts and slides, so you may encounter precipitous detours over loose rock and unexpected fords. It generally stays well away from the creek, limiting your opportunities for water. The lower slopes may be heavily over-grown. Expected campsites may have been buried under rubble or be filled with chaparral. Along the trail in 1990, places combining level open ground and access to water included a bench near 11,000 feet next to the creek and another one near 8700 feet, with a very steep trail of use 75 feet down to the creek. In spite of these difficulties, breather stops allow us to enjoy the spectacular scenery and the patches of very colorful wildflowers that include monkey flower, arnica, milfoil, cinquefoil, pennyroyal, buckwheat, spiraea, gilia and penstemon.

As we descend below the bench near 8700 feet, the route begins to resemble a trail. We ford the creek (difficult in high water) in the middle of a mixed forest cover, and soon embark on another long set of zigzags. These are succeeded by a gentle, sandy descent ending with a few more quick switchbacks down to a last crossing of the rubble-filled main creek. As the trail drops to the creek, one encounters a good sampling of typical east-side Sierra flora including rabbit brush, bitter brush, sagebrush and mountain mahogany. Recent washouts may have erased the trail, but you can escape the creek bed by climbing north over a heap of boulders and picking up a sandy trail that soon dips under black oaks, crosses a tributary, and emerges on a exposed ridge. Descend this ridge past the wilderness boundary to the parking area under the welcome shade of oak trees.

55 Lewis Creek to Kennedy Lakes

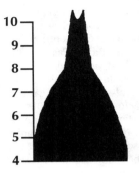

Trip	From Lewis Creek via Kennedy Pass to Kennedy Lakes
Distance	23 miles
Type	Out and back trip
Best season	Mid or late
Topo maps	Cedar Grove, Slide Bluffs 7½′

Grade (hiking days/recommended layover days)

Leisurely	—
Moderate	—
Strenuous	4/0
Trailhead	Lewis Creek Trailhead (17)

HIGHLIGHTS   This steep, little-used route climbs over 6000 feet to well-named Monarch Divide. Ascending the Lewis Creek drainage, the trail passes through many different habitats and plant communities. Since much of this drainage has experienced fire in recent decades, you get an exceptional tour of fire ecology and forest succession.

DESCRIPTION (Strenuous trip)

1st Hiking Day (**Lewis Creek** to **Frypan Meadow**, 6 miles): Ignoring a trail-of-use that leads off to the right and heading north from the parking area, you make a few short switchbacks under shady incense-cedar, ponderosa pine and black oak. Once beyond the mouth of Lewis Creek canyon, the cover diminishes, for much of this drainage was burned, at different times, between 1979 and 1984. As a result, much of this trip crosses areas that are in different stages of forest succession. By the time you reach Kennedy Pass, over 6000 feet above, you will have seen how the plant communities along the way are well-adapted to periodic fires. Along many of the open slopes you can see manzanita and snowbush that was burned to the ground. These same plants have since sprouted new growth from the crowns of their roots.

Climbing moderately, you make two more sets of switchbacks before the grade eases in a Jeffrey-pine forest where fragrant kit-kit-dizze forms an extensive ground cover. Conifers, especially pines, benefit from fires because the heat helps open their cones so seeds can reach the soil, and fire also clears the ground so young trees can get enough sun.

Beyond a junction with the Hotel Creek Trail you stay on the Lewis Creek Trail and descend to cross a small stream whose channel was the path of a debris flow in 1984. The deposits of mud and tree stumps that mark a debris flow will be gone in a few years, but you may see the tell-tale signs elsewhere, since this phenomenon is common in the Sierra. A debris flow, like a conventional flood, indicates excess runoff, but unlike a flood, a debris flow is viscous and slow-moving, being composed not only of water but also dirt, rocks, trees, snow—anything available. Beyond the creek you climb unevenly under canyon live oak, where western fence lizards scurry along the trail as you walk. Soon you reach the ford of Comb Creek (difficult in early season). Beyond the ford you leave shade for a while as you climb through sunny stands of young Jeffrey pines, indicating that you are crossing another burned area.

Shade trees reappear near the ford of Lewis Creek (difficult in early season). Beyond the ford you climb moderately past Jeffrey pines showing signs of a ground fire: their trunks are blackened only near the ground. The route then becomes steep and dusty, but you have good views of Comb Spur to the east and the Great Western Divide in the distance. Just beyond a junction with a trail to Wildman Meadow, the grade eases and you enter Frypan Meadow. Near the upper end of the flowery glade is a well-used campsite under towering white firs. This campsite is just below the Grizzly Lakes Trail junction. Unfortunately, the last California grizzly was shot near Kings Canyon in 1926, but there are still black bears nearby, so hang your food accordingly.

2nd Hiking Day (**Frypan Meadow** to **tarns, upper Kennedy Canyon,** 5½ miles): Between Frypan Meadow and Kennedy Pass the trail climbs 3000 feet in 5 miles, and the last 1600 feet are both waterless and very steep. Initially the trail makes an undulating ascent under tall conifers, fording two creeks and then Lewis Creek.

From here the trail makes several switchbacks and then begins a traverse around the south side of Kennedy Mountain. In ½ mile the forest diminishes and soon you are climbing on a sunny, manzanita-covered hillside. Far to the south are the Great Western Divide and the Kings-Kaweah Divide. The trail then enters an extensive grove of aspens, where many flower-lined creeks provide cool rest stops. Aspens, as well as the flowers you see here, are well-adapted to fire; this verdant hillside was quite charred after a fire in 1980.

Beyond the largest and last creek you leave aspen behind as you begin the last, steep 1600 feet to the pass. As you gain altitude, other tree species are left behind, too, and the end of the climb is through sparse whitebark pines. Upon reaching Kennedy Pass (10,800′) you are greeted by an extensive view over the Middle Fork Kings River canyon into northern Kings Canyon National Park. From the pass you can see several small tarns to the north, where you can find good campsites. The descent to the first tarn is very steep and may be difficult or dangerous if there is a lot of snow.

3rd and 4th Hiking Days: Retrace your steps, 11½ miles.

Lewis Creek to Volcanic Lakes 56

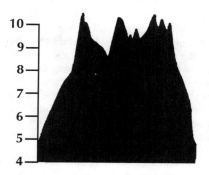

Trip	From Lewis Creek to Kennedy Pass, cross-country to Volcanic Lakes, return via Granite Pass, Granite Lake, Cedar Grove
Distance	54 miles
Type	Shuttle trip
Best season	Mid or late
Topo maps	Cedar Grove, Slide Bluffs, Marion Peak, The Sphinx 7½'

Grade (hiking days/recommended layover days)

Leisurely	—
Moderate	5/1
Strenuous	4/0
Trailhead	Start at Lewis Creek Trailhead (17), end at Cedar Grove Roadend (18)

HIGHLIGHTS   The lofty Monarch Divide separates the gigantic chasms of the South and Middle forks Kings River. The canyon of the Middle Fork is the deepest in North America, and you will be looking right down at a large expanse of it from the top of the Monarch Divide. This bold route, involving cross-country work, is for strong, experienced hikers only.

DESCRIPTION (Strenuous trip)

1st and 2nd Hiking Days: Follow Trip 55 to **tarns, upper Kennedy Creek canyon**, 11½ miles.

3rd Hiking Day (**tarns, upper Kennedy Canyon**, to **Granite Lake**, part cross-country, 5½ miles): The cross-country route to

Granite Pass is short, but one can easily spend a whole day exploring the mostly treeless upper Volcanic Lakes basin. From the tarns near Kennedy Pass follow the switchbacking trail toward Kennedy Creek until you are just above a little lake on your right. Turn right and go past the left side of the lake and straight up the hill to the northwest shore of East Kennedy Lake (poor campsites). Beginning at the outlet of East Kennedy Lake, we skirt the north shore for a few hundred feet and then head uphill. Staying on the left side of the slope, our route passes through the little forested area and arrives at the top of the ridge. A little to the left of the shallow saddle is an excellent viewpoint. From it we can see Mt. Gardiner and the Kings-Kern Divide above the Monarch Divide, and also Arrow Peak, the Palisades, the Black Divide, Mt. Goddard, and the Sierra Crest beyond.

From about 50 feet south of this point the route descends down a grassy gully that leads toward the head of the largest of the Volcanic Lakes. Near the lake, the slabs can be avoided by walking several dozen yards to the right. From the head of the lake, follow the inlet stream toward the highest two Volcanic Lakes, where there are rainbow and golden trout (to 16″). Walk around the rocky north side of the first lake and cross the low saddle to the northeast. It's worthwhile strolling up to the highest lake: nestled under the Monarch Divide, this lake presents a scene of alpine splendor at its finest. Just below the saddle is a fishless lake. Descend to its south shore and walk around the east side to where two points of rock jut into the lake.

From here a grassy gully angles up, right, to the top of the ridge on the east. From this ridgetop contour east to Granite Pass (10,673′). Then from the pass, the rocky-sandy trail descends, steeply at times, to a small meadow filled with lavender shooting stars in early season, where there are several good campsites. Our trail then descends moderately through lodgepole forest to a junction with the spur trail to Granite Lake. Here we turn right (west) and skirt the north side of a meadow to the fair campsites on that lake (10,000′), where fishing is fair for brook trout (to 8″).

4th Hiking Day (**Granite Lake** to **Cedar Grove Roadend**, 10 miles): Reverse the steps of the 1st and 2nd hiking days, Trip 57.

Cedar Grove to Granite Lake   **57**

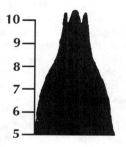

Trip	From Cedar Grove to Granite Lake via Tent Meadows
Distance	20 miles
Type	Out and back trip
Best season	Early or late
Topo maps	The Sphinx, Marion Peak 7½′

Grade (hiking days/recommended layover days)

Leisurely	—
Moderate	3/1
Strenuous	2/0

Trailhead   Cedar Grove Roadend (18)

HIGHLIGHTS   The South Fork Kings River valley is comparable in many ways to Yosemite Valley, but it's much less crowded. Because the valley walls are so steep, this trip climbs out of the canyon fast—5000 feet in 6 miles. Granite Basin is perched on the north rim of this great valley, and the setting here is indeed fit for a king and queen.

DESCRIPTION (Moderate trip)

1st Hiking Day (**Cedar Grove Roadend** to **Lower Tent Meadow**, 4½ miles): The Copper Creek Trail begins on the north side of the parking loop (5036′) under tall pines, but soon you are climbing the hot, dry north wall of Kings Canyon. Canyon live oaks provide intermittent shade for most of the 1¼ miles to the first stream. The canyon walls reflect much sunlight, and on a summer's day the trail can be like a glaring furnace. Even so, this route has been well-used for centuries.

The first set of switchbacks gains 1400 feet, and then you swing into Copper Creek canyon. The trail is now partly shaded under

Jeffrey pine, sugar pine, incense-cedar and white fir. Beyond a small creek the forest cover increases, and along the dusty trail you might see dismantled white-fir cones, chewed apart by chickarees. These small, squirrel-like rodents emit a rapid-then-slowing series of high-pitched squeaks (like an alarm running down), and are more often heard than seen. Where the trail descends to cross a flower-lined creek, you encounter the first aspens. Soon you pass a large campsite by a seasonal stream, and ¼ mile beyond, you come to the dashing creek in Lower Tent Meadow (7825'). Campsites are on the east side of the creek, but bears can find you anywhere, so hang your food accordingly.

2nd Hiking Day (**Lower Tent Meadow** to **Granite Lake**, 5½ miles): Climbing moderately, the trail crosses an area burned in 1980. After two long switchbacks you near the creek in a wide avalanche path where only low-lying bushes and a multitude of wildflowers grow. The trail switchbacks again and nears the creek for the last time—fill your bottle here. Now the trail enters shady red-fir forest and begins a long series of switchbacks that climb 1300 feet up a moraine to the divide between Copper Creek and Granite Creek. En route, you cross the belt of western white pines, and then the ridgetop is shaded by lodgepole pines. From here you can see two prominent peaks to the east, Mt. Clarence King, on the left, and Mt. Gardiner.

As the trail descends into aptly named Granite Basin, it is at first steep and rocky. After many switchbacks it turns north to make a winding, rolling ascent under lodgepole pines, passing several small ponds and meadows. A mile or so up the basin you top a low ridge, and from it you can see the bowl to the northwest that holds Granite Lake. Skirting a large meadow, you soon arrive at the signed lateral to the lake. Here you turn left, cross a creek, and then wind up an easy slope to the north side of beautiful Granite Lake (10,000'). Good campsites can be found above the lake here. Fishing for brook trout is fair (to 8"). Since the environment around this heavily used lake is delicate, please use your best environmental ethics in order to minimize your impact.

3rd Hiking Day: Retrace your steps, 10 miles.

Cedar Grove to State Lakes **58**

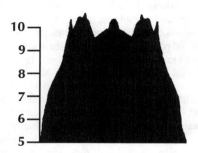

Trip	From Cedar Grove Roadend to State Lakes via Granite Basin and Granite Pass
Distance	34 miles
Type	Out and back trip
Best season	Mid or late
Topo maps	The Sphinx, Marion Peak 7½′

Grade (hiking days/recommended layover days)

Leisurely	—
Moderate	5/2
Strenuous	4/2
Trailhead	Cedar Grove Roadend (18)

HIGHLIGHTS   Once past the initial 5000-foot climb, the route to State Lakes stays high and elevation change is small. Traveling along the aptly named Monarch Divide, this route overlooks the mighty Middle Fork Kings River Canyon, the deepest in North America. Side trips to Glacier and Horseshoe lakes offer more fine angling potential

DESCRIPTION (Moderate trip)

1st and 2nd Hiking Days: Follow Trip 57 to **Granite Lake**, 10 miles.

3rd Hiking Day (**Granite Lake** to **lower State Lake**, 7 miles): You begin this hiking day by retracing your steps to the Granite Pass trail, where you turn left to climb moderately under lodgepole pines. Beyond a meadow you leave the creek and the forest cover, and then the trail switchbacks steeply up a narrow, rocky gully. The last ¼ mile to the pass is easy, and the good views southward soon give way to the extensive panorama at Granite Pass (10,673′). From the pass the oversize trail descends moderately, and then skirts a meadow where it has been rerouted to allow the turf to recover.

You then head down a small canyon, where the stream's straight course is determined by fractures in the bedrock. The grade eases at a second glacial-lake-turned-meadow. Just beyond, you pass a drift fence and descend rocky switchbacks to the forested environs along the Middle Fork Dougherty Creek. After a gentle ¾-mile descent and three creek fords, you meet the trail to Kennedy Pass, but you continue north, soon fording a small creek at 9493 feet. In another ½ mile the trail climbs over a ridge, where you pass another drift fence and get a good view of the Dougherty Creek drainage.

Turning east, the trail makes a short descent, passes a seasonal pond and then passes a junction with a trail to Simpson Meadow. Your lodgepole-pine-shaded trail then climbs around a low ridge before crossing the small creek in Glacier Valley (wet in early season). Turning north, you cross the cascading outlet from lower State Lake (difficult in early season) and switchback steeply up before leveling off in the meadowy environs near lower State Lake (10,300'). Wildflowers adorn these wet meadows, and one may see shooting star and cinquefoil near the good campsite on the north side of the lake. Fishing is good for golden trout (to 12"). The easy, shaded trail to the next State Lake (fishless) passes many currants and gooseberries (ripe in late summer), and the shores of the middle lake are a lovely place to see State Peak reflected in still waters on a quiet evening.

4th and 5th Hiking Days: Retrace your steps, 17 miles.

Douglas phlox

Jeff Schaffer

Cedar Grove to South Lake **59**

Trip	From Cedar Grove Roadend to South Lake via Granite Basin, Granite Pass, State Lakes, Simpson Meadow, Middle Fork Kings River, Dusy Basin and Bishop Pass
Distance	49½ miles
Type	Shuttle trip (trans-Sierra)
Best season	Mid or late
Topo maps	**Mt. Goddard** 15′; The Sphinx, Marion Peak, North Palisade, Mt. Thompson 7½′

Grade (hiking days/recommended layover days)

Leisurely	—
Moderate	7/3
Strenuous	6/1

Trailhead	Start at Cedar Grove Roadend (18), end at South Lake (8)

HIGHLIGHTS   This awesome trans-Sierra route is little-used between Granite Lake and the John Muir Trail. The Middle Fork Kings River runs, in its entirety, through wilderness, and you will follow this stream through its mighty canyon for much of its length. Leaving this canyon, you will cross the Sierra Crest at the north end of the Palisades, which are the most ruggedly alpine peaks in all the range.

DESCRIPTION (Strenuous trip)

1st and 2nd Hiking Days: Follow Trip 58 to **State Lakes**, 17 miles.

3rd Hiking Day (**lower State Lake** to **Simpson Meadow**, 8 miles): This hiking day entails a descent of 4400 feet in 7 miles, and can put a tremendous strain on your legs. The first mile, however, is an easy ascent past the grassy fringes of middle State Lake to a junction with the trail to Horseshoe Lakes. From this junction your trail gently descends a forested ridge for 1¼ miles to a junction with a trail (left) back to Dougherty Creek. Here you turn right, and soon begin the big drop into the Middle Fork Kings River canyon. The long descent today will reflect elevation loss by the appearance of 11 different tree species along the way. At first you see whitebark and lodgepole pine. As you descend, you leave those trees behind and pass western white pine and Sierra juniper. Tall red fir is plentiful by the time you reach another trail coming in on the left from Dougherty Creek. (There is a year-round stream ⅓ mile along this trail.)

The dusty trail then descends steeply. Much of your route from here to the east side of Simpson Meadow was burned in varying degrees during a lightning fire that burned slowly for weeks in 1985. Sequoia-Kings Canyon National Park policy now recognizes fire as a normal part of forestry ecology, and allows natural fires to run their course in the backcountry. Indeed, many trees, such as the giant sequoia, require fire for reproduction. Cones of various trees, especially some pines, release their seeds if heated, and young trees usually grow better after a fire because fire clears the soil and opens the ground to sunlight. Fire also releases nutrients from dead plant matter back into the soil.

Even if most of the trees are killed in a fire, enough usually survive to reseed an area quickly. Hardwood plants such as manzanita, aspen and black oak, even if burned to the ground, can sprout new foliage from the crown of their roots. Sometimes, large trees literally explode when water in their trunks is superheated by fire. Depressions you see along the trail mark the sites of large trees whose roots were burned below ground level. Trees with thick bark, such as Jeffrey pine and incense-cedar, usually won't burn unless fire gets under the bark and starts burning the trunk.

The downward grade eases temporarily on a moraine at 8000 feet—2000 feet to go. The next few hundred feet are extremely steep and rocky. Soon you meet the first white fir, and then aspen and incense-cedar. The grade eases again on an open slope where there are sugar pines, and you can see Windy Peak to the northeast, now high above. By the time the trail levels off on the canyon floor, you can feel the warm, oxygen-rich air here at 6000 feet. After you cross an open area, you pass a junction with the trail to Tehipite Valley. The bridge ½ mile downstream washed out in 1982, and those who don't mind rattlesnakes and wish to visit Tehipite Valley may have to make a wet ford near this junction or else upstream. Around Simpson Meadow, you can find unburned campsites near the trail on this side of Horseshoe Creek, ¼ mile up-canyon, or farther up, near the river. Anywhere you camp, a hungry bear can find your food, so hang it accordingly. Fishing in the Middle Fork Kings River is good for rainbow trout (to 12″).

4th Hiking Day (**Simpson Meadow** to **Grouse Meadows**, 10 miles): Starting at the junction with the trail to Tehipite Valley, you head east, soon ford Horseshoe Creek, and cross more burned area. The trail skirts a meadow and then contours around the base of Windy Peak. The Middle Fork Kings River flows nearby, tucked against the base of Windy Peak, opposite Goddard Creek canyon. The river channel here has been pushed to this side of the canyon by the sediments deposited by Goddard Creek as it debouches from its canyon. This process is widespread; farther upstream the Middle Fork Kings River flows on the north side of the canyon floor opposite the alluvial fan at the base of Windy Canyon.

As you gently ascend this shadeless alluvial fan there are many black oaks, indicating a high water table, and there are more of these trees as you approach Windy Canyon Creek, where the water table is at the surface. Beyond this creek the main canyon turns north, becoming steep and narrow. Your trail steepens, too, as it winds up through thickets of black oak. Soon you pass a drift fence and then cross Cartridge Creek on a wood bridge.

From here to Palisade Creek the rocky canyon is very steep and narrow, and your trail climbs steeply, usually high above falls and pools in the river below. Flowers seen along this stretch are generally of the dry-country variety, including paintbrush, penstemon, Collinsia, forget-me-not, lupine and fleabane.

The trail climbs steeply to the flats just below Devils Washbowl. To the right, the east canyon walls provide a fascinating study in convoluted glacial polish, and the views to the west and northwest of the Great Cliffs and the heavily fractured rock of Devils Crags portend later, equally exciting views of the Black Divide. The trail touches the river briefly near some sandy campsites, and then switchbacks up to awesome Devils Washbowl, a wild, spectacular falls and cataract in a granite gorge setting. Leaving the tumult of the water behind, the trail continues to ascend over rock to the innocuous-looking but treacherous ford of the unnamed creek draining Windy Cliff to the southeast. The flora around these tributary fords deserves the traveler's attention because of both its lushness and the presence of the water birch, rare in westside Sierra canyons though common on the east side. Among the wildflowers one may find at stream crossings are white Mariposa lily, cinquefoil, tiger lily, lupine, columbine and elderberry.

Ascending and descending steeply, the undulating trail is sometimes at river's edge, and other times 200 feet above. The underfooting is very rocky and treacherous until we near the Palisade Creek crossing. This crossing is preceded by a reacquaintance with a timber cover of Jeffrey, lodgepole and western white pine and white fir. There is no longer a bridge connecting our Middle Fork trail with the John Muir Trail, and water cascading over slippery slabs makes fording unsafe near the Middle Fork-Palisade Creek confluence, so turn upstream along Palisade Creek to search for a place to ford the creek safely. Once across, make your way to the John Muir Trail, on which you pass some good campsites beyond the confluence. Continuing north, the trail crosses an easy ridge, fords the unnamed tributary draining the west slopes of Giraud Peak, and arrives at the overused campsites at the east side of Grouse Meadows (8250'). The intimate views are excellent of the lush meadows and the quiet waters of the meandering river. Fishing is good for golden trout (to 11").

5th Hiking Day (**Grouse Meadows** to **Dusy Basin**, 7½ miles): Leaving the pleasant grasslands of Grouse Meadows behind, the trail continues its gentle but steady ascent. On the left, the river abandons the placid temperament of its winding meadow course and resumes its mad, white-water plunge. Beyond the river to the west, The Citadel's granite face stands guard over the south side of an obvious hanging valley and the cascades from Ladder Lake, and the early-morning traveler is often treated to a burst of reflected sunlight from glacially polished surfaces high on the canyon's west wall north of that valley. The trail undulates up and down the east wall, sometimes 80 to 100 feet above the river, sometimes right alongside it, and passes through a drift fence. The thin lodgepole forest cover occurs mostly in stands, with intermittent stretches of grassy pockets, and the underfooting is mostly rocky. Ahead, the canyon narrows, and the trail crosses Dusy Branch Creek via a substantial steel footbridge to meet the Bishop Pass Trail. A few yards north of this junction is the LeConte Ranger Station (emergency services perhaps available).

Our route turns right (east) and begins a steep, switchbacking ascent of the east canyon wall. This ascent is broken into two distinct steps that gain a total of 2000 feet in about 2 miles, but the steepness of the slopes is tamed by the well-graded switchbacks. Touching the creek at strategic intervals (a drink on this climb is welcome), the trail offers magnificent views of the monolithic granite structures on the far side of the canyon. Near the creek, the wildflower lover will find lush shooting star, fireweed, penstemon, pennyroyal and some yellow columbine nestling next to damp, moss-covered rocky grottos. Along the switchbacks, occasional lodgepole and juniper break the monotony of the slab granite. Near the top of the first climb, one particular juniper with a near-record girth stands out, like a beetle-browed sentinel.

Views of the chutes and cascades of Dusy Branch creek reward dusty trail-pounders as they finish the first climb and enter a cooling bower of mixed lodgepole and aspen. The trail crosses the creek on a bridge and continues switchbacking up through a sparse cover of aspen (campsites). This ascent levels out near the lowest of the Dusy Basin lake chain and emerges to open, breathtaking views of Mt. Winchell, Mt. Agassiz, Thunderbolt Peak and Columbine Peak. After rounding the north side of the lower Dusy Basin lake chain, the trail turns north and climbs a series of grass-topped ledges. A short, well-worn spur trail branches right, leading to campsites situated both alongside Dusy Branch creek and on the middle lakes of the Dusy Basin chain.

Our route veers up and away from the creek, and after it rejoins the creek while on an eastward jog, turns right a short cross-country distance and descends through an alpine fell field to the fair campsites near the west side of the northernmost large lake in the basin (11,350'). Fishing for golden and golden hybrids is good (to 8"). This campsite offers the camper a fine base for further explorations of Dusy and Palisades basins, and a granite outcropping just east of the lake provides the finest panoramic viewpoint in the entire basin.

6th Hiking Day (**Dusy Basin** to **South Lake**, 7 miles): Reverse the steps of Trip 45.

Dusy Basin

60   Cedar Grove to Vidette Meadow

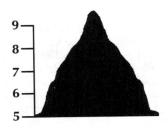

Trip	From Cedar Grove Roadend up Bubbs Creek to Vidette Meadow
Distance	26 miles
Type	Out and back trip
Best season	Early to mid
Topo maps	The Sphinx, Mt. Clarence King 7½′

Grade (hiking days/recommended layover days)

Leisurely	4/1
Moderate	3/0
Strenuous	2/0
Trailhead	Cedar Grove Roadend (18)

HIGHLIGHTS   Climbing 4000 feet, this trip follows an old Indian trade route paralleling Bubbs Creek. Beyond the realm of the Park's dayhikers, the trail climbs the path of an old glacier to beautiful Vidette Meadow, a "high country crossroads." Here in the shadow of the spectacular Kearsarge Pinnacles this route meets the famous John Muir Trail.

DESCRIPTION (Moderate trip)

1st Hiking Day (**Cedar Grove Roadend** to **Charlotte Creek**, 7½ miles): From the paved roadend loop (5036′) the wide, sandy trail heads east through a mixed forest of ponderosa pine, incense-cedar, black oak, sugar pine and white fir. But soon the shade is left behind, and there is only a sparse cover of ponderosas. The balmy climate usually characteristic of the gently sloping canyon floor made this area a favorite of Indians, who had their summer camps here. Foraging parties of Yokuts Indians made their "spur" camps along Bubbs Creek at many of the same spots chosen by today's backcountry travelers.

Soon our trail enters a cool, dense forest of alder, white fir and ponderosa and sugar pine, and we pass the Paradise Valley/Woods Creek Trail branching north just before crossing a large steel bridge over the South Fork. We then pass a trail heading down-canyon and turn east to cross four branches of Bubbs Creek on expertly constructed log-and-plank bridges. The last bridge crossing marks the beginning of a series of steady switchbacks. This climb is hot and dry, so try to get an early start.

Along this climb we find some rare (for this side of the Sierra) piñon pines. This tree, whose fruit provides the delicious pine nut, is of the single-needle group, and may be identified by either its single needle or its distinctive spherical cone. Most noticeable about the cone is its very thick, blunt, four-sided scale. This ascent offers fine views back into the dramatic U-shaped South Fork Kings River canyon. On the south side of the Bubbs Creek canyon the dominating landmark is the pronounced granite point called The Sphinx. To the east its namesake stream cuts a sharp-lipped defile on the peak's east shoulder.

Above the switchbacks, as you angle toward tumbling Bubbs Creek, you re-enter the cool shade of tall conifers and climb past a drift fence. Beside a junction with the Sphinx Creek Trail to Avalanche Pass is a small, one-night campsite. Much of the lower canyon burned in 1976. One of the few noticeable effects of the fire now is the lack of shade. Fire is part of the ecosystem in Sierran forests. The extent to which trees are killed in a fire is partly a function of how hot the fire is. Generally, fires here are relatively cool, and they burn mostly dead wood and brush near the ground. But if dead wood accumulates for a long time due to natural conditions or human fire suppression, the eventual inevitable fire is likely to be hot, and will kill even tall trees. Fire-adapted plants regrow quickly, and on the trail here you see manzanita, black oaks, young Jeffrey pines and white firs. Some of the young trees may eventually produce a mature forest like the one we soon find around Charlotte Creek. There are good campsites several hundred feet beyond this creek under tall white firs (one-night stay only). In nearby Bubbs Creek fishing is good for brown, brook, rainbow and golden-rainbow hybrid trout (to 10″).

2nd Hiking Day (**Charlotte Creek** to **Vidette Meadow**, 5½ miles): From Charlotte Creek the grade alternates between being shady and fern-lined, and being steep, rocky and dusty. The steep southern rampart of Mt. Bago stretches up to the left as we arrive at the campsites at the west end of long Junction Meadow, where there are two major camping areas: at the west end just before a drift fence below the meadow proper, and at the east end across Bubbs Creek along the East Lake Trail. (No grazing.) At the east end of the meadow our route passes the East Lake Trail, begins a steady, rocky climb and soon emerges onto a sparsely forested hillside. Bubbs Creek, on the right, flows down through a steep, narrow gorge, and it is worthwhile to walk over a few yards at one of the right-hand switchback hairpins to look at the spectacular cascades and waterfalls.

The steepest part of the climb ends at the top of these switchbacks, and then the trail proceeds on a moderate ascent past the ruins of a drift fence under an old, weathered foxtail pine. Looking back, one has fine views of the avalanche-scarred north face of West Spur. The ascent is gentle now, and we soon arrive at a junction with the John Muir Trail at lower Vidette Meadow. Here our route turns right, fords the outlet creek from Bullfrog Lake, and arrives at the good campsites (9500') above beautiful Vidette Meadow, scattered along Bubbs Creek. Fishing for brook and rainbow trout (to 8") is fair. Because of the area's heavy use, a pit toilet is located several dozen yards down-canyon from the trail junction, just uphill from the Bubbs Creek Trail.

3rd Hiking Day: Retrace your steps, 13 miles.

Tarn on Bullfrog Lake's outlet stream

Cedar Grove to Charlotte Lake   **61**

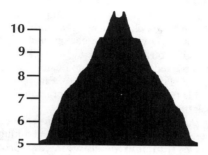

Trip	From Cedar Grove Roadend to Charlotte Lake via Bubbs Creek
Distance	33 miles
Type	Out and back trip
Best season	Mid or late
Topo maps	The Sphinx, Mt. Clarence King 7½′

Grade (hiking days/recommended layover days)

Leisurely	5/1
Moderate	4/1
Strenuous	2/0

Trailhead   Cedar Grove Roadend (18)

HIGHLIGHTS   Striking right into the heart of the high country, this route ascends a lengthy stretch of Bubbs Creek canyon to the charming meadows at the foot of the Kearsarge Pinnacles and the Videttes. The terminus of this trip, Charlotte Lake, is a base-camp location for exploring Charlotte Creek.

DESCRIPTION (Leisurely trip)

1st and 2nd Hiking Days: Follow Trip 60 to **Vidette Meadow**, 13 miles.

3rd Hiking Day (**Vidette Meadow** to **Charlotte Lake**, 3½ miles): First, retrace your steps to the junction of the John Muir Trail and the Bubbs Creek Trail. Following the Muir Trail as it switchbacks up the steep north side of the canyon, the traveler is treated to breathtaking views of the Kearsarge Pinnacles to the east and of the Videttes and snow-necklaced Deerhorn Mountain to the south. It is easy, while viewing this spectacle, to understand the popularity of the Muir Trail. Our route crosses a small creek twice, passes the first of several laterals to Bullfrog Lake (no camping) and continues northwest on a series of switchbacks to a junction with the Charlotte Lake Trail. This trail leaves the Muir Trail at an **X** junction in a sandy saddle (not shown on the 7½′ topo) and, after providing one last look back to the Bubbs Creek drainage and far south into Center Basin, with the Kings-Kern Divide in the background, zigzags down to Charlotte Lake. High on the left of the switchbacks tower the several summits of red-rocked Mt. Bago. Good campsites may be found along the north side of the lake (10,370′). Emergency services are perhaps available from a resident summer ranger. Fishing for rainbow and brook trout (to 10″) is good.

4th Hiking Day (**Charlotte Lake** to **Junction Meadow**, 5 miles): Retrace the steps of the 3rd and part of the 2nd hiking day.

5th Hiking Day (**Junction Meadow** to **Cedar Grove Roadend**, 11½ miles): Retrace the steps of part of the 2nd and all of the 1st hiking day.

Southern rampart of Mt. Bago

Cedar Grove to Sixty Lake Basin

62

Trip	From Cedar Grove Roadend to Sixty Lake Basin via Glen Pass and Rae Lakes
Distance	49 miles
Type	Out and back trip; optional loop trip possible
Best season	Mid or late
Topo maps	The Sphinx, Mt. Clarence King 7½′

Grade (hiking days/recommended layover days)

Leisurely	—
Moderate	7/1
Strenuous	5/0
Trailhead	Cedar Grove Roadend (18)

HIGHLIGHTS   The hiker who values serenity and seclusion amid true alpine surroundings, and is tired of encountering the swarms of hikers and campers who crowd the Muir Trail and other popular routes in the Sierra, will appreciate Sixty Lake Basin. This sanctuary, ringed by granite ridges and sharp peaks, offers a genuine wilderness experience and the option of an exciting cross-country excursion to upper Gardiner Basin.

DESCRIPTION (Moderate trip)

1st, 2nd and 3rd Hiking Days: Follow Trip 61 to **Charlotte Lake**, 16½ miles.

4th Hiking Day (**Charlotte Lake** to **Sixty Lake Basin**, 8 miles):

First retrace your steps to the **X** junction on the sandy saddle. From there take the Muir Trail over Glen Pass to the junction with the Sixty Lake Basin Trail just before the isthmus between the upper Rae Lakes mentioned in the 3rd hiking day of Trip 68.

We leave the junction bearing northward, cross a marshy area, and begin climbing west on switchbacks offering superb views of Rae Lakes. A northwest traverse and some switchbacks bring us to the lakelet just below the unnamed saddle that is our "pass." We round the lakelet on its north, traverse to the saddle (11,200'), and take in the fine view to the west of stark, sharp-peaked Mts. Cotter and Clarence King before descending on steep, rocky switchbacks to the shore of a lake at about 11,000 feet with a sandy campsite near its outlet.

Beyond its outlet we round the ridge that separates upper Sixty Lake Basin into east and west sub-basins, and pause to get our bearings near a good campsite that overlooks the lake at 10,720 feet north of the nose of this ridge. Fin Dome serves as our reference point from most of the basin, which is higher and less forested than adjacent Rae Lakes. This basin is convoluted, particularly at its southern, higher end, and each hollow in the granite holds a pleasant surprise for the rambler: a meadow, a small campsite, a bubbling stream, or a lake or two. Hang food away from bears, gear from marmots.

The "trail" leads northwest from here as a beaten track; look for it or for the occasional duck. Small trout inhabit the northern, lower lakes.

A cross-country trek southwest brings you to the narrow lake southeast of Mt. Cotter, which offers access to upper Gardiner Basin via the Class 2–3 col a mile south of Mt. Cotter. If you are comfortable on Class 2 terrain, you can go high around the lake's west side to avoid cliffs around the bay at its inlet. Then you can work your way up granite ledges to the col. A possible route down to magnificent, desolate Lake 3477 (metric) in upper Gardiner Basin descends talus and sand ledges from about the middle of the col. Further exploration of Gardiner Basin is possible from here. (The old trail over Gardiner Pass has vanished in dense forest and is not recommended.)

5th, 6th and 7th Hiking Days: Retrace your steps, 24½ miles.

(Optionally, make this a loop trip by turning left (north) at the junction just before the isthmus between the upper Rae Lakes, hiking north down Rae Lakes, and reversing the 1st, 2nd and 3rd hiking days of Trip 63, 22½ miles.)

Cedar Grove to Rae Lakes 63

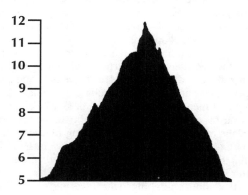

Trip	From Cedar Grove Roadend to Rae Lakes via Paradise Valley and South Fork Woods Creek, return via Glen Pass and Vidette Meadow
Distance	41½ miles
Type	Loop trip
Best season	Late
Topo maps	The Sphinx, Mt. Clarence King 7½'

Grade (hiking days/recommended layover days)

Leisurely	7/2
Moderate	6/1
Strenuous	4/1

Trailhead Cedar Grove Roadend (18)

HIGHLIGHTS This fine trip, known as the Rae Lakes Loop, circles the King Spur. The scenery en route is dramatic enough to challenge the most accomplished photographer or artist as the trail ascends the glacially carved canyon of the South Fork Kings River, visits the exceptionally beautiful Rae Lakes, makes a breathtaking ascent of Glen Pass, circles beneath the Videttes and the Kearsarge Pinnacles, and returns down dashing Bubbs Creek.

Because of very heavy use, camping at Rae Lakes is restricted to a maximum of one night at each of the three lakes, and bears are a serious problem. Store food properly at all times. No wood campfires are permitted.

DESCRIPTION (Moderate trip)

1st Hiking Day (**Cedar Grove Roadend** to **Paradise Valley**, 7 miles): Your trip begins as detailed in Trip 60, heading east from the roadend (5036′) through sparse forest on a sandy trail, then dipping into a damp, dense forest to meet the east-leading Bubbs Creek Trail near a large steel bridge over the South Fork Kings River. In a few days, you'll close the loop here.

For now, you turn north on the Paradise Valley/Woods Creek Trail along the river, here broad and peaceful, and ascend moderately under a mixed cover of conifers, alders, black oaks and live oaks. In sunny spots, there are chaparral shrubs like silk-tassel, mountain mahogany and manzanita. Soon the river swirls, leaps and pools through a narrow channel, and the canyon's walls soar on either side. Granite slabs offer pleasant, open stopping places with excellent views down-canyon to The Sphinx and Avalanche Peak. You soon reach Mist Falls, a series of pretty cascades that are tumbling whitewater in early season, sedate and subdued by late season.

The trail continues climbing to the lower end of Paradise Valley, where the river dashes straight down the canyon. The grade eases to gentle as you curve into Paradise Valley (6640′) through a mixed forest cover of lodgepole pine, red fir, Jeffrey pine and some juniper and aspen. There are good campsites as the valley widens, and fishing for rainbow and brown is fair (to 8″).

2nd Hiking Day (**Paradise Valley** to **Woods Creek Crossing**, 7 miles). Leaving Paradise Valley, you pass through a drift fence, pass the confluence with Woods Creek, curve east, and shortly ford the river, which flows in two channels here. The ford can be difficult in early and mid season. Look for use trails that lead to spots where you can cross on logs or boulders.

Now on the north side of Woods Creek, the trail rises steeply at first and then makes an undulating ascent on a moderate grade up the canyon, crossing two unnamed tributaries. You wind through Castle Domes Meadow, named for the obvious landmarks to the north. Clumps of the water-loving quaking aspen dot the stream banks along Woods Creek. This smooth-barked, whispering tree is the most conspicuous member of the deciduous group found in the high country. Always found near running water or at the edge of porous seepage areas (lava, talus, gravel), it acts as a native water locator, and its ghostly white trunk can be seen for great distances. Hikers who have camped in a grove of aspen will always remember the tree's gentle rustling sound as the leaves, responding to the slightest breeze, tremble against one another.

The underfooting is alternately sandy and rocky as the trail climbs, and the forest cover includes more and more lodgepole as the

Castle Domes

altitude increases. When your trail meets the John Muir Trail, you turn south on it and soon cross Woods Creek (8492′) on a wooden bridge, just below the confluence of its north and south forks— difficult in early season if the bridge is washed out. Fair but overused campsites may be found near the crossing; fishing in the creek is good for brook and rainbow (to 10″).

A few yards above the crossing the sharp-eyed hiker may spot one of this region's most interesting historical landmarks: the ruins of one of fur trapper Shorty Lovelace's unusual line cabins, on the west side of the creek. Those who take time out to examine this structure will soon discern its unique character. Appearing to be almost a miniature replica of the real article, it was erected to suit the needs of its builder—Shorty was indeed short—and would scarcely accommodate the average person, standing or sleeping. It was from this cabin and several others that Shorty worked his trap lines from late fall to spring, before the area became part of Kings Canyon National Park in 1940. Shorty trapped throughout the Sierra for over half a century, mostly alone in his little cabins during the long, bitter winters. The mountains were his salvation from the alcoholism that he fell prey to in civilization. Few of his tiny shelters remain, so it is a privilege to happen upon the ruins of one of them.

3rd Hiking Day (**Woods Creek Crossing** to **Rae Lakes**, 6½ miles): The southbound John Muir Trail curves around the northern-most prominence of the King Spur. Bearing south-southeast, it ascends the west side of the South Fork Woods Creek on a moderate grade, crossing the stream draining Lake 10296 (3144 metric), an unnamed tributary, and then the stream draining Sixty Lake Basin. You pass the unmarked use trail to Baxter Pass—so obscure you may not even notice it—just before rounding the west side of the lowest of the Rae Lakes, Dollar Lake—closed to camping but a favorite photo spot. Between Dollar and Arrowhead lakes, and just west of Diamond Peak, you ford the South Fork Woods Creek and continue up-canyon on the east side of the lake chain. The long black striations seen along the face of Diamond Peak and the continuing ridge to the north are metamorphosed lava, one of the few remaining bits of volcanic evidence to be found in this area.

Distinctive Fin Dome, a familiar landmark in Rae Lakes country, comes into sight, and you pass Arrowhead Lake (campsites), climb high above the creek, and pass the next two large lakes (campsites at each). A summer ranger station half-hidden in the trees above the second-highest lake (10,560′) sometimes provides emergency services. A camp at one of the Rae Lakes will be among the best and longest remembered of this trip because of its views: the rugged granite of Fin Dome mirrored in the still waters of the lake; the jagged King Spur beyond; and, if you're at one of the higher lakes, Painted Lady to the south. Fishing is good for brook trout and some rainbow (to 16″).

4th Hiking Day (**Rae Lakes** to **Vidette Meadow**, 8 miles): Leaving the second-highest Rae Lake, the trail passes an unmarked, unmaintained lateral to Dragon Lake and swings west to cross the narrow isthmus separating the near-rockbound highest lake from the rest of the chain. On the west side, we pass the unmaintained trail that heads west to Sixty Lake Basin and turn south toward Glen Pass. The trail briefly traces the rocky west shore of the highest Rae Lake and then begins a no-nonsense climb toward Glen Pass. Partway up you splash across the outlet stream of a little willow-choked lake, one of a group of small lakes lying on a granite bench below Glen Pass. The grade briefly eases through boulder-strewn, sandy flats and then zigzags up, up, up on rocky switchbacks to the splendid views of the Rae Lakes chain at narrow Glen Pass (11,978′).

From the pass you corkscrew steeply down the south side on a sandy-rocky trail. After about 500 feet, the grade eases, and you pass a couple of lonely, rockbound lakes before rounding a granite promontory where there are fine views west over Charlotte Lake and Charlotte Creek's canyon to impressive Charlotte Dome. The route presently becomes a long, sandy traverse through sparse lodgepole around an outlier of Mt. Rixford. You pass a junction with the eastbound Kearsarge Pass Trail and continue south to an **X** junction on a sandy flat with the trail to Charlotte Lake (west) and a connector to the Kearsarge Pass trail (east). You continue south on the John Muir Trail, passing a spur to Bullfrog Lake—closed to camping—and pause atop the handsome white granite cliffs above Vidette Meadow, where there are excellent views of the Kearsarge Pinnacles to the east, the Videttes to the south, the barren granite of Center Basin, and the distant peaks of the Kings-Kern Divide.

Now you descend into open forest, crossing the outlet of Bullfrog Lake twice, and switchback down to Lower Vidette Meadow (campsites) and a trail junction. Follow the John Muir Trail east and southeast a little less than ½ mile more to beautiful upper Vidette Meadow (9500'), where good campsites are scattered above the meadow along Bubbs Creek. A pit toilet is provided because of heavy use, and fishing for brook and rainbow trout (to 8") is fair.

5th and 6th Hiking Days: Reverse the steps of Trip 60, 13 miles.

Upper Gardiner Basin

64   **Cedar Grove to Lake Reflection**

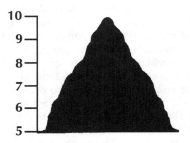

Trip	From Cedar Grove Roadend to Lake Reflection via Bubbs Creek and East Creek
Distance	31 miles
Type	Out and back trip
Best season	Mid or late
Topo maps	**Mt. Whitney** 15′; The Sphinx, Mt. Clarence King, Mt. Brewer 7½′

Grade (hiking days/recommended layover days)

Leisurely	6/1
Moderate	4/1
Strenuous	3/1
Trailhead	Cedar Grove Roadend (18)

HIGHLIGHTS   Those who appreciate the serenity of high, alpine lake basins will find this trip to the upper reaches of East Creek a rewarding choice. Excellent fishing amid spellbinding surroundings makes this a fine angling trip, and if one doesn't fish, it is time well spent just "soaking up the country." Lake Reflection can be very windy.

DESCRIPTION (Moderate trip)

1st Hiking Day (**Cedar Grove Roadend** to **Charlotte Creek**, 7½ miles): Follow the 1st hiking day, Trip 60.

2nd Hiking Day (**Charlotte Creek** to **Lake Reflection**, 8 miles): Proceed to Junction Meadow, as described in part of the 2nd hiking day, Trip 60. At Junction Meadow our trail branches right, fords Bubbs Creek by a log, and starts to ascend East Creek canyon. This ascent is accomplished via rocky switchbacks that zigzag through a sparse-to-moderate forest cover of lodgepole, fir, western white pine and some aspen. The view back to the north is dominated by the red metamorphic rocks of Mt. Bago, with Mt. Gardiner coming into view beyond it. As one tops the first rise of the ascent, peaks of the Kings-Kern Divide come into view. Anglers trying their luck along East Creek will find rainbow and brook trout (to 8″), but the trout are somewhat larger in East Lake.

After a brief stretch of moderate uphill going, the trail crosses East Creek (wet in early season) and then climbs steadily along the

Lake Reflection

creek's east bank. The grade steepens and our route enters a forest of pines and firs. After the ford of an unnamed, fern-lined creek, our trail levels off near the outlet of East Lake. One's first view of these picturesque waters with their grassy fringes may be accompanied by a sighting of one of the many mule deer that frequent the canyon. The trail rounds the lake's east side to the good campsites in dense forest at the head of the lake. The barren, unjointed granite walls that rise on either side—especially Mt. Brewer on the west—are an impressive backdrop for leisure moments spent on the shores of this mountain gem, and it is always with some reluctance that visitors move on.

Beyond the head of East Lake the trail climbs steadily past a drift fence through rock-broken stands of lodgepole and foxtail pine. Just before crossing a 50-yard-wide rockpile, we pass the unmarked start of the Harrison Pass Trail. Beyond the talus slope, the easy grade traverses many wet areas along the east side of East Creek to the good campsites beside the little lake below Lake Reflection and at the northeast end of Lake Reflection (10,005'). The angler will find good fishing for golden, rainbow and hybrids (to 16"). When no breeze stirs the waters of this lake, the tableau of peaks reflected in their depths is a memorable scene of a scope seldom matched in the Sierra. At the head of the cirque basin, all side excursions are up, but the expenditure of sweat and effort required to explore the surrounding lakes and lakelets is repaid by great views and a sense of achievement that has been shared by many mountaineers since the Brewer Party first ascended these heights.

3rd and 4th Hiking Days: Retrace your steps, 15½ miles.

Cedar Grove to Upper Kern River

65

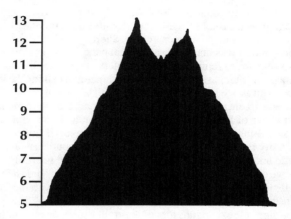

Trip	From Cedar Grove Roadend to Upper Kern River via Bubbs Creek, Forester Pass, return via Harrison Pass, East Lake
Distance	49½ miles
Type	Semiloop trip
Best season	Late
Topo maps	**Mt. Whitney** 15′; The Sphinx, Mt. Clarence King, Mt. Brewer, Mt. Williamson 7½′

Grade (hiking days/recommended layover days)

Leisurely	—
Moderate	7/3
Strenuous	6/2

Trailhead   Cedar Grove Roadend (18)

HIGHLIGHTS   Crossing two high passes, this trip explores the glaciated upper reaches of the Kern trench and circumnavigates a good piece of the Kings-Kern and Great Western divides. This is a long and rugged route that is recommended for the hearty, experienced backcountry traveler possessed of a sense of adventure and a liking for high, barren surroundings. It would be prudent to carry a rope.

DESCRIPTION (Strenuous trip)

1st Hiking Day: (**Cedar Grove Roadend** to **Junction Meadow**, 10 miles): Proceed to Junction Meadow as described in the 1st and part of the 2nd hiking day, Trip 60.

2nd Hiking Day (**Junction Meadow** to **Upper Bubbs Creek**, 6½ miles): Follow the 2nd hiking day, Trip 60, to Vidette Meadow, where our route joins the John Muir Trail and turns southeast, ascending beside Bubbs Creek. About ½ mile above Vidette Meadow our route passes an old trapper's cabin. Shorty Lovelace trapped this country until it was made into a national park, and a network of his cabins remains to remind today's travelers of an era of the not-too-distant past. After passing through a drift fence and making the initial steep ascent above Vidette Meadow, the trail levels out to a moderate but steady ascent along the east bank of the creek through a moderate forest cover of lodgepole and occasional hemlock. Several camp-sites line Bubbs Creek, and those at 10,200 feet offer fine views of University Peak to the east, Center Peak to the southeast, and East Vidette and East Spur to the west. However, to be nearer Forester Pass, we continue passing through another drift fence abreast of East Vidette to the overused campsites near the junction with the Center Basin/Junction Pass Trail. Fishing for brook trout (to 7″) is good. Rewarding side excursions for golden-trout fishing or exploration of lakes can be made via the old Muir Trail route to Center Basin.

3rd Hiking Day (**Upper Bubbs Creek** to **outlet stream of Lake 11440**, 9 miles): From these campsites the trail ascends more steeply over the barren granite west of Center Peak. This climb takes one above timberline as it winds back and forth over the tributary that drains Lake 12248, and over one's shoulder the peaks of the Sierra Crest march away on the northern horizon. After fording the outlet of Lake 12248, the trail climbs the west wall of the canyon and then switchbacks steeply up to the narrow notch in the Kings-Kern Divide that is Forester Pass (13,180′). Views from the pass to the northeast include Mt. Pinchot, University Peak, Mt. Bradley and Mt. Keith. To the south stand Mt. Kaweah, the Kaweah Peaks Ridge, the Red Spur, Kern Point and Black Kaweah. Close by, Caltech Peak is to the west and Junction Peak to the east.

Leaving this windy orientation point behind, the trail descends steeply by numerous short switchbacks, some of which are mere shelves carved into the steep face of the Junction Peak ridge. A few hardy polemonium and some yellow hulsea share the high slope with scurrying conies, and travelers who lift their eyes are sometimes treated to a sighting of a golden eagle soaring high above the granite steeples. After the trail levels off somewhat, the rocky route winds among a number of unnamed lakes that make up the headwaters of this branch of Tyndall Creek. To the east the unusual formation called Diamond Mesa appears as a sheer-walled, flat-topped ridge dangling from the jumbled heights of Junction Peak. Here, the trail passes through "marmot land," and the traveling human intruder is looked upon indulgently as a seasonal part of the scenery—and as a possible source of carelessly guarded food.

Near treeline, our route intersects the Lake South America/ Milestone Creek Trail and turns right onto it. This trail soon turns west, and then ascends gently at treeline for ½ mile to another junction, where the Lake South America Trail turns north and our route veers southwest. At the outlet stream of Lake 11440 (3490 metric), the hiker should turn left and descend cross country to the good campsite (11,200') in foxtail pines at the edge of the meadow ¼ mile south.

4th Hiking Day (**Outlet stream of Lake 11440** to **East Lake**, 10 miles, part cross country): Retrace the steps of the previous hiking day to the Lake South America Trail junction, where this day's route turns north and ascends gently up the east side of a long, boulder-strewn meadow. At the head of this ascent, the trail becomes steeper and switchbacks up 500 feet of barren, broken granite to a saddle which give access to the large cirque basin at the head of the Kern River. Beside a charming little lake that feeds the Kern River our route meets a trail coming up from the river and turns right, toward Lake South America (so called from its shape), where the angler may wish to try the good fishing for golden (to 12″).

From here the trail may be ducked as it climbs toward Harrison Pass. Ahead, locating the pass by visual sighting is difficult, as the lowest point on the headwall of the canyon is nearer Mt. Ericsson than the actual pass is. Our route veers eastward, toward Mt. Stanford, where the best descent on the north side may be had. This descent is often snow-choked until late summer. Views from Harrison Pass to the south include Mt. Kaweah, Kaweah Peaks Ridge, Milestone Mountain and Mt. Guyot. Looking north, Deerhorn Mountain with its avalanche chutes and talus fans stands athwart the view, but Mt. Goddard can be seen far in the distance to the left of it, and Middle Palisade in the distance to its right. From the pass, the route leads north down the talus. (This descent is often snow-choked until late summer.)

Carefully pick your way downward, toward the first lake visible on the cirque floor. Then cross its outlet and veer west to ford the stream connecting the second and third lakes in the cirque. From here the route ascends somewhat and then drops to the outlet of the third lake, passing close under the buff and tan granite cliffs of soaring

Ericsson Crags. In the canyon below the third lake you encounter timber, and also achieve your first view of Mt. Brewer, due west across the canyon of East Creek.

The route then levels off briefly in a meadow and fords the crystal stream to the north side. The white color of the trumpet-shaped flowers of alpine gentian in this meadow tells us we are still quite high; blue gentians lie below. After passing several lovely tarns not shown on the topo map, the sometimes blazed trail easily crosses a little divide on a southbound course and traverses down to attractive Golden Lake, where there is one excellent campsite. From the lake we have a direct view of imposing Lucys Foot Pass, on the Kings-Kern Divide. This pass is Class 3 in places and it is not advised for ordinary backpacking or for inexperienced mountaineers. Due to all the loose "garbage" on the north side, the best passage is south-to-north.

From Golden Lake the route has a short level segment and then it descends steeply on a rocky-dusty, ill-maintained trail down poorly built switchbacks to the East Creek Trail, meeting it at a junction a few yards north of a rockslide. Here we turn right (north) and descend gently, sometimes moderately, for 1 mile to the good campsites at the south end of East Lake (9445'), described in the 2nd hiking day, Trip 64.

5th Hiking Day (**East Lake** to **Charlotte Creek**, 6½ miles): Descend to Junction Meadow, reversing part of the 2nd hiking day, Trip 64, then retrace your steps to Charlotte Creek.

6th Hiking Day (**Charlotte Creek** to **Cedar Grove Roadend**, 7½ miles: Reverse the 1st hiking day, Trip 60.

Great Western Divide seen from upper Tyndall Creek

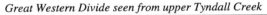

Onion Valley to Flower Lake   6

```
10 ┐
    │   ⬛
 9 ┘
```

Trip	From Onion Valley to Flower Lake
Distance	5 miles
Type	Out and back trip
Best season	Early or mid
Topo maps	Kearsarge Peak 7½′
Grade (hiking days/recommended layover days)	
Leisurely	2/0
Moderate	Day
Strenuous	½ day
Trailhead	Onion Valley (13)

HIGHLIGHTS   A short hike over well graded trail and a mere 1300 feet of elevation gain bring you to the justly popular lakes that compose the headwaters of Independence Creek. Angling is good and the scenery grand.

DESCRIPTION (Leisurely trip)

1st Hiking Day (**Onion Valley** to **Flower Lake**, 2½ miles): The trail leaves the road a few yards north of the Onion Valley campground and switchbacks up a dry, manzanita-covered slope. Switchbacks always seem to come in bunches, and this ascent is no exception. The first set of switchbacks is relatively open and exposed, offering fine views back onto Onion Valley and south to the heavily diked summit of Independence Peak. After about ⅓ mile there is a short level stretch where one may study the distinctive shapes of the large foxtail pines nearby. Found only at high altitudes in the mountains of California, foxtail pines have distinctive dark, purple cones that take two years to mature. The densely needled (in clusters of five) branches do look like tails and do look inviting to touch—but you'll probably get sticky fingers if you do. Then the trail enters John Muir Wilderness and switchbacks steadily again, until after a mile it comes close enough to tumbling Independence Creek that only a few steps are needed to reach the wildflower-lined stream bank and slake one's thirst.

After this draught, on a more gradual slope, our path crosses many runoff rills in early and mid season, where a neophyte botanist may identify specimens of Queen Anne's lace, paintbrush, wallflower, tiger lily, columbine, shooting star and whorled penstemon. At the

tle grade is Little Pothole Lake, not much for camping,
wo beautiful, willow-lined cascades pouring into its
..ᴜᵼ bays.

After another set of rocky switchbacks, the trail levels off in a slightly ascending groove across glacial moraine and then reaches small, round Gilbert Lake (10,417'). Poor-from-overuse campsites dot the shores of this fine swimming lake, and fishing for rainbow and brook trout is good in early season. This small lake absorbs much of the day-hiking impact from people camping at Onion Valley, as does Flower Lake, at the top of the next set of switchbacks. There are many highly used campsites along the north and east sides of this shallow lake (10,531'). Less used and more scenic are Matlock and Bench lakes, the first reached by an unmarked trail that leads south from the east side of Flower Lake, and the second, cross country west from the first. Fishing for rainbow and some brook trout is fair in Flower Lake, but serious anglers will hike to the more distant lakes in the timbered cirque basin to the south.

2nd Hiking Day: Retrace your steps, 2½ miles.

Gilbert Lake

Onion Valley to Charlotte La

Trip	From Onion Valley to Charlotte Lake via Kearsarge Pass
Distance	16 miles
Type	Out and back trip
Best season	Mid or late
Topo maps	Kearsarge Peak, Mt. Clarence King 7½′

Grade (hiking days/recommended layover days)

Leisurely	3/1
Moderate	3/0
Strenuous	2/0
Trailhead	Onion Valley (13)

HIGHLIGHTS   Kearsarge Pass, because of its relatively low elevation and its proximity to an east-side roadend, is a justly popular way to reach the John Muir Trail. Because of this popularity, many of the lakes and meadows en route have been overrun, and Park officials have felt it necessary to close these "impacted" areas to grazing and camping.

DESCRIPTION (Leisurely trip)

1st Hiking Day: Follow Trip 66 to **Flower Lake**, 2½ miles.

2nd Hiking Day (**Flower Lake** to **Charlotte Lake**, 5½ miles): From Flower Lake the Kearsarge Pass Trail turns north and ascends steeply to a viewpoint overlooking Heart Lake. Now the trail switchbacks up to another overlook—this time the lake is the nearly perfect blue oval of Big Pothole Lake. From the trail high above the water, the lake, with its backgrounding granite finger, is particularly photogenic. Continuing, the trail rises above timber, except for a few hardy whitebark specimens, and then makes two long-legged traverses across an exposed shaley slope to the low saddle of Kearsarge Pass (11,823′). To the west, the impressive view encompasses the Kearsarge Lakes, Bullfrog Lake and the serrated spires of the Kearsarge Pinnacles.

On the west side of the pass our route descends easily on a traverse high above the basin holding the Kearsarge and Bullfrog lakes. After passing a spur trail branching left to the Kearsarge Lakes (one-night stay limit) and Bullfrog Lake (no camping), the route continues westward on a gentle descent into sparse timber. Crossing several small runoff streams in early season, the rocky-sandy trail contours high on the viewful slopes above Bullfrog Lake.

Now descending steadily through sparse-to-moderate whitebark and foxtail pine, the trail offers fine views south to Center Peak and Junction Peak. On this viewful slope we reach a fork whose branches both go to the John Muir Trail. We take the left fork southwest. Our route descends gently onto a sandy flat in a broad saddle overlooking Charlotte Lake, where at an **X** junction (not shown on the 7½′ topo) we take a trail west that switchbacks down moderately-to-steeply for a short mile to Charlotte Lake (10,370′). Good campsites line the north shore, and fishing for rainbow and brook trout (to 10″) is fair. Emergency services are perhaps available from the resident summer ranger on the north shore.

3rd Hiking Day: Retrace your steps, 8 miles.

Kearsarge Lakes and Kearsarge Pinnacles

Onion Valley to Rae Lake

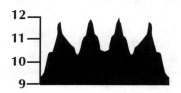

Trip	From Onion Valley to Rae Lakes via Kearsarge Pass, Charlotte Lake and Glen Pass
Distance	27 miles
Type	Out and back trip
Best season	Mid or late
Topo maps	Kearsarge Peak, Mt. Clarence King 7½′

Grade (hiking days/recommended layover days)

Leisurely	5/2
Moderate	4/1
Strenuous	4/0
Trailhead	Onion Valley (13)

HIGHLIGHTS　From the high desert surroundings of the Onion Valley trailhead, this trip ascends to the alpine "moonscape" of rugged Kearsarge Pass, descends to the forested shores of bright blue Charlotte Lake, and then joins the John Muir Trail to climb over Glen Pass and visit the justly famous—and consequently well-visited—Rae Lakes. It's an exciting mix of varied scenery and good angling.

Because of very heavy use, camping at Rae Lakes is restricted to a maximum of one night at each of the three lakes, and bears can be a serious problem. Store food properly at all times. Wood campfires are not permitted.

DESCRIPTION (Leisurely trip)

1st and 2nd Hiking Days: Follow Trip 67 to **Charlotte Lake**, 8 miles.

3rd Hiking Day (**Charlotte Lake** to **Rae Lakes**, 5½ miles): Retrace your steps to the **X** junction with the John Muir Trail and turn left (north) toward Glen Pass. The trail makes a long, steady, rocky ascent that rounds a granite promontory with fine views of Charlotte Lake, the Charlotte Creek canyon, Charlotte Dome and Mt. Brewer; then it descends slightly and veers east. As the headwall of Glen Pass comes into view, it is hard to see where a passable trail could go up it. And indeed the last 500 feet up to the top are steeply switchbacking—but never on the edge of a cliff. At the pass (11,978'), one can look north down on the unnamed glacial lakes immediately to the north, and to several of the Rae Lakes below.

The descent from the pass is by zigzagging, rocky switchbacks down to the granite bench holding the unnamed lakes seen from the pass. Bad underfooting here requires care in placing one's feet, and the upper part of this side of the pass may be snow-covered until late season. After crossing the outlet stream of the lakes on the bench, the trail resumes its switchbacking descent, re-enters a pine forest cover and skirts the west shore of upper Rae Lake. Just before the trail crosses the narrow isthmus separating the upper lake from the rest of the chain, we pass a spur trail branching west to Sixty Lake Basin.

After crossing the sparsely timbered isthmus, the route swings north, passes the unmarked, unmaintained lateral to Dragon Lake, and arrives at the many good campsites near the east shores of middle and lower Rae Lakes (10,560'). Fishing is good for brook trout and some rainbow (to 16"). Views from these campsites across the beryl-green lake waters to dramatically exfoliating Fin Dome and the King Spur beyond are among the best and longest remembered of the trip, along with sun-up views of Painted Lady in the south. A summer ranger is stationed on the east shore of the middle lake.

4th and 5th Hiking Days: Retrace your steps, 13½ miles.

Fin Dome over Dollar Lake

Onion Valley to Symmes Creek Trailhead   **69**

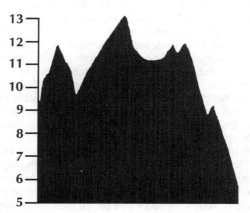

Trip	From Onion Valley to Symmes Creek Trailhead via Vidette Meadows, Forester Pass, Wright Lakes, Shepherd Pass and Anvil Camp
Distance	41 miles
Type	Shuttle trip
Best season	Mid or late
Topo maps	**Mt. Whitney** (15′); Kearsarge Peak, Mt. Clarence King, Mt. Brewer, Mt. Williamson 7½′

Grade (hiking days/recommended layover days)

Leisurely	9/3
Moderate	7/2
Strenuous	4/0

Trailhead	Start at Onion Valley (13), end at Symmes Creek Trailhead (22)

HIGHLIGHTS   This unusual trip is for the hiker who likes to explore very high country: most of the days are spent at or above treeline. Beginning with a 2800-foot elevation gain to enter the high country via Kearsarge Pass (11,978′), you then cross Forester Pass (13,180′), the highest pass on the John Muir Trail, visit spacious, alpine Wright Lakes (about 11,200′), and return via Shepherd Pass (12,050′).

This trip is ideal if you like to hike up and down. Be prepared for nothing but, along with cross-country stretches.

DESCRIPTION (Moderate trip)

1st and 2nd Hiking Days (**Onion Valley** to **Vidette Meadow**, 9.5 miles): Follow Trip 67 to the sandy-flat John Muir Trail junction in the second hiking day. Here you turn left (southeast) and almost immediately descend 1400 feet, the upper part of which is very steep and eroded from heavy stock travel. You repeatedly cross several streams, colorful with myriad wildflowers. You look down into beautiful meadows; to the south you can see into Vidette Creek canyon across Bubbs Creek canyon. At the bottom you meet the trail coming up from Cedar Grove. You turn left, uphill, ford the outlet creek from Bullfrog Lake for the last time, and within half a mile come to hardened, improved campsites (9600') above upper Vidette Meadow. Excellent and less crowded camping continues over the next mile up-canyon.

3rd Hiking Day (**Vidette Meadow** to **Upper Bubbs Creek**, 4.8 miles): The trail ascends steadily and moderately through a lodge-pole-pine forest alongside Bubbs Creek. Take advantage of this short day's hike to explore the creek's smooth granite ledges and irresistible pools. In 2.8 miles you pass the Center Basin/Junction Pass Trail going east. This was part of the old John Muir Trail, which went over Junction Pass before the Forester Pass section was built in 1932. There are good campsites here, and Golden Bear Lake, $1\frac{1}{4}$ miles and 700 vertical feet up the Center Basin Trail, offers good fishing and is one of the gems of the Sierra. However, to be nearer Forester Pass, your hike continues south and uphill another 2 miles to treeline. A number of campsites have been carved out of the rock among the whitebark pines on the west side of the trail. Or, just past this point, at the top of the rise where the trail turns due east, there is ample exposed camping (11,200').

4th Hiking Day (**Upper Bubbs Creek** to the **lake at 11,400'**, 7.2 miles): This entire day you hike above treeline, often with vast views. From your starting point, you climb along a wall with the outflow from Lake 12248 splashing down beside you, and then cross the stream several times. The trail then ascends the west wall of the canyon, reaches the south wall and switchbacks steeply up to the visible notch of Forester Pass (13,180'). As you near the pass, Junction Peak is a near-perfect pyramid due east of you just $\frac{1}{4}$ mile away. Views from the pass to the northeast include Mt. Pinchot, University Peak, Mt. Bradley and Mt. Keith. To the south are Mt. Kaweah, Kaweah Peaks Ridge, Red Spur, Kern Point, and Black Kaweah. Close by, Caltech Peak stands out to the west. Delicate blue-purple sky pilot, denizen of the sky-high country, grows in crevices in the rocks around the pass.

From here, the trail descends in steep switchbacks, some blasted out of the rock. The first 20 feet of descent make you wish the trail builders had made it a little wider. Below you, to the south you can see the two lakes immediately to the west of Diamond Mesa, a distinctive flat-topped table with sheer walls as its sides. These two lakes are set in open granite slabs and sand, and provide unlimited, extremely exposed campsites. After you pass them and Diamond Mesa, spectacular views open up of the Tyndall Creek headwaters and Mt. Tyndall in the east. Near timberline, shortly past the outflow of a small lake, you reach the signed Lake South America/Milestone Creek Trail to the west. Leave the trail at this junction and follow the outflow up to this lake (11,400'), where you will find beautiful camping in the nearby foxtail pines on the north shore.

5th Hiking Day (**Lake at 11,400'** to **Wright Lakes**, 6 miles): Return to the trail junction and continue southward on the Pacific Crest/John Muir Trail. Within a short half mile you cross Tyndall Creek, and then pass the Shepherd Pass Trail going northwest along the west side of Tawny Point. After passing the steeper slopes of Tawny Point, look for an unmarked trail eastward that crosses the Bighorn Plateau's margin into the Wright Lakes basin. Here you cross a vast meadow, sloping upward, to reach Wright Lakes, which are tucked under Peak 13540 west of Mt. Versteeg. You will find fair campsites at about 11,200 feet, where the outlet stream of Lake 11952 meets the other two outflows draining the upper basin. Occasional foxtail pines and granite erratics provide wind shelter for camping. You may hear a coyote pack howl, and you will probably share the basin with mule deer, for they summer here. A layover day here lets you explore these lakes which, unusual in the Sierra, are set in a vast expanse rather than hemmed in by mountain walls. You could take another unforgettable layover day to visit Wallace Lake, where scenery and fish compete to tempt you to a long stay.

6th Hiking Day (**Wright Lakes** to **Anvil Camp**, 6.5 miles): Walk northwest cross-country toward the northwestmost lakelet shown on the topo map. An obvious fisherman's trail works up the northeast wall of the western shoulder of Peak 13540. The saddle between Peak 13540 and Peak 12345 is visible for your entire ascent. The panoramic view from this saddle includes the noble series of summits of the Great Western Divide: Junction Peak; Mts. Keith, Brewer, Kaweah, Guyot and Young; and the top of Mt. Whitney, as well as the Kern River trench. From the saddle, head straight down; it does not help to try to contour northeastward. Only when you have left very steep terrain should you begin to contour northeastward, planning to meet the Shepherd Pass Trail near the tarn shown at 11,600 feet on the topo map. Beyond the tarn this trail ascends gently and steadily toward Shepherd Pass. The lake just a few feet before the pass has several chilly, windy campsites: this lake is often half frozen even in midsummer. At Shepherd Pass (12,050') views of the Great Western Divide spread out behind you; and before you, 8000 feet below, you can see Owens Valley.

The trail down the first 500 feet of Class 3 talus was rebuilt in 1989 but has deteriorated rapidly. Often this north-facing slope is covered by a snowfield well into summer, so that you descend a ladder of snow pockets rather than unstable talus. When the steepest part of the descent ends, the trail continues through a jumble of huge boulders. Just below treeline you reach The Pothole and pass a trail going northwest to Junction Pass. In another mile, descending over rough, rocky trail, you cross Shepherd Creek for the first time, and in the welcome foxtail-forest cover you reach good campsites at Anvil Camp (10,000') on either side of the creek. No wood fires are permitted.

  7th Hiking Day (**Anvil Camp** to **Symmes Creek Trailhead**, 7.5 miles): Leaving Anvil Camp, you descend on good trail through talus. Abruptly, the foxtails end and you begin a long series of gentle switchbacks through east-side terrain—mountain mahogany and sage, plants of dry slopes—which brings you to Mahogany Flat (9000'). There are several campsites here, and water if you leave the trail and descend to the creek. Continuing your switchbacking descent, you cross the only year-round creek between Mahogany Flat and Symmes Creek. You then pass the burned remaining stubs that were once a mountain mahogany "forest" of very large shrubs. A final stream crossing at 8700 feet (often dry by midsummer) marks the beginning of a discouraging 500-foot ascent. The first steep section of climbing carries you to a small ridge; there is a dry campsite with views that make up for the absence of water. Shepherd Creek has carved a steep canyon to the south, capped by towering Mt. Williamson, the only 14,000-foot peak in the Sierra not on the crestline.

The trail then traverses from Shepherd Creek Canyon to the Symmes Creek watershed by crossing two small ridges, continuing to ascend over slopes so steep they seem to exceed the angle of repose. Frequent rockslides take out sections of this trail. You reach a final welcome but waterless saddle (9200') with ample campsites set in the trees. From this saddle the trail descends and descends, moderately steeply, through western white pine and red fir on switchback after switchback 2240 feet to Symmes Creek, the first water since Shepherd Creek. You ford Symmes Creek four times as the steep canyon narrows—easy in a dry year or in late summer, but sure to wet your feet and threaten your footing most of the rest of the time. Between crossings, the trail is overgrown by alders, willows, creamberry bushes and cottonwoods. A scant quarter mile after the last crossing, the stock trail leaves to your left, and you continue another ½ mile to the Symmes Creek Trailhead (6250′).

Junction Peak

Bubbs Creek to Lower Kern

This stretch of country is the least visited, least known, and least trampled region in the southern Sierra. Much of it owes its integrity not to any lack of scenic or recreational potential, but rather to the presence of a fortuitously placed series of natural barriers—the Great Western Divide, the Kings-Kern Divide and the Sierra Crest. Joined together in a U, they protect the first 24 miles of the Kern River watershed with a wall of mountains crossed only by 1) people who have business here (rangers, packers, etc.), 2) people who have a love for the high country, and 3) people who fly over. There's no need to take aircraft over this region, and low-flying supersonic jets especially detract from one's wilderness experience. Within the mountainous U shape, the Kern River flows through a 30-mile section of straight, glacier-scoured canyon. This deep, spectacular canyon is very unusual for the Sierra in that it runs north-south instead of east-west.

The main area described in this region that sits outside this protective cup of divides and ranges is west of the Great Western Divide. Remoteness from roads and a convoluted terrain guarantee its sanctuary. And sanctuary it is, for in the remote headwaters of the Roaring and Kaweah rivers a hiker can walk for one, two, or even three days without seeing a soul.

This high region has a delicate balance between plant and animal life, which is nowhere more manifest than in the alpine fell fields over Cottonwood Pass just west of Horseshoe Meadow, or around the subalpine meadows just south of Little Claire Lake over the divide from Mineral King. Here, in an incredibly brief 6–7-week span, some 40 varieties of hardy-yet-vulnerable grasses, sedges and flowering plants grow, bud, blossom, seed, and are harvested, running their appointed course under the daily threat of killing frost, and before the juggernaut deadline of the first winter snows. Caught in the complex web of life, year-round resident animals like the cony, the marmot and the pocket gopher stake their very existence on the plants' short summer tenure. Inexorably linked in the ecological chain, the migrating and hibernating carnivores, such as coyote, mountain lion, black bear, red fox, marten, weasel and wolverine, would perish without their dependable rodent and squirrel food supply. So fragile and tenuous is this balance that the trampling by people and their livestock of a high, grassy meadow—particularly during the early, wet days of spring—can have and has had catastrophic effects upon the food chain.

This is not to argue that we do not have a place in this setting. Our trails, within strict practical and esthetic limitations, are as legitimate as those of the deer. We have the right to share the fish of the streams and the berries of the hillside with the bear. Like the marmot, we have our place in the sun—preferably a big flat rock where we too can laze away a warm afternoon. Our propensity for mountaintops and places of quiet solitude is as valid as the bighorn sheep's. And, like the hermit thrush at nesting time or the Brewer blackbird at sundown, we have the right to sing of our exultation at being alive and here.

But, because we know the devastation wrought by large, concentrated numbers of our species upon wilderness, we should try to expand rather than decrease the size of wilderness areas, and to disperse our impact upon them. Implicit within both of these obligations should be a profound respect for the ecological chain, of which we are a part, for this respect will give birth to a deeper knowledge and appreciation of the re-creating benefits of a region such as this.

The authors hope that, beyond sharing their appreciation of and passion for this grand part of the Sierra, they might, with this modest guide, call the attention of the prospective traveler to the less traveled byways and thereby contribute, in small measure, to the distribution of human impact. Because many of the routes described here are the lesser traveled, they are therefore sometimes faint, but that is as it should be. The passes are sometimes steeper than those used on the more traveled routes, but the rewards of scenery and solitude are commensurate.

As the quality of the wilderness experience is important, so is the quantity. For it is only through public support that requisite public legislation and administrative decisions will reflect our desire and need for wild areas. The more people that are introduced to basic wilderness values, perhaps through guidebooks like this, the greater will be the demand for more and better wilderness areas and national parks. If pieces of untrammeled country like that between the Kings-Kern Divide and the lower Kern River remain bastions of peace and solitude, it will be not so much because government officials discourage and restrict wilderness travel as because more wilderness alternatives are created for people to use. The sooner people recognize this fact, the sooner the trend to wilderness attrition will be reversed.

Wood fires are *prohibited* in the following places: Kings Canyon National Park above 10,000 feet; Kern River drainage above 11,200 feet and in Nine Lake Basin; Kaweah River drainage above 9000 feet and at Hamilton Lakes; Cottonwood, Cirque, South Fork, and Rocky Basin lakes; anywhere within ¼ mile of Chicken Spring Lake. *Use a gas stove.*

70 Whitney Portal to Outpost Camp

Trip	From Whitney Portal to Outpost Camp
Distance	7 miles
Type	Out and back trip
Best season	Mid or late
Topo maps	**Mt. Whitney** 15′; Mt. Langley, Mount Whitney 7½′
Grade	(hiking days/recommended layover days)
Leisurely	2/0
Moderate	Day
Strenuous	½ day
Trailhead	Whitney Portal (23)

HIGHLIGHTS   This overnight trip offers an experience of the high country in the shadow of Mt. Whitney. Outpost Camp can be used as a base camp for climbing Mt. Whitney or for exploring the spectacular surrounding country.

DESCRIPTION (Leisurely trip)

1st Hiking Day (**Whitney Portal** to **Outpost Camp**, 3½ miles): From just east of the small store at road's end, our route follows the old stock trail from the defunct pack station as it steadily climbs on seemingly endless, dusty switchbacks through a moderate forest cover of Jeffrey pine and red fir. After ½ mile the trail crosses the North Fork Lone Pine Creek and shortly it enters John Muir Wilderness. Soon the forest cover thins, and the slope is covered with a chaparral that includes mountain mahogany, Sierra chinquapin and sagebrush. This steep slope can get very hot by mid-morning, and the trip is best begun as early as possible. (Carry water.) Breather stops on this trail section provide a view down the canyon framing the Alabama Hills. Then the trail levels off somewhat through several willow-covered pockets having a moderate forest cover of lodgepole and foxtail pines, and passes fields of corn lilies, delphinium, tall lupine and swamp whiteheads as, in 1½ miles, it approaches a ford of Lone Pine Creek.

Beyond this log ford is a junction with the lateral that leads east to pretty Lone Pine Lake, visible from the junction. The route leads up a barren, rocky wash, then switchbacks up another slope through a moderate lodgepole tree cover to Outpost Camp (toilets) (10,365'), a willow-covered meadow that was once a lake. Before Congress made this area part of John Muir Wilderness, a packer's wife ran a little camp here, renting tents and selling meals. A very large abandoned stove—now gone—remained for some years near the upper end of this park as evidence of the camp, which had to be removed when the area was made wilderness.

There are many fair campsites here in Outpost Camp, but wood fires are forbidden, as they are on all of the Mt. Whitney Trail. Those bound for the summit of Mt. Whitney or for Crabtree Meadows and beyond may have enough steam left to climb on to overused Trail Camp (toilets), almost 3 miles ahead, the last legal camping place on the trail, which is above treeline.

2nd Hiking Day: Retrace your steps, 3½ miles.

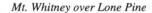

Mt. Whitney over Lone Pine

71 Whitney Portal to Crabtree Ranger Station

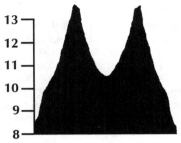

Trip	From Whitney Portal to Crabtree Ranger Station via Trail Crest
Distance	30 miles
Type	Out and back trip
Best season	Mid to late
Topo maps	**Mt. Whitney** 15′; Mt. Langley, Mount Whitney 7½′

Grade (hiking days/recommended layover days)

Leisurely	—
Moderate	5/1
Strenuous	4/0

Trailhead	Whitney Portal (23)

HIGHLIGHTS   Despite the elevation at Trail Crest, where this route crosses the Sierra Crest, it is actually one of the easier routes into the Upper Kern Basin. This route follows the Mt. Whitney Trail and passes within 2 trail miles of the highest point in the contiguous US. Permits for the trail are much sought-after.

Summer weekends bring out huge crowds to dayhike to Whitney's summit. Don't be too disappointed if you find yourself part of a continuous stream of traffic all the way to the summit.

DESCRIPTION (Strenuous trip)

1st Hiking Day: Follow Trip 70 to **Outpost Camp**, 3½ miles.

2nd Hiking Day: (**Outpost Camp** to **Crabtree Ranger Station**, 11½ miles): (This hiking day is a long one, since you do not camp short of Crabtree Ranger Station, and it involves an ascent of 3400 feet. Start early.) Your trail veers away from the waterfall that tumbles down into Outpost Camp from the southwest, fords Lone Pine Creek and begins a short series of switchbacks beside the cascading creek past blossoming creambush, Indian paintbrush, Sierra chinquapin, mountain pride, currant, pennyroyal, fireweed and senecio. Just after the trail crosses the outlet stream on rocks, it arrives at unattractive Mirror Lake (10,640'), cradled in its cirque beneath the south face of Thor Peak. This cold lake has fair fishing for rainbow and brook trout, but camping has been forbidden here since 1972, after severe overuse had created a montane slum.

Leaving Mirror Lake, the trail ascends the south wall of the cirque via rocky switchbacks. Ascending steeply under the north flanks of Mt. Irvine, the rocky trail crosses the south fork of the Middle Fork Lone Pine Creek and winds up past giant blocks and granite outcroppings. In the cracks in the boulders the hiker will find ivesia, cinquefoil, creambush, currant and much gooseberry, and looking across the canyon one will see the cascading outlet of Consultation Lake. Beside a rock bridge that crosses the stream are specimens of the moisture-loving shooting star. After ascending again, the trail arrives at the last campsites before the crest, Trail Camp (12,000') (toilets). The toilets may be closed on weekdays, due to overuse. When they're closed, use standard backpacking sanitation techniques (see page 5). There are numerous level campsites, lots of campers, and the last reliable water in late season. As the trail begins exactly 100 switchbacks (100 unless trail crews have done some remodeling) to Trail Crest Pass, Mt. Whitney disappears behind its needles. The steep, rocky slope up to the crest is not entirely barren, for in season one may see a dozen species of flowering plants, climaxed by the multiflowered, blue "sky pilot." The building of this trail involved much blasting with dynamite, and the natural fracture planes of the granite are evident in the blasted slabs. Finally, the 1800-foot ascent from Trail Camp ends at Trail Crest (13,580'), and you suddenly have vistas of a great part of Sequoia National Park to the west, including the entire Great Western Divide. To the east, far below, are several small, unnamed lakes, lying close under the steep faces of Mts. Whitney and Muir. These lakes may be ice-covered well into summer.

From Trail Crest the route descends for a short 100 yards to a junction with the 2-mile lateral to Mt. Whitney (14,491'). The highest mountain in the United States until Alaska was admitted as a state, this peak was first climbed on August 18, 1873, by three fishermen, who made the ascent up the southwest slope. The present trail between this junction and the summit lies close to the crest on the west side of it, and is an easy hike if you don't try to fight bad weather and take proper clothing. If a storm breaks, stay out of the summit hut and get off the peak!

As your switchbacking descent on the west side of the Sierra Crest begins, you leave the crowds behind and can make out the

Hitchcock Lakes below in a cirque basin that has been changed but little since its glacier melted. The parallel avalanche chutes on the northeast wall of Mt. Hitchcock all terminate at the upper limit of glacial erosion. Along the switchbacks, the most prominent flower is the yellow, daisylike hulsea, or alpine gold. After the long switchbacks end, the trail follows a moderate descent on a traverse of the "back" side of Mt. Whitney, descends to a bench with two tiny lakes and some small, exposed campsites, and then levels off at campsites overlooking Guitar Lake (11,600'). Guitar Lake becomes very overused late in the season, and you may prefer camping near the tiny lakes on the bench above it, along Arctic Lake's outlet, or on the rise above the "guitar neck."

From these campsites your route crosses the outlet of Arctic Lake, descends on a moderately steep, rocky trail into a sparse cover of lodgepole, and arrives at Timberline Lake (no camping or grazing, but fair fishing for golden to 7"). After skirting the shore of this lake (viewpoints for focusing the camera on Mt. Whitney and its reflection), the trail passes a lovely meadow, and then descends the valley of Whitney Creek to a junction with the trail to Crabtree Ranger Station (10,640') and the fair campsites nearby. Emergency services are sometimes available at the ranger station. Fishing in Whitney Creek is fair for golden (to 7"). (During times of heavy trail traffic, the hiker who wants more solitude may choose to camp at Upper Crabtree Meadow, ½ mile southwest of the ranger station, or Lower Crabtree Meadow, 1 mile southwest. These sites are reached by taking the Rock Creek Trail at the junction west of the ranger station.)

3rd and 4th Hiking Days: Retrace your steps, 15 miles.

Mt. Hitchcock

Whitney Portal to Wallace Lake

72

Trip	From Whitney Portal to Wallace Lake via Trail Crest, Crabtree Ranger Station and Wallace Creek
Distance	47 miles
Type	Out and back trip
Best season	Mid to late
Topo maps	**Mt. Whitney** 15′; Mt. Langley, Mount Whitney 7½′

Grade (hiking days/recommended layover days)

Leisurely	—
Moderate	8/1
Strenuous	6/0

Trailhead   Whitney Portal (23)

HIGHLIGHTS   Wallace Lake, lying in the heart of the Mt. Whitney region, is thought by many to be the finest fishing lake in the region. Well off the "beaten track," it is also a base from which to climb Mts. Barnard and Russell.

DESCRIPTION (Strenuous trip)

1st and 2nd Hiking Days: Follow Trip 71 to **Crabtree Ranger Station**, 15 miles.

3rd Hiking Day (**Crabtree Ranger Station** to **Wallace Lake**, 8½ miles): From Crabtree Ranger Station our route branches right (north), fords Whitney Creek (last reliable water till Wallace Creek in a dry year) and climbs the north slope of Whitney Creek canyon into a foxtail-pine forest. On an overcast day, this foxtail forest, with its dead snags, fallen trees, and lack of ground cover, has an eerie, gloomy, otherworldly quality. The trail then switchbacks up to a junction with the justly famous Pacific Crest Trail. These switchbacks offer the hard-breathing hiker views of Mts. Hitchcock, Pickering and Chamberlain, and the flanks of Mt. Whitney, whose summit is over the horizon. From the ridge the route descends gently on a sandy trail through a moderate cover of lodgepole and foxtail to a ford (10,636') of an unnamed creek. Beginning here the trail skirts what is called Sandy Meadow on the topo map. Small meadowy sections of trail lie beside several little streams not shown on the topo map, and in season they are graced with the yellow blossoms of senecio and monkey flower.

After these crossings the trail ascends a moderate slope with a lodgepole canopy and a heavy lupine ground cover to the saddle marked 10964 on the topo map. From this saddle the route descends gently on a sandy trail around the west shoulder of Mt. Young. Leveling off, the trail winds among some massive boulders that make up a lateral moraine, and then leads down a rocky hillside from which the traveler has fine views of Mt. Ericsson, Tawny Point, Junction Peak, the flank of Mt. Tyndall, Mt. Versteeg, Mt. Williamson, and, farthest right, Mt. Barnard. Beyond the ford of a tributary of Wallace Creek the descent becomes gentle again, through a moderate cover of lodgepole, foxtail and whitebark pines. Beyond the next tributary ford the descent steepens, and the trail switchbacks ¼ mile down to Wallace Creek. Just past the ford (very difficult in early season) the High Sierra Trail and the John Muir Trail, which have been conjoined from the top of Mt. Whitney to here, diverge. The High Sierra Trail turns left (west) toward Giant Forest and the Muir Trail continues north toward Yosemite.

Our route turns right (east) up Wallace Creek canyon on an unmarked use trail on the creek's north side. Under a forest cover of sparse-to-moderate lodgepole the trail ascends gently amid sprinklings of western wallflower, penstemon, senecio, yarrow milfoil and Labrador tea. You are also likely to see deer. At the meadow where the outlet of Wales Lake joins Wallace Creek, the trail fords the creek and then fords the tributary, staying on the south side of Wallace Creek. Here the ascent becomes moderate for a short distance, and then reverts to a gentler grade. This beautiful route up Wallace Creek canyon is sometimes indistinct and sometimes confused by multiple trail sections and inadequate ducking. Careful negotiation of the indistinct sections will bring one to the fair campsites at treeline (11,400') about ½ mile below Wallace Lake. The lake lies beneath the ridge that connects Mt. Barnard with Tunnabora Peak. Fishing in Wallace Lake is good for golden (to 14").

4th, 5th and 6th Hiking Days: Retrace your steps, 23½ miles.

Whitney Portal to Milestone Basin

73

Trip	From Whitney Portal to Milestone Basin via Trail Crest, Crabtree Ranger Station, Wallace Creek, Junction Meadow and Upper Kern River
Distance	59 miles
Type	Out and back trip
Best season	Mid to late
Topo maps	**Mt. Whitney** 15′; Mt. Langley, Mount Whitney, Mt. Kaweah, Mt. Brewer 7½′

Grade (hiking days/recommended layover days)

Leisurely	—
Moderate	10/2
Strenuous	8/1
Trailhead	Whitney Portal (23)

HIGHLIGHTS   This trip samples both well-traveled trails and little-used trails, country above timberline and dense forests. Milestone Basin, set under the giant finger of Milestone Mountain, encompasses countless small lakes bounded by large, rounded boulders and connected by cascading streams. These lakes are devoid of people but full of fish.

DESCRIPTION (Strenuous trip)

1st and 2nd Hiking Days: Follow Trip 71 to **Crabtree Ranger Station**, 15 miles.

3rd Hiking Day (**Crabtree Ranger Station** to **Upper Kern River**, 8½ miles): Follow the 3rd hiking day, Trip 72, to the junction of the John Muir Trail and the High Sierra Trail at Wallace Creek.

Taking the High Sierra Trail from this junction, our route proceeds down Wallace Creek canyon on sandy underfooting, with views ahead of Mt. Kaweah and the Kaweah Peaks Ridge. The trail veers away from Wallace Creek and then meets it again after a short, moderate descent on an exposed slope. Our trail passes campsites lining both sides as it winds among sparse-to-moderate lodgepole and a great variety of wildflowers (in midsummer), including 3-foot-tall, bright pink fireweed, paintbrush, arnica, sulfur flower, wild buckwheat, pennyroyal, mountain pride and creamberry. After fording Wright Creek (difficult in early season), the trail descends more steeply through sparse lodgepole mixed with some foxtail pines.

As the canyon widens and the trail veers more westward, the timber cover diminishes almost to nothing, and the slope (hot in afternoon) is covered with manzanita, creambush, hollyleaf redberry, mountain mahogany and Sierra chinquapin. The main splash of color in this chaparral is the red penstemon, or mountain pride. This exposed slope offers views down the great trough of the Kern River, south to Mt. Guyot and west to Kaweah Peaks Ridge.

The descent now reaches the Canadian life zone as Jeffrey pines are seen, along with mountain juniper. Here our route turns northward and traverses down the Kern Canyon wall to meet the Kern River Trail, onto which it turns right (north), leaving the High Sierra Trail. One mile up the canyon our route passes a decaying roofless cabin. Beginning here there are several good campsites along the river, where fishing is good for golden (to 10").

4th Hiking Day (**Upper Kern River** to **Milestone Basin**, 6 miles): Once past the cabin, the trail ascends less steeply and soon reaches a ford of Tyndall Creek (difficult in early season). Beyond the ford, the trail becomes sandier and drier, and the red fir and aspen gradually disappear, leaving a forest cover of lodgepole and some foxtail that is sparse on the hillsides and moderate on the river terraces. There are numerous campsites along this stretch of trail, including a large campsite ½ mile beyond the junction with the Tyndall Creek Trail. Beyond this trail, our route becomes more exposed, with considerable sagebrush. After the trail fords the outlet stream of Lake 11440, we soon come to a dell thick with lodgepole trunks. The prolific, varied wildflower display in this large dell is dominated by senecio, but also includes tiger lilies, swamp onions and red columbine. The trail ascends above the dell and passes through a bank of shield ferns, Queen Anne's lace and bush chinquapin, staying on the east side of the river. Here the rocky trail ascends steeply through a sparse lodgepole cover on a rocky trail over granite slabs that rise 600 feet to the upper Kern plateau. After the trail levels off, it soon reaches a junction with the Milestone Basin Trail, where you turn left (west). (This is an indistinct junction but the path should be clear west of the river.) If the ford here is too hard, there may be a log to cross on at the outlet of the unnamed lake about 200 yards north. After fording the river, the trail contours to meet Milestone Creek and then veers west up a rocky slope away from the creek. After another ½ mile it rejoins the creek at a bench where, beside a waterfall, there is a good campsite (11,110′). Fishing in Milestone Creek is good for rainbow (to 10″). Those who wish to camp as high as possible may climb to the high lake (11,900′) just to the right of the words *Midway Mtn.* on the topo map. Follow a route that turns right up the north fork, passes through a defile, skirts a small lake barren of fish, and traverses up to the high lake, where fishing is good for golden (to 12″). There are fair campsites below this lake on the outlet stream.

5th, 6th, 7th and 8th Hiking Days: Retrace your steps, 29½ miles.

Milestone Mountain

74 Whitney Portal to Kern-Kaweah River

Trip	From Whitney Portal to the Kern-Kaweah River via Trail Crest, Crabtree Meadow, Wallace Creek and Junction Meadow
Distance	61 miles
Type	Out and back trip
Best season	Mid to late
Topo maps	**Mt. Whitney** 15'; Mt. Langley, Mount Whitney, Mt. Kaweah 7½'

Grade (hiking days/recommended layover days)

Leisurely	—
Moderate	10/2
Strenuous	8/1
Trailhead	Whitney Portal (23)

HIGHLIGHTS   This route combines the high, rocky country along the Whitney crest with the alluvial meadows on the Kern River and the intimate camping in the little-visited Kern-Kaweah River canyon. These latter campsites are about as far "away from it all" as you can get.

DESCRIPTION (Strenuous trip)

1st and 2nd Hiking Days: Follow Trip 71 to **Crabtree Ranger Station**, 15 miles.

3rd Hiking Day (**Crabtree Ranger Station** to **Junction Meadow**, 9½ miles): Follow the 3rd hiking day, Trip 73, to the junction of the High Sierra Trail and the Kern River Trail, and turn left (south). From here the rocky trail descends steeply to Junction Meadow

(8036′) through stands of aspen and past occasional Jeffrey and lodgepole pines, winding through a ground cover of manzanita and currant. As the trail levels off, it enters a parklike grove of stalwart Jeffrey pines that provide the setting for the poor campsites near the Kern River. Fishing is good for rainbow and some brook trout (to 10″).

4th Hiking Day (**Junction Meadow** to **Kern-Kaweah River**, 6 miles): This day's route is irregularly maintained, but a backpacker with experience will have no trouble staying on the route. Soon after the ford of the Kern River (very difficult in early season) the trail begins the steep ascent up the west Kern canyon wall to the hanging valley above. Veering away from the Kern-Kaweah River, it ascends to the north side of a granite knob, or spine, and passes through what has been called Kern-Kaweah Pass. This difficult climb is repaid by the delightful valley above it, one of the finest in the Sierra. From the "pass" the trail makes a very steep, loose and rocky—but mercifully short—descent, a moderate ascent and finally a slight descent to what is left of Rockslide Lake (9040′)—two wide pools of crystal-clear, emerald-green water in the river.

Beyond the lake, the canyon widens into a granite amphitheater, where two tributary streams merge and dash into the main canyon over a rocky ledge to meet the main river below the fall by which the river arrives at the bowl. From here the ascent through a sparse-to-moderate lodgepole cover is moderate as the route threads the deep canyon lying between Kern Point and Picket Guard Peak. One more steep ascent is required to reach the bowl that contains what is left of Gallats Lake (10,000′), a lovely oxbow in a large, wet meadow (fishing is good for golden to 8″). Fair campsites are here, but better ones lie about 1 mile ahead where the trail turns away from the river toward Colby Pass. These campsites are a good explorer's base for excursions into the lightly visited headwaters of the Kern-Kaweah River and into Milestone Bowl. Fishing is excellent for golden (to 7″).

5th, 6th, 7th and 8th Hiking Days: Retrace your steps, 30½ miles.

75 Whitney Portal to Symmes Creek Trailhead

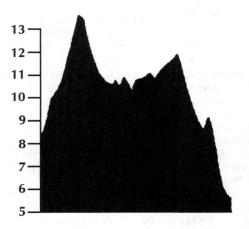

Trip	From Whitney Portal to Symmes Creek Trailhead via Trail Crest, Crabtree Meadow, Tyndall Creek and Shepherd Pass
Distance	39 miles
Type	Shuttle trip
Best season	Mid to late
Topo maps	**Mt. Whitney** 15′; Mt. Langley, Mount Whitney, Mt. Williamson 7½′

Grade (hiking days/recommended layover days)

Leisurely	—
Moderate	6/2
Strenuous	5/0
Trailhead	Start at Whitney Portal (23), end at Symmes Creek (22)

HIGHLIGHTS   This high trip loops around "the Whitney group," the culmination of the Sierra spine, with five peaks standing over 14,000 feet. A spur trail can take the hiker to the highest point in the contiguous 48 states, 14,494 feet above sea level. The vast panoramas of the upper Kern basin along this route are unequaled in the Sierra.

DESCRIPTION (Strenuous trip)

1st and 2nd Hiking Days: Follow Trip 73 to **Crabtree Ranger Station**, 15 miles.

3rd Hiking Day (**Crabtree Ranger Station** to **Tyndall Creek Tributary**, 9 miles): Follow the 3rd hiking day, Trip 72, to the junction of the John Muir Trail and the High Sierra Trail. From Wallace Creek, this day's route continues north on the Muir Trail. The sandy and rocky trail ascends moderately through a sparse-to-moderate forest cover, to a spectacular overlook of the Great Western Divide. Here the trail becomes quite level as it crosses a sandy flat bearing a forest cover of lodgepole and foxtail pines. The trail crosses Wright Creek via a rocky ford (difficult in early season) and passes some campsites east of the trail.

Several short but taxing ascents separated by level stretches bring the hiker onto Bighorn Plateau, where the panoramic view begins with Red Spur in the southwest and sweeps north along the Great Western Divide, then east along the Kings-Kern Divide to Junction Peak. In addition, one can see, to the southeast, Mts. Whitney, Young and Russell. A small lake west of the trail presents great photographic possibilities in the morning, and any time of day is good for photographing the lateral moraine of the Tyndall Creek glacier, which follows a contour along the west side of the plateau. A large field of vivid purple lupine sweeps up the slope to the east. From here a gentle descent on a rocky trail through a sparse foxtail cover leads to the good campsites (11,100') where the trail crosses the outlet of Tyndall "Frog Ponds," which offer good swimming in mid and late season. (More campsites—poor ones—are located ½ mile farther north just across Tyndall Creek.)

4th Hiking Day (**Tyndall Creek Tributary** to **Anvil Camp**, 7½ miles): As this hiking day begins, the John Muir Trail descends gently on a rocky course through a forest cover of mixed lodgepole and foxtail pines to a junction with the Shepherd Pass Trail. Your route turns right (east) onto the Shepherd Pass Trail and begins a long, steady ascent up the meadowy, vast, open, boulder-strewn upper basin of Tyndall Creek. Views improve constantly as you gain elevation, and the peaks of the Great Western Divide take on new aspects as they are seen from new angles. To the north, the southern escarpment of Diamond Mesa hides an upper surface that is one of the most level areas in this region. The traveler who has read the incredible first chapter of Clarence King's *Mountaineering in the Sierra Nevada* may speculate on where King and Richard Cotter crossed the Kings-Kern Divide and traversed this basin on their way to ascending Mt. Tyndall—which, in naming it, they believed to be the highest Sierra peak until they were on top of it and saw other, higher ones nearby.

The appearance of Lake 12002 heralds the approach to Shepherd Pass (12,050'), which from this side of the crest is merely the end of a long, gentle ascent. The east side of the pass is a total contrast, with some Class-3 steep scree and talus slopes, which are often snow covered until August. In 1989 a trail crew worked for the entire summer to repair and rebuild the route from Shepherd Pass to the Symmes Creek trailhead, transforming it into a pleasure walk. Since then, the harsh conditions at 12,000 feet have taken their toll on the upper sections, returning the trail to a flow of loose scree.

From the pass, the trail, such as it is, switchbacks down a 500-foot scree slope into a gigantic, barren bowl scooped out by the plucking action of the Shepherd Creek glacier. After winding among boulders and topping a slight rise, the trail begins a moderate descent to treeline and a poor campsite near a junction with the Junction Pass Trail. Our rocky trail continues to descend moderately through a cover of whitebark pines, soon replaced by foxtails and lodgepoles, to a ford of Shepherd Creek and the good campsites at Anvil Camp (10,000'), where fishing for rainbow (to 9") is fair. No wood fires are permitted.

5th Hiking Day (**Anvil Camp** to **Symmes Creek Trailhead**, 7½ miles): Follow the 7th hiking day, Trip 69.

Mt. Tyndall guards Shepherd Pass

Lodgepole Campground to Ranger Lake **76**

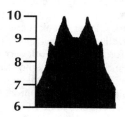

Trip	From Lodgepole Campground to Ranger Lake via Silliman Pass
Distance	20 miles
Type	Out and back trip
Best season	Mid to late
Topo maps	**Triple Divide Peak** 15′; Lodgepole, Mt. Silliman 7½′

Grade (hiking days/recommended layover days)

Leisurely	3/1
Moderate	2/1
Strenuous	2/0
Trailhead	Lodgepole Campground (19)

HIGHLIGHTS Crossing the Silliman crest on the boundary between Sequoia and Kings Canyon parks, this trip terminates at picturesque Ranger Lake. En route, the trail passes through sedate fir forests, skirts flower-splashed meadows, traces rambling brooks, and passes between a pair of shallow lakes whose waters, on a sunny day, invite the dusty hiker in for a refreshing swim.

DESCRIPTION (Moderate trip)

1st Hiking Day (**Lodgepole Campground** to **Ranger Lake**, 10 miles): The trail begins north of a bridge of the Marble Fork Kaweah River (6800′), and curves west to skirt the campground on a moderate ascent through a dense forest cover of fir, pine and cedar, understoried by abundant stickweed, pennyroyal, lupine, gilia and pussy paws. These woods teem with wildlife, and the traveler is very apt to see a few mule deer, many squirrels, and a host of birds. This ascent, over alternating rocky and sandy stretches, crests the moraine we have been walking on, then turns north and levels to a ford of Silliman Creek. After passing shooting-star-fringed Cahoon Meadow, the trail continues the moderate ascent over duff-and-sand underfooting through patchy, dense stands of red and white fir and some meadow sections, crossing several streamlets, to Cahoon Gap. The trail then descends moderately to ford the unnamed tributary just south of the East Fork Clover Creek (campsite). One fourth mile beyond this ford the trail veers east as the trail to JO Pass goes north (campsite) and then fords the East Fork Clover Creek.

The sometimes gentle, sometimes moderate ascent up the East Fork Clover Creek introduces lodgepole and mountain white pine into the forest cover, and as the trail approaches Twin Lakes, open stretches between the trees are a tide of colors. In season, one will find rank, knee-high corn lily, blue and white lupine, white mariposa lily, orange wallflower, purple larkspur, lavender shooting star, white cinquefoil, violet aster and golden senecio. The last mile to the heavily timbered flats around Twin Lakes is a steep ascent, and the traveler may well contemplate a quick swim in the largest lake, whose shallow waters quickly warm to a midsummer's sun.

Continuing toward Silliman Pass, the view of the two large boulder stands of exfoliating granite (Twin Peaks) dominates the horizon during the steep progress to the pass' saddle. This ascent sees the end of the fir, and almost exclusive domination of lodgepole pine. At the pass (10,165') one has a good view of flat-topped Mt. Silliman to the south, the heavily wooded Sugarloaf Creek drainage to the northeast, the Great Western Divide to the east, and the barren flats of the Tableland to the southeast.

From the pass the trail drops steeply and then turns north to the nose of a granite ridge before switchbacking down. From the switchbacks one has fine views of Ball Dome and much of the Kings River watershed, including the Monarch Divide. At the foot of the switchbacks a level duff trail leads north to Ranger Lake, and to the excellent campsites on the southwest side of the lake (9180'). Anglers working their way around the shallow lake plying their art on the fair-to-good fishing for rainbow trout (8–12") will also enjoy the carpet of shooting stars and the rose-purple blossom of heather. A layover day spent in this pleasant environment will allow the traveler to visit the nearby scenic settings of Beville (rainbow and brook) and Lost (brook) lakes.

2nd Hiking Day: Retrace your steps, 10 miles.

Lodgepole Campground to Roaring River   **77**

Trip	From Lodgepole Campground to Roaring River Ranger Station via Silliman Pass, Ranger Lake and Sugarloaf Valley
Distance	46 miles
Type	Out and back trip
Best season	Mid to late
Topo maps	**Triple Divide Peak** 15'; Lodgepole, Mt. Silliman, Sphinx Lakes 7½'

Grade (hiking days/recommended layover days)

Leisurely	7/2
Moderate	6/2
Strenuous	4/1
Trailhead	Lodgepole Campground (19)

HIGHLIGHTS   Take the scenic delights of Trip 76 and add the pleasure of strolling along Sugarloaf Creek, the fine camping near Roaring River Ranger Station, and the outstanding dayhiking from there—exploring remote Deadman and Cloud canyons and scaling viewful Moraine Ridge. Together, they make an unforgettable trip of great beauty—and one less-traveled because of its remoteness.

DESCRIPTION (Moderate trip)

1st Hiking Day: Follow Trip 76 to **Ranger Lake**, 10 miles.

2nd Hiking Day (**Ranger Lake** to **Comanche Meadow**, 5½ miles): First, return to the marked junction with the Silliman Pass Trail and on it go east, then north, toward Comanche Meadow. Our trail passes the turnoff to Lost Lake and circles Ball Dome. Passing through a moderate-to-heavy forest cover, the trail emerges at a meadowed crossing of the outlet stream from Seville Lake. Beyond this crossing is the marked junction of the Seville Lake/Marvin Pass Trail. Going east on the northwest side of Sugarloaf Creek, our route descends sometimes steadily and sometimes moderately over duff-and sand underfooting. This descent crosses an unnamed tributary, and a short distance beyond passes another trail to Marvin Pass. About 100 yards farther on, the trail passes the Kanawyer Gap Trail (which leads north and then west to Marvin Pass), and then fords the rocky creek emptying Comanche Meadow (7680'). Good campsites will be found on Sugarloaf Creek before and after this ford, and fishing for brook trout (to 8") is fair.

3rd Hiking Day (**Comanche Meadow** to **Roaring River**, 7½ miles): Beginning ¼ mile after the ford, the trail drops moderately on sandy underfooting over a heavily forested slope that shows the effects of a 1974 fire. As the trail levels out on the floor of Sugarloaf Valley, it follows the course of an old glacier. Through the trees, you can see the round, smooth, 1000-foot-high Sugarloaf Dome. More resistant than the surrounding rock, this granite island withstood the onslaught of the ice. The trail passes Sugarloaf Meadow and parallels and then fords Sugarloaf Creek.

On the south side of this wide, shallow ford, the trail passes more campsites before crossing a series of sharp wrinkles in the terrain to reach Ferguson Creek and still more campsites. After fording this creek via logs or rocks, the trail rounds a long, dry, timbered ridge nose before dropping down a steady slope to the drift fence below Scaffold Meadows, a pasture reserved for grazing animals. The signed SCAFFOLD MEADOWS TOURIST PASTURE across the river is also reserved for grazing. Living up to its name, Roaring River can be heard a few yards to the left, and with this pleasant accompaniment the trail ascends the last, gentle mile to the good campsites near Roaring River Ranger Station (7430') (toilet), fording the Barton Peak stream on the way. Fishing for rainbow and some golden trout (to 10") is fair to good. Emergency services are perhaps available from the resident summer ranger, whose cabin is nearby. These campsites make a fine base camp for further explorations of the surrounding headwaters of Deadman Canyon Creek, Roaring River and Brewer Creek.

4th, 5th and 6th Hiking Days: Retrace your steps, 23 miles.

Lodgepole Campground to Crescent Meadow   **78**

Trip	From Lodgepole Campground to Crescent Meadow via Silliman Pass, Ranger Lake, Comanche Meadow, Roaring River Ranger Station, Deadman Canyon, Elizabeth Pass and Bearpaw Meadow
Distance	51 miles
Type	Shuttle trip (see 6th hiking day for loop idea)
Best season	Late
Topo maps	**Triple Divide Peak** 15′; Lodgepole, Mt. Silliman, Sphinx Lakes, Triple Divide Peak 7½′

Grade (hiking days/recommended layover days)

Leisurely	—
Moderate	6/2
Strenuous	4/2

Trailhead	Start at Lodgepole Campground (19), end at Crescent Meadow (20)

HIGHLIGHTS   The climax of this trip is the high, wildflower-filled meadows at the head of Deadman Canyon. This glaciated canyon—a perfect example of the geological formation that John Muir called a "yosemite" with a small "y"—nestles against the craggy summits of Glacier Ridge in solitary splendor. It's named for the grave in its lower reaches, that of a sheepherder whose tomb, as visitors have noted, far surpasses in its natural magnificence that of any mere human monument.

The trail to Elizabeth Pass is seldom maintained, and its condition may resemble a cross-country route more than an established trail. Cross-country travel experience and navigating skills will be helpful.

DESCRIPTION (Moderate trip)

1st, 2nd and 3rd Hiking Days: Follow Trip 77 to **Roaring River**, 22 miles.

4th Hiking Day (**Roaring River** to **Upper Ranger Meadow**, 7 miles): Leaving Roaring River, the Elizabeth Pass Trail leads south, veering away from the river on a gentle-to-moderate ascent past well-charred Jeffrey pines. Views back over one's left shoulder include a fine example of a lateral moraine in the form of Moraine Ridge, the northeast wall of the canyon. About 1½ miles above the Roaring River bridge, our route ascends past the upper drift fence and several campsites. At the right time of summer, flowers seen during this short stretch include buckwheat, sagebrush, Indian paintbrush, Mariposa lily, pennyroyal, penstemon and shooting star. Past the drift fence, the trail fords Deadman Canyon creek, and in 1½ miles reaches a campsite. About 50 yards southeast of the campsite at the north end of a large wet meadow lies the gravesite from which Deadman Canyon got its name. The citation on the grave reads: "Here reposes Alfred Moniere, sheepherder, mountain man, 18– to 1887."

From this grave our ascent continues, offering good views up the canyon of the spectacularly smoothed, unjointed, barren walls. Soon the trail refords the creek and then climbs alongside a dramatic, green-water, granite-slab chute. The trail levels out in a dense stand of lodgepole and fir, and, passing a campsite, emerges at the north end of the open grasslands of Ranger Meadow. The precipitous canyon walls dominate the views from the meadow, and the cirque holding Big Bird Lake is clear on the west wall. By midsummer this meadow is a colorful carpet of purple and red wildflowers, including shooting star, penstemon and red heather.

From Ranger Meadow the trail resumes its steady ascent over duff and sand through stands of lodgepole and clumps of aspen. Just before the Upper Ranger Meadow flat, the route fords the creek to the east side. Here one has awesome glimpses of the headwall of the Deadman Canyon cirque, and this view continues to rule the skyline from the good campsites just beyond the drift fence at the north end of Upper Ranger Meadow (9200'). Fishing for rainbow, brook and hybrids is good (to 10"). A cross-county route to Big Bird Lake takes off west across the creek here, becoming a well-worn tread as it ascends the slope south of the lake's outlet and takes the traveler to a bench overlooking the main lake and several small ones.

5th Hiking Day (**Upper Ranger Meadow** to **Bearpaw Meadow**, 11 miles, part cross country): This day's hike is a long one, and you must get a very early start. It begins with a 2100-foot ascent, mostly cross country, to Elizabeth Pass, continues with a 3300-foot descent from the pass, and ends with a short but steep and exposed ascent and a shady descent to Bearpaw Meadow.

As we leave our campsite in Upper Ranger Meadow, our trail ascends gently through boulders, with Upper Ranger Meadow to the west. Low-growing willows line the stream, and clumps of wildflowers dot the green expanse. The ascent steepens to a moderate grade; then, as we begin the steep ascent of the headwall, we parallel a dramatic series of cascades and falls. Near the top of the falls, we reach a bench and cross the stream above a long, dashing granite chute, and then we climb steeply by a faint route up the southwest wall of the cirque. The light-colored granite slabs contrast with the darker metamorphic rocks (around an old copper mine site) seen to the east, and this contrast is even more marked from the tiny saddle of Elizabeth Pass (11,380′). Views to the southwest from the pass include parts of the Middle Fork Kaweah River watershed, Moose Lake, and the jumbled peaks of the southernmost prominences of the Tableland divide.

From the pass, the trail initially descends steeply by switchbacks, then by a moderate traverse, and then again by a series of rocky switchbacks. At the foot of these zigzags, our route passes a spur trail to Tamarack Lake. Travelers ready to stop for the night may want to take the spur trail from the first junction a short way up Lone Pine Canyon, to the first wooded area near the creek. In ¼ mile you reach a second junction where your route, the right fork, swings southwest to make a steep and mostly shadeless ascent across the sparsely timbered nose of the ridge above Bearpaw Meadow.

The descent from this ridge is steep, rocky and dry as it passes through stands of lodgepole and red fir and joins the High Sierra Trail 150 yards west of a ranger station and backcountry lodge that share a magnificent view over the Middle Fork Kaweah country. The view is worth a visit! Emergency services are probably available at the ranger station. Meals and lodging at Bearpaw Lodge are by reservation only, but there is a tiny "store" where you can buy film, freeze-dried food and trail snacks (supplies very limited). Turn left onto the High Sierra Trail, go a few yards, and then turn right to reach a very overused campground under heavy forest cover (piped, treated water, toilets). Open fires are not allowed around here.

6th Hiking Day (**Bearpaw Meadow** to **Crescent Meadow**, 11 miles): Reverse the 1st hiking day, Trip 79.

(Ambitious hikers can make this trip a loop by (1) using one of the many dayhiking trails between Crescent Meadow and Lodgepole or (2) leaving the High Sierra Trail short of Crescent Meadow and taking the Wolverton Cutoff trail or the Trail of the Sequoias to pick up one of those dayhiking trails. Allow an extra day on the High Sierra Trail, stopping at, say, Mehrten Creek Crossing.)

79   Crescent Meadow to Whitney Portal

Trip	From Crescent Meadow to Whitney Portal via the High Sierra Trail—with a slight detour: Bearpaw Meadow, Hamilton Lakes, Kaweah Gap, Moraine Lake, Kern Hot Spring, Junction Meadow, Wallace Creek, Crabtree Ranger Station, Mt. Whitney, Trail Crest and Outpost Camp
Distance	68½ miles
Type	Shuttle trip (trans-Sierra)
Best season	Mid to late
Topo maps	**Triple Divide Peak, Mt. Whitney** 15′; Lodgepole, Triple Divide Peak, Mt. Kaweah, Chagoopa Falls, Mount Whitney, Mt. Langley 7½′

Grade (hiking days/recommended layover days)

Leisurely	—
Moderate	8/3
Strenuous	6/2
Trailhead	Start at Crescent Meadow (20); end at Whitney Portal (23)

HIGHLIGHTS   This dramatic trans-Sierra route follows the High Sierra Trail. From Crescent Meadow, the High Sierra Trail winds eastward high above the Middle Fork Kaweah

River, crossing the Great Western Divide at Kaweah Gap. After dipping into Big Arroyo, it crosses the lightly visited Chagoopa Plateau, detours to lovely Moraine Lake, and descends to the great trench of Kern Canyon. Heading up-canyon, it passes the Sierra's most remote—but nevertheless well-visited—hot spring, Kern Hot Spring. Turning east, it climbs the gentler west side of Mt. Whitney and finally descends the steeper east face, where there are stunning views of vast, quiet Owens Valley. This is the quintessential Sierra crossing—*and* there's plenty of fine fishing on the way.

Bears are a serious problem on most stretches of this popular trail. Store your food properly at all times.

DESCRIPTION (Strenuous trip)

1st Hiking Day (**Crescent Meadow** to **Bearpaw Meadow**, 11 miles): From the parking loop, we circumvent the meadow on asphalt and begin climbing steadily through a forest of giant sequoias, sugar pines and white firs. Soon after passing a trail leading to Giant Forest, we break out into the open above the Middle Fork Kaweah River. In a few hundred yards, at Eagle View Overlook, the view is indeed awesome. Moro Rock pokes up in the west, far below is the river, and to the east are the heavily glaciated peaks of the Great Western Divide.

Our trail does not follow a "natural" route, but instead stays high on the north wall of the Middle Fork Kaweah River canyon. However, it is not a level traverse: frequently, the trail undulates over 400-foot rises, only to drop down into a secondary tributary canyon, and then emerge to climb again.

The trail is nearly level and mostly shady as we continue up-valley in a forest of ponderosa and sugar pine, black oak, incense-cedar, and white fir, mixed with manzanita, whitethorn scrub and much fragrant kit-kit-dizze. Across the canyon, those impressive sentinels of the valley, Castle Rocks, fall slowly behind as we march on. After negotiating three switchbacks, we resume strolling and soon pass a cutoff to Wolverton Corral in the north, used mostly by stock. Innumerable spring-fed streams cross the trail in this vicinity late into the season. Yellow-throated gilia and mustang clover are abundant along the trail until rather late in the year. Beyond Sevenmile Hill, a prominent ridge jutting out in the canyon below, we pass a junction with a trail that leads up to the Alta Trail 1300 feet above.

From the Alta Trail junction, the trail descends to ford an unnamed tributary and then climb steeply. Views are to the south and southeast, where the spectacular granite-dome formations of Sugarbowl Dome and Castle Rocks rise above the timbered valley floor. At each ford of the unnamed tributaries flowing from the slopes of Alta Peak, the trail passes precariously perched campsites. Then it rounds a hot, dry, sparsely timbered slope and reaches the Buck Creek bridge.

From here the route ascends through dense fir forest cover to the signed turnoff to a campground 200 yards south. Here, very overused campsites (7700') have toilets and piped, treated water. Emergency services are usually available from the ranger station just east of the campground turnoff. No open fires are allowed.

2nd Hiking Day (**Bearpaw Meadow** to **Big Arroyo Trail Junction**, 11 miles): Returning to the High Sierra Trail, our route turns right (east), and soon passes expansive, green Bearpaw Meadow. Today, most of the meadow is devoted to the outbuildings of Bearpaw Lodge (advance reservations for bed and board are essential and should be made on January 2 of the year you plan to go). Just across the trail from the lodge is the ranger's cabin. The magnificent views from the meadow and the subsequent trail include Mt. Stewart and Eagle Scout Peak on the Great Western Divide, Black Kaweah beyond, the Yosemite-like depths of Hamilton Creek and the Middle Fork Kaweah River, and the Cliff Creek drainage below.

Continuing past Bearpaw Ranger Station, the trail descends moderately through mixed, sparse forest stands. As the trail rounds the slope and descends toward River Valley, it traverses a section blasted from an immense, exfoliating granite slab. Views of clearcut avalanche chutes on the south wall of the canyon accompany the descent to the culvert fording wild, turbulent Lone Pine Creek. This stream cascades and plunges down a narrow granite chasm below the culvert. The force of the torrent and the narrow **V** of the chasm are clear evidence of the cutting power of the water. From the creek, the trail ascends an exposed slope, passing a side trail to Tamarack Lake and Elizabeth Pass (good campsites at this junction).

Continuing the steady ascent, the traveler is overwhelmed by the gigantic scale of the rock sculpting by ice, rock and snow to the east and southeast. The final climb to the ford of Hamilton Creek is overshadowed by the mighty rock on all sides: the sheer granite wall to the north called Angel Wings, the sharply pointed granite sentinels atop the south wall, and the wall's avalanche-chuted sides—all are a constant source of wonderment and awe.

Under these heights you boulder-hop across the stream a few hundred yards below the lowest lake of the Hamilton Lakes chain. From this ford the trail climbs steeply over shattered rock to the good campsites at the northwest end of Lake 8235. Views from the campsites, including the silver waterfall ribbon at the east end, are superlative, and fishing for brook, rainbow and golden (to 10") is fair to good, but the lake is highly overused, and we head for Kaweah Gap. Besides, two of the camping areas here were closed indefinitely in 1987 for rehabilitation, and there is a two-night limit on camping at any of the Hamilton Lakes.

The 2500-foot steep climb to Kaweah Gap is an engineering marvel of trail construction, which has literally blasted the way across vertical cliff sections. Beginning at the northwest end of Lake 8235, the trail ascends steadily up the juniper-and-red-fir-dotted slope with constant views of the lake and its dramatic walls. Despite the rocky terrain, many wildflowers line this ascent and among the manzanita and chinquapin one will find lush lupine, yellow columbine, penstemon, Indian paintbrush, white cinquefoil, false Solomon's seal and Douglas phlox.

After some doubling back, the trail turns south on a steep ascent to a point just above the north shore of Precipice Lake (10,200'), at the foot of the near-vertical north face of Eagle Scout Peak. The jagged summits of the peaks of the Great Western Divide dominate the skyline to the east during the final, tarn-dotted ascent to U-shaped Kaweah Gap, but as one approaches the gap one can see the equally spectacular summits of the Kaweah Peaks Ridge beyond. This colorful ridge dominates the views from Kaweah Gap (10,700'), and one can see the Nine Lake Basin watershed to the north. Hikers with a bent for exploring barren high country, or interested in the good brook-trout fishing, may elect to detour across granite slab-and-ledge routes north to the Nine Lake Basin.

Our trail continues its steady-to-moderate southward descent along the west side of the headwaters of Big Arroyo Creek, fording over to the east side midway down. (In 1987, CCC crews were rerouting the trail away from the vulnerable banks of the creek onto the harder soils of the sides of Big Arroyo.) This descent crosses unjointed granite broken by substantial packets of grass and numerous runoff streams even in late season. Open stretches afford fine views of the U-shaped, glacially wrought Big Arroyo below, and the white, red and black rocks of Black Kaweah and Red Kaweah peaks to the east. The trail then reenters timber cover and arrives at some good campsites along the stream (9600'). These campsites and an abandoned trail-crew cabin are about ¼ mile above the Little Five Lakes/Black Rock Pass Trail junction. Fishing for brook trout (to 7") is fair to good. For those anglers with extra time, the 2-mile side trip to Little Five Lakes offers fine angling for golden trout.

3rd Hiking Day (**Big Arroyo Trail Junction** to **Moraine Lake**, 8 miles): Continuing past the Little Five Lakes Trail junction, the High Sierra Trail begins a long, moderate ascent along the north canyon wall of Big Arroyo. This route parallels the course of a trunk glacier that once filled Big Arroyo, overflowed the benches on either side, and contributed to the main glacier of Kern Canyon. Our route climbs the wall of this trough, and the timber cover of this ascent is sparse, but there is no shortage of wildflowers tucked among the sage, manzanita and chinquapin. Most colorful are yellow columbine, bright red Indian paintbrush and purple lupine.

The trail levels off near a small, mirror-faced tarn, and, swinging away from the lip of Big Arroyo, it begins a gradual descent through alternating timbered and meadowed stretches. Tree-interrupted views of the jagged Great Western Divide skyline accompany the descent to a trail junction in a meadow on the south side of a tributary of Chagoopa Creek. At this junction our route leaves the High Sierra Trail, and branches right (south) through meadows with clumps of shooting stars. This descent becomes steeper over coarse granite sand, through dense stands of lodgepole and foxtail pine, with superlative views down into Big Arroyo and across the arroyo to the drainages of Soda and Lost Canyon creeks. This steadily down-winding trail brings one to the wooded shores of Moraine Lake (9290'). Good campsites on the south side of the lake provide lake-fronted views back to the Kaweah Peaks, and gardens of wild azalea in season.

4th Hiking Day (**Moraine Lake** to **Kern Hot Spring**, 7 miles): After traversing a moraine just east of Moraine Lake, the trail descends moderately, then gently, passing an old stockman's cabin before reaching superb Sky Parlor Meadow. Views back across this flower-filled grassland to the Great Western Divide and the Kaweahs are excellent. Shortly beyond the ford of Funston Creek at the east end of the meadow, the route rejoins the High Sierra Trail and begins the moderate, then steep descent to the bottom of the Kern Trench. The initial descent sees the lodgepole being replaced by the lower-altitude white fir and Jeffrey pine; and still lower down, the trail descends steeply through manzanita and snow bush that are over-shadowed by an occasional juniper and oak. The unmistakably U-shaped Kern Trench is typical of glacially modified valleys. The final climb down to the valley floor is accomplished via a series of steep, rocky switchbacks generally paralleling the plunging drop of Funston Creek.

On the Kern Canyon floor our route turns north, upstream, on the Kern River Trail, drops into a marshy area, and then crosses two meadows on wooden walkways. Then the trail leads gently upward through a forest of Jeffrey pine and incense-cedar. High on the western rim of the canyon one catches glimpses of Chagoopa Falls, a fury of plunging white water when full. Past a manzanita-carpeted open area the trail crosses the Kern on a fine bridge and arrives at the south fork of Rock Creek. Then, around a point, we arrive at the delightful mountain spa of Kern Hot Spring (6880′)—a treat for the tired, dusty hiker. To the traveler, the crude, cemented bathtub here becomes a regal, heated pool. Just a few dozen yards away, the great Kern River rushes past. If camping near the spring, you must stay in the campground just north and east of it. The sites are, unfortunately, very close together and very overused, but the spring and the setting are worth it. Fishing is good for rainbow and golden-rainbow hybrids (to 10″).

5th Hiking Day (**Kern Hot Spring** to **Junction Meadow**, 8 miles): Continuing north, we ford the upper fork of Rock Creek and traverse the gravelly canyon floor below the immense granite cliffs of the canyon's east wall. Past the confluence of Red Spur Creek this route ascends gently, sometimes a bit stiffly, beside the Kern River, heading almost due north. The U-shaped trough of the Kern River, called the Kern Trench, is remarkably straight for about 25 miles as it traces the Kern Canyon fault. The fault, a zone of structural weakness in the Sierra batholith, is more susceptible to erosion than the surrounding rock, and this deep canyon has been carved by both glacial and stream action. Many times glaciers advanced down the canyon, shearing off spurs created by stream erosion and leaving some tributary valleys hanging above the main valley. The glaciers also scooped and plucked at the bedrock, creating basins in the granite which became lakes when they melted and retreated.

The walls of this deep canyon, from 2000 to 5000 feet high, are spectacular, and a number of streams cascade and fall down these walls. (The fords of the stream draining Guyot Flat, of Whitney Creek and of Wallace Creek can be difficult in early season.) Beyond the ford of Wallace Creek the trail enters a parklike grove of stalwart Jeffrey pines that provide a noble setting for the overused campsites at Junction Meadow (8036′) on the Kern River, where fishing is good for rainbow and some brook trout (to 10″).

6th Hiking Day (**Junction Meadow** to **Crabtree Ranger Station**, 8½ miles): Our trail leaves the parklike Jeffrey pines of Junction Meadow and ascends steeply on rocky underfooting over a slope covered by manzanita and currant. Views down the Kern Trench improve constantly, as the occasional Jeffrey, lodgepole and aspen offer frames for the photographer who would compose a shot of the great cleft. After one miles we arrive at the junction of the Kern River Trail and the High Sierra Trail, where our route turns right (southeast), back toward Wallace Creek canyon. At 10,400 feet you reach a junction with the John Muir Trail. Turn right (south) onto it— here, it's also the Pacific Crest Trail and the High Sierra Trail. You immediately ford Wallace Creek (difficult in early season), pass some campsites and then continue southward on generally gentle gradients through sporadic stands of lodgepole and foxtail pine. At 10,800 feet the John Muir Trail and the Pacific Crest Trail diverge: you take the left fork, the John Muir Trail, toward Crabtree Ranger Station and the fair campsites (10,700') nearby. Emergency services are sometimes available at the ranger station. Fishing in Whitney Creek is fair for golden (to 7").

7th and 8th Hiking Days: Reverse the 2nd and 1st hiking days, Trip 71, to **Whitney Portal**, 15 miles.

Kern River Canyon

USGS

Crescent Meadow to Mt. Whitney   **80**

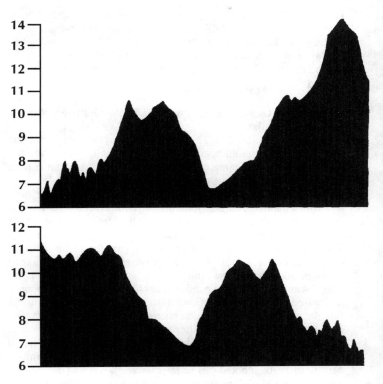

Trip	From Crescent Meadow to Mt. Whitney via Hamilton Lakes, Kaweah Gap, Big Arroyo, Junction Meadow, Wallace Creek, Crabtree Ranger Station, return via Tyndall Creek, Upper Kern River to Junction Meadow
Distance	136 miles
Type	Semiloop trip
Best season	Mid to late
Topo maps	**Triple Divide Peak, Mt. Whitney** 15′; Mt. Kaweah, Mount Whitney, Mt. Brewer, Chagoopa Falls 7½′

Grade (hiking days/recommended layover days)

    Leisurely   —
    Moderate   14/3
    Strenuous   10/1
Trailhead   Crescent Meadow (20)

HIGHLIGHTS   Many people plan for years to climb Mt. Whitney from Giant Forest, via the well-named High Sierra Trail. This trip repays the planning, and adds the dividend of getting off the main track during a looping return from the great peak. A food cache at Crabtree Ranger Station is almost a must.

DESCRIPTION (Moderate trip)

First 6 Hiking Days: Follow Trip 79 to **Crabtree Ranger Station**, 53½ miles.

Layover Day, 18 miles: This "layover" day is the most strenuous of the trip. You should begin as early as possible. To shorten the distance, you might camp on the Mt. Whitney Trail, about ½ mile above Crabtree Ranger Station in a small meadow on Whitney Creek, or hike after dinner to Guitar Lake and sleep there.

From Crabtree Ranger Station our route ascends the narrow canyon of Whitney Creek. Past a small meadow we arrive at Timberline Lake (no camping, but fair fishing for golden trout). Then the trail ascends somewhat steeply past the last pine trees, crosses the outlet of Arctic Lake, and traverses above Guitar Lake to a wet meadow where the "fun" begins. Switchback is piled upon steep switchback until the panting hiker has to stop for breath, only to confront another series of switchbacks. Little windbreaks at the few flat places tell of westbound hikers who were too tired to make it down to Crabtree. Finally, after more than 1500 feet of climbing, we reach the side trail that leads to Whitney's summit. If, while on top, you should wonder how John Muir felt the first time he climbed Mt. Whitney, be it noted that he later wrote, "I reached the summit needles about 11 o'clock that night and danced most of the time until morning, as the night was bitterly cold and I was in my shirtsleeves." If a storm breaks, stay out of the summit hut and get off the peak.

7th Hiking Day (**Crabtree Ranger Station** to **Tyndall Creek Tributary**, 9 miles): Follow the 3rd hiking day, Trip 75.

8th Hiking Day (**Tyndall Creek Tributary** to **Lake on Upper Kern River**, 4½ miles). From the ford we descend gently on a rocky trail through a forest cover of mixed lodgepole and foxtail pine to a junction with the Shepherd Pass Trail. Immediately beyond is a ford of Tyndall Creek (difficult in early season). Then, one eighth of a mile later, we turn left onto the Lake South America Trail. Then, a half mile farther on across alpine fell fields, we turn left again, onto the Milestone Basin Trail. Views in this upper Kern basin are at all times panoramic, and travelers will mentally record pictures of the skyline they will not soon forget.

At the outlet stream of Lake 11440 the angler may wish to veer north and sample that lake's waters for the good fishing for golden (to 12"). The trail then skirts along the north side of a small lake, and makes a short, rocky climb to a ridge where the descent to the Kern River begins. From the ridge the traveler has closer views of Thunder Mountain, Milestone Mountain, Midway Mountain—all on the Great Western Divide—and Kern Ridge and Red Spur in the south. Past this viewpoint the trail descends moderately through rocky and meadowy sections with a moderate cover of foxtail, lodgepole and some whitebark pine, and arrives at a picturebook lake that is fast (geologically speaking) turning to meadow. One may regret that all these high lakes are doomed, but one may enjoy the blend of meadows and lakes existing in the time to which one was born.

After climbing slightly, our route begins the last, steep descent to the Kern River, where it emerges at an unnamed lake at 10,650 feet elevation (good fishing for golden and rainbow-golden hybrids to 10").

9th Hiking Day (**Lake on Upper Kern River** to **Junction Meadow**, 6 miles): Your trail proceeds south along the east shore of the lake, where red penstemon, or mountain pride, is especially abundant in the broken granite slopes. After 200 yards you pass the Milestone Basin Trail branching right, and soon you begin the steep 600-foot descent of a granite-slabbed slope down which the young river cascades and falls. In the shade of lodgepole pines, one may see yarrow milfoil, paintbrush, penstemon, fleabane, and red mountain heather. As the descent begins to level off, the trail passes through a bank of shield ferns among which grows the delicate, white-headed Queen Anne's lace. At the foot of the descent our route enters a thick stand of trees. Yellow senecio flowers dominate the ground cover under these pines, complemented by the hues of orange tiger lily, purple swamp onion and red columbine.

After fording the stream from Lake 11440, the trail begins a dusty section where the sagebrush is spottily shaded by a few lodgepole and foxtail pines. Shortly before the junction with the Tyndall Creek Trail there is a good campsite beside the river, and here one begins to see red fir and aspen, indicating arrival in the Canadian life zone. The sandy, exposed trail continues its gentle descent to the Tyndall Creek ford (difficult in early season). Beyond this ford, the canyon becomes steeper, and the trail becomes more dufflike and tree-shaded. The first Jeffrey pines of this trip appear, along with a few mountain junipers. One short mile beyond a roofless, decaying cabin our route meets the High Sierra Trail coming down from Wallace Creek, and from here down almost to Upper Funston Meadow the Kern River Trail and the High Sierra Trail are conjoined.

From this junction it is a steep descent of 1 mile to Junction Meadow (8036'). Views on this descent are good down the Kern Canyon, an immense U-trough which was given that shape by the main Kern glacier, which left the tributary valleys hanging. The forest cover on this descent is sparse lodgepole and Jeffrey, along with clumps of aspen, on a slope dominated by manzanita and currant. As the trail levels off, it enters a parklike grove of stalwart Jeffrey pines that provide a noble setting for the overused campsites near the Kern River. Fishing is good for rainbow and golden-rainbow hybrids (to 10").

10th–14th Hiking Days (**Junction Meadow** to **Crescent Meadow**, 45 miles): Retrace the steps of the first five hiking days.

Mt. Whitney from the northwest

Cottonwood Lakes Trailhead to 81 South Fork Lakes

Trip	From Cottonwood Lakes Trailhead to South Fork Lakes, return via cross country down South Fork Cottonwood Creek
Distance	10¼ miles
Type	Loop trip
Best season	Mid to late
Topo maps	Cirque Peak 7½'

Grade (hiking days/recommended layover days)

Leisurely	2/1
Moderate	—
Strenuous	Day
Trailhead	Cottonwood Lakes (24)

HIGHLIGHTS   A fine weekend loop trip, this route offers grand scenery and delightful camping opportunities. The relatively small elevation gain makes this a good warm-up trip if you are not in good condition, or not well acclimated. No wood fires in Cottonwood Lakes Basin or at South Fork Lakes.

DESCRIPTION (Leisurely trip)

1st Hiking Day (**Cottonwood Lakes Trailhead** to **South Fork Lakes**, 5¼ miles): (The first 1½ miles of trail for this trip don't appear on the *Cirque Peak* topo, though the new trail*head* does.) From the trailhead (10,040') the trail leads west, then north on a gentle and brief ascent through an open stand of lodgepole and foxtail pine, passes a spur to the equestrian area, and soon enters Golden Trout Wilderness. The sandy trail soon begins to descend gently, then levels out. In about 1 mile we cross the South Fork Cottonwood Creek. It's often willow-choked, but the more open stretches are ideal for fly-rod action.

In another ½ mile we pick up the trail as it's shown on the topo; the junction is imperceptible, the old trail south of it overgrown. We skirt the west side of the meadows along Cottonwood Creek and ascend steadily, passing privately-operated Golden Trout Camp. Soon we enter John Muir Wilderness and cross Cottonwood Creek.

Beyond this crossing the trail swings west, with the creek and its meadows to our southwest. The ascent levels during these stretches. At the next trail junction, we turn left and cross Cottonwood Creek. Now the trail climbs moderately above the creek. Beside a large meadow, we reach another junction. Here we take the right fork for New Army Pass, instead of the left fork to South Fork Lakes, because we're heading for the westernmost, highest South Fork lake, which is slightly closer via the right fork. We ascend a forested moraine to a junction at the meadowed west end of the lowest Cottonwood Lake, Cottonwood Lake #1, and to a fine view of Cottonwood Basin and Mt. Langley. Cottonwood Lakes #1 through #4 and their tributaries are closed to fishing, but Lake #5 is open.

Taking the left fork here, we pass Cottonwood Lake #2 and then veer southwest through a jumbled area of near-white granite blocks. From the point where the trail turns west-northwest, a short spur trail descends a few yards to the good campsites at the west end of the westernmost South Fork Lake (11,000'). These campsites are located in a sparse grove of foxtail pines with fine views of Cirque Peak to the southwest. Anglers will fare better at the easternmost South Fork lake (good campsites), Cirque Lake, Long Lake (good campsites) and High Lake (very limited camping).

2nd Hiking Day (**South Fork Lakes** to **Cottonwood Lakes Trailhead**, 5 miles, part cross-country): From the west side of the westernmost South Fork Lake, our route heads south and then east toward the easternmost lake, skirting the large talus area between the two lakes. We round the south side of the easternmost lake (golden to 7") and pick up a trail (not shown on the topo) that leads downstream from its outlet. Keeping on the north and then the east side of the outlet stream, this route descends over heavily fractured granite past foxtail and lodgepole pines on a slope where the dashing stream cascades and falls from one rocky grotto to the next. Clumps of shooting star topped by showy yellow columbine and orange tiger lily line the stream.

The trail levels off in a meadow and then descends into a larger meadow, where the outlet of Cirque Lake joins the South Fork Cottonwood Creek. Following the creek's course, we swing east and descend steeply in lodgepole forest to traverse another meadow. Beyond this meadow the trail drops steeply again, passing an old notched-log cabin where there are two cement fireplaces. The trail veers away from the South Fork Cottonwood Creek and rounds the moraine between this fork and the main fork. Then our trail goes up the west side of the main fork for ⅓ mile to join the trail described in the 1st hiking day. Now our route fords Cottonwood Creek and turns south to retrace the steps of part of the 1st hiking day.

Cottonwood Lakes Trailhead to 82 Upper Rock Creek

Trip	From Cottonwood Lakes Trailhead to Upper Rock Creek Lake via South Fork Lakes and New Army Pass
Distance	23½ miles
Type	Out and back trip
Best season	Mid or late
Topo maps	**Mt. Whitney** 15′; Cirque Peak, Mount Whitney, Johnson Peak 7½′

Grade (hiking days/recommended layover days)

Leisurely	4/3
Moderate	3/2
Strenuous	2/1
Trailhead	Cottonwood Lakes Trailhead (24)

HIGHLIGHTS Beautiful Rock Creek and its spectacular headwaters are the goals of this high-country trip. The
tiny, unnamed lake at the end of this trip makes a fine base camp for
further exploration of Miter Basin and Soldier Lakes.

A way from the trail, especially in Miter Basin, map-and-compass
skills and some boulder-scrambling experience are needed. No
wood fires in Cottonwood Lakes Basin or at South Fork Lakes.

DESCRIPTION (Leisurely trip)

1st Hiking Day: Follow Trip 81 to **South Fork Lakes**, 5¼ miles.
2nd Hiking Day: (**South Fork Lakes** to **Upper Rock Creek**, 6½
miles): From the westernmost South Fork Lake, the trail ascends
westward through thinning timber to Long Lake. After skirting the
south shore, our route begins a long, steadily rising traverse that
takes the traveler above the campsites at the west end of the lake.
Views of the lake are photographers' favorites, but save some film
for the panoramic shots farther up. This traverse brings one above
treeline as the trail skirts a wet area covered with grass, willows and
wildflowers. Where the trail touches the south edge of High Lake, a
pause will brace one for the upcoming rocky switchbacks.

The trail soon begins a series of long, gently graded zigzags that climb the cirque wall up to New Army Pass (12,300'). The higher one climbs up, the better are the views to the east of the lakes immediately below and of the Cottonwood Creek drainage.

Descending from New Army Pass into Sequoia National Park, the trail crosses a long, barren slope of coarse granite sand sprinkled with exfoliating granite boulders. A half mile north of the pass our route passes an unmaintained trail (not shown on the topo map) that branches right to Old Army Pass, the original pass built by the army in the 1890s. Beyond this junction our route swings west and descends steeply over rocky tread to level off on a more gentle descent in a barren cirque. The trail crosses to the north side of the unnamed stream in the cirque and re-enters moderate forest cover. About 2 miles from New Army Pass the trail meets a trail to Siberian Pass, and there are good campsites on the south side of the stream just south of this junction.

Our route turns right (north), continuing to descend through denser lodgepole pine. When the forest gives way to the open spaces of a lovely meadow, our trail fords a little tributary of Rock Creek and turns left on the Rock Creek Trail. (If you turned right, in ¼ level mile you'd reach excellent campsites on both sides of the lower of the unnamed Soldier Lakes—3290 meters, just southwest of The Major General.) This trail descends steeply alongside a willow-infested tributary of Rock Creek until the rocky slope gives way to a meadow just above the lake on Rock Creek at 10,440 feet. Around these meadows one may sight the relatively rare white-tailed jackrabbit. There are fair campsites at the head of this meadow, others are located at the lake's outlet, and more primitive ones are to be found on the south side of the lake. Fishing for golden (to 8″) in the lake and adjoining stream is good.

This marshy-meadowed lake makes a grand base camp for side trips to the rugged Miter Basin and adjoining unnamed Soldier Lakes, the lower of which was mentioned above. Fishing for golden trout in most of the lakes below The Miter and The Major General is good. A trail of use to Miter Basin makes a hard-to-spot exit along the north side of the large, overused campsite just east of our lake's meadow. This trail is easy to follow to the place where Rock Creek cascades out of the basin; from there, it's cross-country. Other fine side trips include a looping cross-country exploration of the Boreal Plateau via Siberian Outpost, or if you are a hardy and experienced backpacker with a yen for adventure, taking the Pacific Crest Trail to Crabtree Meadow and then scrambling cross-country over Crabtree Pass, rounding Mt. Chamberlin, Mt. Newcomb, Mt. Pickering and Joe Devel Peak, and returning via Miter Basin.

3rd and 4th Hiking Days: Retrace your steps, 11¼ miles.

Cottonwood Lakes Trailhead to **83** Upper Rock Creek

Trip	From Cottonwood Lakes Trailhead to Horseshoe Meadow via South Fork Lakes, New Army Pass, Upper Rock Creek Lake, Chicken Spring Lake and Cottonwood Pass
Distance	22¼ miles
Type	Loop trip
Best season	Mid or late
Topo maps	**Mt. Whitney** 15′; Cirque Peak, Mount Whitney, Johnson Peak 7½′

Grade (hiking days/recommended layover days)

Leisurely	4/3
Moderate	4/1
Strenuous	3/0
Trailhead	Start at Cottonwood Lakes Trailhead (24), end at Horseshoe Meadow Trailhead (25), closing the loop either on the road between the parking lots or via a short trail between the trailheads

HIGHLIGHTS   One of the finest circuits in the Sierra, this route travels up an elegant cirque past spectacular peaks, visits lonely alpine lakes and soft-meadowed ponds, traces streams that now dash, now meander through green forests and open meadows, and climbs past treeline into desolate "moonscapes." All who take this trip will come away with a sense of accomplishment and inner peace.

Away from the trail, especially when exploring Miter Basin, map-and-compass skills and some boulder-scrambling experience are needed. No wood fires in Cottonwood Lakes Basin, at South Fork Lakes or within ¼ mile of Chicken Spring Lake.

DESCRIPTION (Leisurely trip)

1st and 2nd Hiking Days: Follow Trip 82 to **Upper Rock Creek**, 11¾ miles.

3rd Hiking Day (**Upper Rock Creek** to **Chicken Spring Lake**, 6 miles): You begin this hiking day by retracing your steps for 1 mile to the meadowed Siberian Pass Trail junction passed during the 2nd hiking day. Fill your canteens here; this is the last reliable water source before Chicken Spring Lake. From the junction this trail ascends southward gently over a moderate-to-densely forested slope of foxtail and lodgepole pine. Our route crosses a barren area, climbs over an easy ridge and, 1 mile south of the last junction, turns left onto the famous Pacific Crest Trail. We now reverse the first part of the 2nd hiking day, Trip 89, to Chicken Spring Lake.

4th Hiking Day (**Chicken Spring Lake** to **Horseshoe Meadow**, 4½ miles): Reverse the 1st hiking day, Trip 89.

Siberian Outpost

Cottonwood Lakes Trailhead to 84
Whitney Portal

Trip	From Cottonwood Lakes Trailhead to Whitney Portal via South Fork Lakes, New Army Pass, Rock Creek, Crabtree Meadow, Mt. Whitney and Outpost Camp.
Distance	37¼ miles
Type	Shuttle trip
Best season	Mid or late
Topo maps	**Mt. Whitney** 15′; Cirque Peak, Johnson Peak, Mount Whitney, Mt. Langley 7½′

Grade (hiking days/recommended layover days)

Leisurely	—
Moderate	5/1
Strenuous	4/0
Trailhead	Start at Cottonwood Lakes Trailhead (24), end at Whitney Portal (23)

HIGHLIGHTS This wonderfully scenic trip is one of the favorite alternatives to a simple—and relatively dull—stomp up and down Mt. Whitney, the highest peak in the contiguous 48 states. On *this* trip, you stay at alpine lakes, fish dashing streams, thrill to fine cross-country dayhiking, and savor the far southeastern corner of Sequoia National Park.

Away from the trail, especially when exploring places like Miter Basin, map-and-compass skills and some boulder-scrambling experience are needed. No wood fires in Cottonwood Lakes Basin or at South Fork Lakes.

DESCRIPTION (Moderate trip)

1st Hiking Day: Follow Trip 82 to **South Fork Lakes**, 5¼ miles.

2nd Hiking Day (**South Fork Lakes** to **Lower Rock Creek Ford**, 10½ miles): Follow the 1st part of the 2nd hiking day, Trip 82, to Upper Rock Creek Lake. The rest of this day is an easy 4-mile stroll down lovely Rock Creek canyon, passing through a drift fence ¼ mile below the lake. This sometimes-tumbling rill slows to a murmuring brook in the meadow flats, and its fresh-from-the-source waters are crystal clear and icy cold. The dense green canopy of lodgepoles overhead allows only clumps of shade-loving gooseberry to grow along the trail, but the virile willow maintains its verdant stream-bank growth, shade or sun. Willow growth is synonymous with birdlife, and Rock Creek has its share of robins, white-crowned sparrows, chickadees, juncos, woodpeckers and olive-sided flycatchers. It is often the *"oh-see view"* call of this flycatcher that reminds the passerby of the beauty of the surroundings—surroundings that on this canyon descent include a chain of lovely meadows. Unfortunately, this native tour guide leaves these environs in August, and late-season travelers are left to rely on their own devices.

Just before reaching a large meadow, our trail meets the Pacific Crest Trail and then veers away from the stream. Most anglers ignore the waters of this tiny creek and thereby miss some fine fishing for golden trout. The fish are not large, but there are several in every hole. The trail crosses a large meadow where a sign points north to a summer ranger station, and in 1 mile reaches the ford of lower Rock Creek (9500'), where fishing is good for golden (to 8").

3rd Hiking Day (**Lower Rock Creek Ford** to **Crabtree Ranger Station**, 7 miles): Beyond logs over the stream, the trail climbs steeply up the north wall of the canyon, then levels somewhat to the ford of Guyot Creek (campsite; last water for more than 4 miles). The jumbled, symmetrical crest of Mt. Guyot takes up the skyline to the west, and highly fractured Joe Devel Peak looms to the east as the trail begins another steep ascent through a moderate forest cover of lodgepole and foxtail pine. This bouldery climb culminates at a saddle—sometimes called Guyot Pass—from which there are good views north across the Kern Canyon to the Kern-Kaweah drainage and of Red Spur, Kern Ridge and the Great Western Divide. From the saddle, the trail descends moderately to the large, sandy basin of Guyot Flat, then traverses the forest east of the flat. Like the Chagoopa Plateau across the canyon, this flat and the subsequent "shelf" traversed later in this hiking day were part of an immense valley floor in preglacial times. However, much of the granular sand deposits are a result of later weathering and erosion of the granite peaks to the east.

Beyond Guyot Flat the trail undulates through a moderate forest cover, bobbing over a pair of sandy ridges, before dropping steeply on very rocky switchbacks into the Whitney Creek drainage. The descent into this drainage affords views eastward to Mt. Whitney—the long, flat-topped, avalanche-chuted mountain that towers over the nearer, granite-spired shoulder of Mt. Hitchcock. This descent concludes over a barren, rocky stretch to lower Crabtree Meadow, where, just beyond a good campsite, our route fords Whitney Creek and turns right (east) along its north bank, leaving the Pacific Crest Trail. A half mile of gentle ascents ends at Upper Crabtree Meadow, where the route passes the unmarked Crabtree Lakes Trail. (This unmaintained trail leads to the good fishing on Crabtree Lakes for golden, to 14″). Continuing northeast beside Whitney Creek, the trail ascends gently, fords the creek, and meets the John Muir Trail beyond another ford of Whitney Creek. Northeast of this ford is the Crabtree Ranger Station (10,640′) (emergency services perhaps available) and fair campsites. To shorten the next day a little, you could camp in a meadow about ½ mile up Whitney Creek, or continue to Guitar Lake by reversing part of the 2nd hiking day of Trip 71.

4th and 5th Hiking Days: Reverse the 2nd and 1st hiking days, Trip 71, 15 miles.

High Lake, near New Army Pass

85 Cottonwood Lakes Trailhead to Mineral King

Trip	From Cottonwood Lakes Trailhead to Mineral King via New Army Pass, Siberian Pass, Kern River, Rattlesnake Creek and Franklin Pass
Distance	55¾ miles
Type	Shuttle trip (trans-Sierra)
Best season	Mid or late
Topo maps	**Mineral King** 15'; Cirque Peak, Mount Whitney, Johnson Peak, Kern Peak, Kern Lake, Chagoopa Falls, Mineral King 7½'

Grade (hiking days/recommended layover days)

   Leisurely —
   Moderate 8/4
   Strenuous 7/3

Trailhead	Start at Cottonwood Lakes Trailhead (24), end at Mineral King (21)

HIGHLIGHTS This excellent trans-Sierra route visits the finest fishing lakes and streams of the lower Kern River drainage, then surmounts the Great Western Divide in the notch at Franklin Pass. The severe altitude changes in the route make this a trip for experienced hikers only.

DESCRIPTION (Strenuous trip)

1st and 2nd Hiking Days: Follow Trip 82 to **Upper Rock Creek**, 11¾ miles.

3rd Hiking Day (**Upper Rock Creek** to **Big Whitney Meadow**,

7 miles): Follow the 3rd hiking day, Trip 83, for the route to Siberian Outpost. Fill your canteens at the Siberian Pass Trail junction; this is the last reliable water before Big Whitney Meadow in a dry year. From where the Pacific Crest Trail turns east, our route crosses the east end of Siberian Outpost and ascends gently past a snowmarker site to the easy rise called Siberian Pass (10,920′) where we leave Sequoia National Park and enter Golden Trout Wilderness.

Our gently graded, switchbacking trail crosses the headwaters of Golden Trout Creek (may be dry) midway down the descent from the pass, and then crosses a few ridges before descending a moderate slope to the west edge of Big Whitney Meadow. The underfooting of most of this descent has been dust and some rock, but as we near the meadow it is mostly sand. The gently descending trail may seem to vanish in the sand on the east side of this wash, but it reappears in the forest edge on the west side as we approach the north tip of the grassy area. Mats of yellow monkey flower color the forest floor, and as the trail emerges in the opener sections, one sees much lupine, penstemon, cinquefoil and sagebrush. Keeping to the forest fringes on the west side of the very large grassland, our trail passes the Cottonwood Pass Trail, and a few hundred yards beyond arrives at the fair campsites at the Rocky Basin Lakes Trail junction (9760′). The meadow is a cattle-grazing allotment; expect bovine company here.

4th Hiking Day (**Big Whitney Meadow** to **Little Whitney Meadow**, 8 miles): The winding meadow trail continues south over rolling terrain. Many wildflowers line the route through the southern arm of the meadow and onward, including shooting star, monkey flower, mountain aster, scarlet gilia, and pussy paws. The sandy surface of the meadow trail continues into the moderate-to-dense forest cover of lodgepole and foxtail pine below. Shortly after re-entering forest cover, the trail fords Barigan Stringer and passes several nearby campsites. There are many good campsites along Golden Trout Creek. Now the sandy, rocky canyon walls narrow, and the stream quickens for about ½ mile, and then as the canyon opens somewhat, our trail passes the Barigan Stringer Trail to Rocky Basin Lakes. This creek was the original source for golden trout used in subsequent plantings throughout the higher lakes and streams of the Sierra.

Beyond the Barigan Stringer Trail junction our trail continues a moderate sandy descent past several more campsites to the ford of Golden Trout Creek. Mounting a sandy shelf above the creek, the trail meets the Bullfrog Meadow Trail above the South Fork Kern River (flowing only 300 yards from Golden Trout Creek) and descends gradually past Tunnel Ranger Station and one of its fenced administrative pastures (emergency services perhaps available). The final descent to the guard station affords views of Kern Peak and of the red-topped volcanic hills to the southwest. Beyond the Tunnel Ranger Station our route passes the Kern Peak/Ramshaw Meadows Trail branching east, then turns west to ford Golden Trout Creek, and passes another fenced administrative pasture. Fishing on Golden Trout Creek is restricted to artificial lures.

Across sandy, moderately forested, level terrain, the faint trail, heavily trampled by horses, mules and cattle, stays well north of the creek, and passes a trail to Volcano Meadow. Multiple tracks diverge and converge here; blazes mark the main trail. Rejoining the creek, the trail continues westward, winding along the northernmost edge of a large late Pleistocene volcanic flow (post-glacial) called Malpais Lava. The largest single concentration of volcanic action in the upper reaches of the Kern, this basalt flow shows itself near the trail in brilliant displays of the colored rock. Predominant in the volcanic rock is a deep red, sometimes mixed with ochres and shades of tan.

These colorful displays accompany the traveler all the way down this drainage, but the interested rockhound can see extensive fields of this rock by fording the creek and exploring the mile-wide strip of old lava flow to the south. Just east of Little Whitney Meadow, the more obvious trail curves north, passes through a drift fence and, south of the cabins of still-active Little Whitney Cow Camp, fords Johnson Creek. (A less obvious fork curves south across Golden Trout Creek.) We may notice, in passing, an unsigned, unmaintained trail north to Salt Lick Meadow. There are beautiful campsites in the forested edges of this 8420-foot meadow, which is no longer a cattle-grazing allotment but attracts travelers with stock. Expect equine company here. (Cattle grazing in nearby meadows may wander back here, so bovine company is possible too.)

5th Hiking Day (**Little Whitney Meadow** to **Rattlesnake Creek/ Kern River**, 11 miles): Our trip skirts the south end of beautiful Little Whitney Meadow, climbs a rise, and passes through another drift fence. Descending steadily over a dusty granite-sand surface, the trail then refords Golden Trout Creek. Then, as the route continues its steady descent, the trail surface becomes pumice, and the forest cover of lodgepole gives way to Jeffrey and juniper. Large concentrations of wildflowers daub the opener stretches with yellows (monkey flower), whites (Mariposa lily), mixed blues and purples (larkspur and penstemon), and reds (red dogwood). Leveling out to a moderate descent, the trail then recrosses a tributary of Golden Trout Creek via a natural bridge of basalt. Easily eroded, this pink rock shows extensive water cutting and sculpting.

After Natural Bridge, the grade of the trail steepens to a steady descent over pumice and sand through a forest cover of Jeffrey, white fir and some lodgepole. At the switchbacks dropping to the Kern Canyon floor, one can see the clearly delineated volcanic overlay with its subsurface of granite. The underlying rock has been laid bare by subsequent stream cutting that has knifed through the basalt layer and exposed a rainbow of blacks, reds, tans and whites. Some columnar basalt formations, usually associated with these lava flows, may also be seen to the north. Our trail provides a good view of Volcano Falls as we twine steeply down over pumice and rock (poor footing).

With the lower altitude come sugar pine and, on the canyon floor, quaking aspen, birch, black oak and incense-cedar. When you reach the canyon floor, you have your first views of domelike Tower Rock to the south. Through a sparse forest cover and clumps of sage, manzanita, willows and chinquapin, the trail veers south to cross the Kern River (footbridge), leaving Inyo National Forest (Golden Trout Wilderness) and entering Sequoia National Park, passes a spur trail to a natural soda spring, and meets the Kern River Trail a few hundred yards north of the Kern Canyon Ranger Station (emergency services usually available).

Our route turns right onto the Kern Canyon Trail and ascends the canyon by a series of moderate ups and downs. The forest cover is usually dense, and tiny wet sections with dense concentrations of bracken fern make passage difficult. Their luxuriant growth is commonly associated with canyon bottoms, and they are frequently found in conjunction with riverside stands of alder, laurel, aspen and birch. The approach to Lower Funston Meadow is heralded by the lower drift fence, and then the trail begins a steady climb over the alluvial fan that results from Laurel Creek's contribution of silt and rock on the canyon floor. Fording Laurel Creek is accomplished via two crossings, each marked by a campsite; during high water, the second ford is sometimes hazardous.

Fishing in the Kern River, particularly near the confluences of the many tributary streams, is excellent. Angling is sometimes made difficult by the thickets of willows lining the river, but the rewards in rainbow trout (to 20") more than make up for the casting problems. Anglers, or those who simply enjoy the view from streamside, should keep a sharp eye out for beavers that work this section of the river. It is not surprising that wild animal sightings are frequent in this glacially carved trench. Animals, like people, are "channeled" down its steep-walled course, and within the canyon's relatively confined course, the hiker is apt to see bear, coyote, deer and the aforementioned beaver.

From Laurel Creek the trail continues north through a moderate forest. Mostly duff, the trail surface makes pleasant walking, and the distance to the Rattlesnake Creek Trail junction is rapidly covered. At this junction and just across the sometimes difficult ford of Rattlesnake Creek are excellent campsites (6600'). (Note: Yes, there are rattlesnakes in this area.)

6th Hiking Day (**Rattlesnake Creek/Kern River** to **Upper Rattlesnake Creek**, 8 miles): Reverse the 2nd hiking day, Trip 100.

7th Hiking Day (**Upper Rattlesnake Creek** to **Mineral King**, 10 miles): Reverse the 1st hiking day, Trip 96.

Big Whitney Meadow

Cottonwood Lakes Trailhead to 86
Symmes Creek Trailhead

Trip	From Cottonwood Lakes Trailhead to Symmes Creek Trailhead via Upper Rock Creek Lake, Crabtree Meadow, Milestone Basin and Shepherd Pass
Distance	54 miles
Type	Shuttle trip
Best season	Mid or late
Topo maps	**Mt. Whitney** (15′); Cirque Peak, Mount Whitney, Johnson Peak, Mt. Kaweah, Mt. Langley, Mt. Williamson, Mt. Brewer (7½′)

Grade (hiking days/recommended layover days)

Leisurely	10/4
Moderate	8/2
Strenuous	6/0
Trailhead	Start at Cottonwood Lakes Trailhead (24), end at Symmes Creek Trailhead (22)

HIGHLIGHTS   The early part of this shuttle trip explores well-traveled Upper Rock Creek and Crabtree Meadows. Once you turn toward the Upper Kern and Milestone Basin, you are likely to have campsites—even whole lakes—to yourself. The many lakes of Milestone Basin are full of fish and offer fascinating terrain to explore.

DESCRIPTION (Moderate trip)

1st and 2nd Hiking Days (**Cottonwood Lakes Trailhead** to **Upper Rock Creek**, 12 miles): Follow the 1st and 2nd hiking days of Trip 82 to Upper Rock Creek Lake. Take one or more layover days here to explore the glorious hanging lakes in Miter Basin.

3rd Hiking Day (**Upper Rock Creek** to **Crabtree Meadow**, 9 miles): Follow the 2nd hiking day of Trip 84 down Rock Creek Canyon and then the 3rd hiking day of Trip 84 northward on the Pacific Crest Trail as far as lower Crabtree Meadow. Cross Whitney Creek; immediately, you pass a signed trail to your right to Mt. Whitney. (About 1.5 miles up that trail is a manned ranger station.) Excellent camping can be found here along the west side of lower Crabtree Meadow. Bears frequent this area; store food properly.

4th Hiking Day (**Crabtree Meadow** to **Upper Kern River**, 7.4 miles): Continue north on the Pacific Crest/John Muir Trail. The trail climbs through a foxtail and lodgepole forest, fords an unnamed creek and skirts Sandy Meadow. You continue to ascend gently on a sandy trail around the west shoulder of Mt. Young to a very pretty saddle at 10,964 feet. The trail winds among some massive boulders of a lateral moraine, and then descends a rocky hillside from where you have fine views of Mt. Ericsson, Tawny Point, Junction Peak, the flank of Mt. Tyndall, Mt. Versteeg, Mt. Williamson, and, farthest to the right, Mt. Barnard. You ford a tributary of Wallace Creek, then Wallace Creek itself (difficult in early season; campsites), and reach a junction where the High Sierra Trail turns west. Now you follow the High Sierra Trail west, as described in the 3rd hiking day of Trip 73, to the Kern River Trail and then go up the river on it.

(*Shorter trip:* If you are yearning for civilization and wish to curtail your trip, leave Crabtree Meadow and continue north on the John Muir Trail, past the Wallace Creek junction with the High Sierra Trail and past Tawny Point, to the junction with the Shepherd Pass Trail. Turn right on that trail, which gently ascends Tyndall meadows to Shepherd Pass. Then follow Trip 69, 6th and 7th hiking days, to the Symmes Creek Trailhead.)

5th Hiking Day (**Upper Kern River** to **Milestone Basin**, 6 miles): Follow the 4th hiking day, Trip 73, up the Kern River Trail and then west to Milestone Basin. Take a layover day to visit the many private lakes in this basin. Or climb Milestone Mountain (13,641'); the view of the Kaweahs from the top is unforgettable.

6th Hiking Day (**Milestone Basin** to the **lake at 11,400'**, 4.6 miles); Retrace your steps to the Kern River Trail and turn north for only about 200 yards to a junction on the east shore of an unnamed lake (10,650'). From here you can choose a shorter or a longer 6th hiking day to the same destination:

Shorter 6th hiking day (4.6 miles): Turn east at the above junction. The trail climbs through forest to a second picturesque unnamed lake that is rapidly turning to meadow. From here you make a progressively rockier ascent out of the forest into open terrain, where a few windwhipped foxtails tell of past storms. Looking back westward, you see the magnificent Great Western Divide, with Thunder, Table, Midway and Milestone mountains. Kern Ridge and Red Spur can be seen to the south. The view to the southeast encompasses the highest section of the Sierra Crest, capped by Mt. Whitney. Continuing eastward, in about 2 miles you cross the outflow of lake 11,440. (Anglers may wish to veer north and sample this lake's water for its good fishing for golden—to 12".) A generous quarter mile past the outflow you pass a trail going left to Lake South America. Your trail skirts south of a small lake at 11,400 feet. There is good camping in the trees along its north shore and more exposed camping all around it.

Longer 6th hiking day (6.7 miles): A longer day's hike with more elevation changes takes you through more of the upper Kern. When you reach the junction beside the unnamed lake at 10,650 feet, continue north up the Kern River toward Lake South America. At the next lakelet your trail veers northeast, and you ascend through moderate forest cover to the beautiful unnamed lakes at timberline. The trail then climbs over granite ledges with abundant marmots and wildflowers, and turns east to a small lake just southwest of Lake South America (named for its shape, not for its climate). Continue upward east-southeast over barren terrain to the 12,170-foot saddle, from which a quick, steep descent down a trail eroded by stock brings you to a small lake in a meadow that was visible from the saddle. Continue south around the lake on its east side to intersect the Milestone Basin Trail. Now go cross-country a scant quarter mile to the lake at 11,400.

7th Hiking Day (**Lake at 11,400′** to **Anvil Camp**, 7.5 miles): Regain your trail just to the south, and continue ¼ mile east to where you meet the John Muir/Pacific Crest Trail. Turn south on this trail for a scant ½ mile, down a gentle open slope to a ford of Tyndall Creek. Beyond, at a junction with the Shepherd Pass Trail, turn east. Your route ascends gently to moderately up beautiful Tyndall meadows. The meadow is huge, strewn with boulders, some of which are bright red-brown. In the north you see the unusual table formation of Diamond Mesa; Mt. Tyndall stands out to the northeast. As you ascend further, Mt. Williamson becomes visible. Next, following the latter part of the 6th hiking day of Trip 69, continue up to Shepherd Pass (12,050′) and downward to Anvil Camp (10,000′).

8th Hiking Day (**Anvil Camp** to **Symmes Creek Trailhead**, 7.5 miles): Follow the 7th hiking day of Trip 69.

87 Horseshoe Meadow to Rocky Basin Lakes

Trip	From Horseshoe Meadow to Rocky Basin Lakes via Cottonwood Pass and Big Whitney Meadow
Distance	27 miles
Type	Out and back trip
Best season	Mid
Topo maps	Cirque Peak, Johnson Peak 7½'
Grade (hiking days/recommended layover days)	
Leisurely	—
Moderate	4/2
Strenuous	2/1
Trailhead	Horseshoe Meadow (25)

HIGHLIGHTS The fine angling enjoyed at the culmination of this trip should make it a top choice for the intermediate hiker who wants good recreation as well as a varied route. Dayhiking from Rocky Basin Lakes to destinations like Johnson Lake and Funston Lake offers further adventure as well as spectacular scenery.

The trail is fair except for the boulder-scrambling needed on the FOOT TRAIL fork. Away from it, especially when exploring Johnson Lake, Funston Lake, and the Boreal Plateau, map-and-compass skills and some cross-country experience are required. No wood fires at Rocky Basin Lakes.

DESCRIPTION (Moderate trip)

1st Hiking Day (**Horseshoe Meadow** to **Stokes Stringer Campsites**, 4 miles): The trail leaves the parking lot at the end of the Horseshoe Meadow Road and in a mere 150 yards enters Golden Trout Wilderness. Breaks in the lodgepole and foxtail pine forest permit south- and westward views of Mulkey Pass, Trail Pass, Trail Peak and Cottonwood Pass. The rerouted trail along the forest margin is giving the overrutted meadows a chance to recover something like their pre-human condition—although ecological changes never exactly reverse themselves. On the long, gradual ascent west near the meadow, hikers who get an early start are sure to come upon a few late-grazing deer, and along with many other birds they may well sight a long-eared owl, a resident of these grasslands. Usually this predatory bird is seen while swooping down on its prey—meadow mice, deer mice and other rodents—but in very early season it is sometimes seen in family groups among the willows near the stream.

At the head of the meadow, our trail makes two quick stream crossings. A gentle incline brings us to a meadow dense with willows, paintbrush, columbine and penstemon. Then about a dozen switchbacks suffice to mount a rocky saddle, Cottonwood Pass (11,200'). Views eastward include the Inyo and Panamint ranges, and to the west the more Sierralike Great Western Divide. A few feet west of the pass, we cross the famous Pacific Crest Trail, and from this junction our route descends sagebrush-covered slopes southwest for ½ mile to the several fair campsites to the right of the trail above Stokes Stringer.

2nd Hiking Day (**Stokes Stringer Campsites** to **Rocky Basin Lakes**, 9½ miles): About 20 steep switchbacks are required to get down to a ford of Stokes Stringer. Then the trail zigzags down a more gentle slope to the eastern precincts of Big Whitney Meadow. Most of the tiny creeks meandering through this enormous grazeland are as unhealthy as they look; purify the water, as usual. After fording Stokes Stringer again, the trail crosses a forested ridge and descends to a muddy ford or two of an unnamed creek. The trail tops another little rise before we arrive at a jump-across ford of upper Golden Trout Creek (last reliable water before Rocky Basin Lakes). Now the sandy path enters forest cover and reaches the Siberian Pass Trail. Here we veer left and stroll 300 yards southwest to a junction from where the Rocky Basin Lakes Trail leads west.

Our westbound trail begins a moderate ascent through open-to-moderate stands of pine trees. This ascent makes many easy switchbacks on its southwestward traverse of the moraine just west of Big Whitney Meadow, then descends on more switchbacks to a junction and turns right onto the Barigan Stringer Trail. The ascent beyond this junction is gentle, then moderate over increasingly rocky underfooting. The foxtail and lodgepole pine forest cover lining either side of this ravine ascent is a favorite habitat for a great variety of birdlife, including the long-eared owl, Steller jay, robin, chickadee, junco, calliope hummingbird, and Clark nutcracker. In 1989 a sign at a crossing of Barigan Stringer indicated FOOT TRAIL northwest and HORSE TRAIL west. The indistinct foot trail offers a shorter but steeper scramble over a rocky, foxtail-clad ridge above the outlet stream of the largest Rocky Basin lake, past a wedge-shaped lakelet, to that outlet. The distinct, longer horse trail, shown on the topo map, winds over a ridge and emerges at the east end of the westernmost Rocky Basin lake. From there it rounds the middle lakes and descends to the west side of the largest lake (10,771′). Three more secluded campsites are on the northeast side of the lake. Fishing is good for rainbow (to 14″). The north and west walls of this cirque basin are heavily fractured granite, and are a haven for marmots.

To visit nearby Johnson and Funston lakes, where fishing is good, work up the draw that leads southwest from the southwest end of the westernmost Rocky Basin lake. Johnson Peak and Lake are visible from the saddle at the top of that draw. To go directly to Funston Lake, climb out of the draw over the ridge northwest of it and onto the Boreal Plateau, staying near treeline, and traverse over another gentle ridge, bearing generally northwest. Johnson Peak provides a reference point until you descend toward Funston Lake. The views of the Great Western Divide, of Kaweah Peaks Ridge, and north toward Mt. Whitney from that second ridge are worth the scramble! To reach Johnson Lake, descend to it from the saddle. To get to the Boreal Plateau and Funston Lake from Johnson Lake, work your way up the rocky slopes on Johnson Lake's north shore.

3rd and 4th Hiking Days: Retrace your steps, 13½ miles.

Horseshoe Meadow to Mt. Whitney   **88**

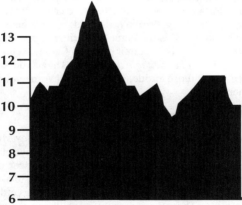

Trip	From Horseshoe Meadow to Mt. Whitney via Cottonwood Pass, Big and Little Whitney Meadows, Lower Funston Meadow, Kern Hot Spring, Junction Meadow, Wallace Creek, Whitney Creek, return via Guyot Creek, Upper Rock Creek Lake and Chicken Spring Lake
Distance	83½ miles including the 10-mile round trip to the summit of Mt. Whitney
Type	Loop trip
Best season	Late
Topo maps	**Mt. Whitney** 15′; Cirque Peak, Johnson Peak, Kern Lake, Chagoopa Falls, Mt. Kaweah, Mount Whitney 7½′

Grade (hiking days/recommended layover days)
> *Leisurely* —
> *Moderate* 11/3
> *Strenuous* 9/1

Trailhead   Horseshoe Meadow (25)

HIGHLIGHTS   On this outstanding loop trip, you sample the high meadows of the Kern Plateau, visit colorful lava flows, cross a creek on a natural bridge, descend into spectacular Kern Canyon and walk up its most scenic segment, soak in the Sierra's most remote natural hot spring, bag the highest peak in the contiguous 48 states as a dayhike, and then wander back on a route that offers excellent views of the rugged Great Western Divide. Along the way, there's fine fishing in Golden Trout Creek, the Kern River and Rock Creek for anglers, and there's exciting dayhiking for all.

The many stream crossings may be hazardous early in the season. Under no circumstances should you attempt to cross a major stream like the Kern River or Big Arroyo if the bridges have been washed out; turn back and take this trip some other time. If a storm breaks while you're at or near the summit of Mt. Whitney, scurry down immediately. *Do not take shelter in the hut*, as its metal roof conducts lightning strikes to those inside, and hikers have been killed by lightning there.

DESCRIPTION (Moderate trip)

1st Hiking Day (**Horseshoe Meadow** to **Big Whitney Meadow**, 8¼ miles). Follow the 1st and part of the 2nd hiking days of Trip 87 to Big Whitney Meadow. Campsites in the forest edges near the junction with the Rocky Basin Lakes Trail offer places to hang your food, and the tree trunks offer a slight barrier to roaming cattle in this grazing allotment. The morning view south down the meadow toward Kern Peak is a treat!

2nd Hiking Day (**Big Whitney Meadow** to **Little Whitney Meadow**, 8 miles). Follow the 4th hiking day, Trip 85.

3rd Hiking Day: (**Little Whitney Meadow** to **Lower Funston Meadow**, 8 miles): Follow the 5th hiking day, Trip 85, as far as the campsites between the trail and the river at Lower Funston Meadow.

4th Hiking Day (**Lower Funston Meadow** to **Kern Hot Spring**, 7 miles): Continue your northward trek on the Kern River Trail. You are likely to make wild animal sightings while traveling up the glacially carved trench of mighty Kern Canyon. Animals, like people, are "channeled" up and down its steep-walled course, and within the canyon's relatively confined course, you are apt to see bear, coyote and deer, not to mention your fellow travelers. From

Laurel Creek the trail continues north through a moderate forest. Mostly duff, the trail surface makes pleasant walking, and the distance to the Rattlesnake Creek Trail junction is rapidly covered. At this junction, and just across the sometimes difficult ford of Rattlesnake Creek, there are possible campsites. Depending on the season and the previous winter's wetness, the pink granite of the canyon's 1500-foot walls may be splashed here and there by ribbons of spray—some nameless streams' abrupt plunges from the hanging valleys and plateaus above. You cross Big Arroyo on a steel bridge, pass Upper Funston Meadow and soon meet the High Sierra Trail where it levels out near Funston Creek.

From here, follow most of the 4th hiking day of Trip 79.

5th Hiking Day (**Kern Hot Spring** to **Junction Meadow**, 8 miles): Follow the 5th hiking day, Trip 79. The fords of the stream draining Guyot Flat and of Whitney and Wallace creeks can be difficult in early season.

6th Hiking Day (**Junction Meadow** to **Guitar Lake**, 11 miles): This is a long, tough day that also includes almost 3500 feet of net elevation gain, so an early start is in order. Here's the tradeoff: Staying at Guitar Lake instead of Crabtree Ranger Station makes your next day's round-trip climb of Mt. Whitney 6 miles shorter even though it makes *this* day's hike 3 miles longer and adds a net 800 feet of elevation gain.

First, follow the 6th hiking day, Trip 79, a mile up Kern Canyon to the junction where the High Sierra Trail turns southeast. Ascend on it to meet the John Muir Trail/Pacific Crest Trail at Wallace Creek's pleasant campsites. Turn south toward Mt. Whitney at this junction and climb over the saddle west of Mt. Young, passing Sandy Meadow, to the junction where the John Muir Trail turns east to Mt. Whitney and the Pacific Crest Trail continues south to Mexico. Turn east with the John Muir Trail, ascending past the turnoff to lower Crabtree Meadow, Crabtree Ranger Station's possible campsites and closed-to-camping Timberline Lake. Ascend to Guitar Lake (11,483'), now a popular staging area for bagging Mt. Whitney. In late season, when Guitar Lake may be overused, consider the areas near Guitar Lake as suggested in the 2nd day of Trip 71. Wood fires are prohibited throughout this high basin.

7th Hiking/"Layover" Day (**Guitar Lake** to **Mt. Whitney summit**, 10 miles out and back): With daypacks instead of backpacks, follow the rest of the "Layover Day" of Trip 80 up the John Muir Trail, ascending the west side of Mt. Whitney. The unfolding panorama to the west is stunning, more than taking your mind off the stiff ascent. At the junction with the trail to the summit, turn north. Your trail eventually becomes indistinct in the loose scree of the gentle summit plateau. Views down the sheer east face of Mt. Whitney to the Owens Valley 11,000 feet below are breathtaking. The scope of the scene in all directions, especially from the summit, is unparalleled in the Sierra. Remember: if a storm breaks, *get off the peak—stay out of the summit hut!*

Retrace your steps to your camp at Guitar Lake.

8th Hiking Day (**Guitar Lake** to **Guyot Creek**, 7¼ miles): First, retrace your steps past Crabtree Ranger Station to the turnoff to lower Crabtree Meadow. From here, you reverse part of the 3rd hiking day of Trip 84 by turning left (southwest) on this spur, soon passing pretty lower Crabtree Meadow, and rejoin the Pacific Crest Trail where it fords Whitney Creek just below its confluence with Crabtree Creek—last water before Guyot Creek in a dry year. Turn south on the Pacific Crest Trail and ascend rocky switchbacks into the broken forest cover and sandy underfooting of a low, unnamed saddle. With flat-topped Mt. Guyot beckoning you south, you descend slightly and curve around sandy Guyot Flat in open forest. Then you ascend the saddle east of Mt. Guyot (sometimes called Guyot Pass) and descend to a ford of pleasant Guyot Creek and its small campsite (10,400').

9th Hiking Day (**Guyot Creek** to **Upper Rock Creek**, 5½ miles): Continuing your reversal of the 3rd and 2nd hiking days of Trip 84, you descend moderately and then steeply to lower Rock Creek ford (difficult in early season). Now on the south side of Rock Creek, you make an easy ascent, alternately through grassy meadows and dense forest. Where the Pacific Crest Trail veers southeast, you stay on the Rock Creek Trail, perhaps taking advantage of the fishing opportunities, and eventually fording it back to the north side (difficult in early season). Campsites along the north side of idyllic, meadowed upper Rock Creek Lake (10,476') and the creek above and below it offer a chance to explore adjacent Miter Basin as well as to fish.

10th Hiking Day (**Upper Rock Creek** to **Chicken Spring Lake**, 6 miles): Continue a short, willow-choked way up Rock Creek to a **T** junction—north to lower Soldier Lake, south to New Army Pass and Siberian Pass. Turn south (right), soon meeting the New Army Pass Trail, which turns east up the cirque; for an alternative, see the "Longer Trip" suggestion below.

You continue south, fording a tributary of Rock Creek that is the last reliable water before Chicken Spring Lake. In a little less than a mile, you rejoin the Pacific Crest Trail and continue south-southeast on a long, sandy traverse around the base of Cirque Peak toward Chicken Spring Lake and Cottonwood Pass. Now you leave Sequoia National Park and re-enter Golden Trout Wilderness, curve through a small cirque, swing around a ridge, and descend to the outlet of Chicken Spring Lake (11,270')—good campsites; no wood fires within ¼ mile of the lake—on a couple of switchbacks. To shorten your trip by a day, see the "Shorter Trip" suggestion below.

Shorter Trip (**Upper Rock Creek** to **Horseshoe Meadow**, 10½ miles). Follow the 10th hiking day of this trip to Chicken Spring Lake. From there, you can end the trip on this same day by continuing 4½ more miles over Cottonwood Pass to the trailhead at Horseshoe Meadow, as described in Day 11, below.

Longer Trip (**Upper Rock Creek** to **Cottonwood Lakes Trailhead**, 11¾ miles). Alternatively, you can lengthen your trip by a day. Take the New Army Pass Trail to South Fork Lakes and then to the Cottonwood Lakes Trailhead by reversing Trip 82. Close the loop on the road or on the spur trail linking the Cottonwood Lakes and Horseshoe Meadow trailheads.

11th Hiking Day (**Chicken Spring Lake** to **Horseshoe Meadow**, 4½ miles): This last, easy day calls for a late start and lingering farewell to the high country. Returning to the Pacific Crest Trail, you stroll through moderate forest cover to meet the Cottonwood Pass Trail just west of Cottonwood Pass. Turn east on the Cottonwood Pass Trail and retrace the steps of Day 1 to the Horseshoe Meadow Trailhead.

Chicken Spring Lake

89   Horseshoe Meadow to Whitney Portal

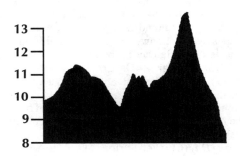

Trip	From Horseshoe Meadow to Whitney Portal via Cottonwood Pass, Chicken Spring Lake, Rock Creek, Crabtree Meadow, Mt. Whitney and Outpost Camp
Distance	36 miles
Type	Shuttle trip
Best season	Mid or late
Topo maps	**Mt. Whitney** 15'; Cirque Peak, Johnson Peak, Mount Whitney, Mt. Langley 7½'

Grade (hiking days/recommended layover days)

Leisurely	6/2
Moderate	5/1
Strenuous	4/0
Trailhead	Start at Horseshoe Meadow (25), end at Whitney Portal (23)

HIGHLIGHTS   Like Trip 84, this adventure is another superb alternative to the old stomp up and down Mt. Whitney. This trip differs by starting with a lovely hike up to Cottonwood Pass and a scenic traverse around Cirque Peak. The views over Siberian Outpost to the Great Western Divide will long be remembered.

The trail is good. Away from it, especially when exploring places like Miter Basin, map-and-compass skills and some boulder-scrambling experience are needed. No wood fires within ¼ mile of Chicken Spring Lake.

DESCRIPTION (Moderate trip)

1st Hiking Day (**Horseshoe Meadow** to **Chicken Spring Lake**, 4½ miles): Follow the 1st hiking day, Trip 87 to Cottonwood Pass. At the pass you meet the Pacific Crest Trail and turn right onto it for ⅔ easy mile on level, dynamited footing to the outlet of Chicken Spring Lake (often dry by late season). Follow the outlet upstream toward the good campsites east and the fair campsites west of foxtail-rimmed Chicken Spring Lake.

2nd Hiking Day (**Chicken Spring Lake** to **Lower Rock Creek Ford**, 9½ miles): Except in early season there is no water until Rock Creek, so fill your canteen. The Pacific Crest Trail switchbacks westward up the wall of the Chicken Spring Lake cirque and then levels off over sandy slopes at the headwaters of Golden Trout Creek. After contouring above a meadow in another cirque, our route enters Sequoia National Park at an unnamed point (11,350') on a ridge west of Cirque Peak. At the next junction, turn left (west), staying on the Pacific Crest Trail. As the trail descends through the moderate-to-dense forest of lodgepole and foxtail pine, we get good views of Mt. Kaweah and the Great Western Divide, as well as large, bleak Siberian Outpost.

The trail descends steadily past a junction with the Siberian Pass Trail before the grade eases and our route begins a long, rolling descent along the forested ridge atop the south wall of Rock Creek canyon. Where the trail is close to the right side of the ridge, it is well worth stepping off to the right a few hundred feet to get the excellent views of the peaks surrounding Miter Basin. After 2½ miles from the junction our route makes a steep descent toward Siberian Pass Creek, but turns north before reaching it. Then it drops via rocky switchbacks through a dense forest down the south wall of Rock Creek canyon. When the underfooting turns to duff, our route meets and turns left onto the Rock Creek Trail and descends one mile down the creek to the overused campsites at the ford of lower Rock Creek (9480'), where fishing for golden trout (to 8") is good.

3rd, 4th and 5th Hiking Days: Follow Trip 84, the 3rd through the 5th hiking days, 22 miles.

90
Mineral King to Upper Cliff Creek

Trip	From Mineral King to Upper Cliff Creek via Timber Gap
Distance	17 miles
Type	Out and back trip
Best season	Mid
Topo maps	**Mineral King** 15'; Mineral King 7½'

Grade (hiking days/recommended layover days)

Leisurely	—
Moderate	2/1
Strenuous	—
Trailhead	Mineral King (21)

HIGHLIGHTS   This is one of the easiest hikes into National Park wilderness in the western High Sierra, but still tough enough that hikers will feel they have earned the fine subalpine scenery that awaits on the banks of Cliff Creek and the pleasure of a swim in Pinto Lake.

DESCRIPTION (Moderate trip)

1st Hiking Day (**Mineral King** to **Upper Cliff Creek**, 8½ miles): From the Timber Gap/Sawtooth Pass trailhead one mile beyond the Ranger Station in Mineral King Valley, our route ascends the manzanita-and-sagebrush-flanked Sawtooth Pass Trail for 1 mile, and then diverges left at a junction. Our trail fork begins a 1600-foot climb, ascending relentlessly up a southwest-facing slope that is warm indeed in midsummer, but blessed by some shade from juniper and red-fir trees. After a steep series of 10 switchbacks, we traverse almost on the level across a treeless, flower-dotted hillside, and then enter a cool stand of red fir, which comes to include lodgepole and foxtail pine.

This ascent tops out at Timber Gap (9400'), and we begin to drop steeply in red-fir forest. During early summer in this forest, hikers may hear the thumping of blue grouse and the melodic flutings of hermit thrushes. As we descend above Timber Gap Creek, we find the rivulets on the slope sometimes disappearing into the loosely consolidated metamorphic rock. Although Timber Gap Creek is virtually inaccessible, there's plenty of drinking water in the rivulets that lace this high garden. Soon we reach a mile-long flower garden, one of the largest and best in the whole Sierra. Then the trail rounds the nose of the ridge on the east and switchbacks down to Cliff Creek through dense coniferous forest.

Beyond a ford of Cliff Creek (difficult in early season) are tiny Cliff Creek Campground and a 3-way junction with trails to Mineral King, Redwood Meadow and Black Rock Pass. After turning right, uphill, through the campsites, on the Black Rock Pass Trail, our route climbs steadily through alternating brush and trees to reach a very verdant area watered in part by cold little streams that issue from the ground. In early summer the fine wildflower displays near the creek include Mariposa lily, rein orchid, wild strawberry, monkey flower, wallflower, corn lily, delphinium, yellow-throated gilia and buck-wheat.

Beyond a grove of fir trees our route goes out onto what looks like an abandoned stream bed, and leads us toward the base of the prominent falls of Cliff Creek. Here we veer away from the falls and turn toward the cascading outlet of Pinto Lake. Now we climb the steep slope to the left through dense willow, sagebrush, whitethorn and bitter cherry. Then our trail crosses the outlet stream of Pinto Lake, tops a small rise in ½ mile, and arrives at another three-way junction. The left fork is the trail to Black Rock Pass, and the right fork is a short spur to good campsites (8620') near Cliff Creek on forested knolls. Just to the north, screened by willows, is little Pinto Lake, an excellent swimming pool much warmer than you'd expect.

2nd Hiking Day: Retrace your steps, 8½ miles.

91 Mineral King to Little Five Lakes

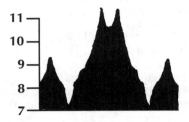

Trip	From Mineral King to Little Five Lakes via Cliff Creek and Black Rock Pass
Distance	31 miles
Type	Out and back trip
Best season	Mid or late
Topo maps	**Mineral King** 15′; Mineral King 7½′

Grade (hiking days/recommended layover days)

Leisurely	5/2
Moderate	4/1
Strenuous	—

Trailhead	Mineral King (21)

HIGHLIGHTS   Next to the Sierra Crest itself, the Great Western Divide is the most spectacular feature in Sequoia National Park. This trip crosses that sky-piercing divide at Black Rock Pass and leads to a large number of lakes, all of them close under the colorful cliffs and soaring peaks of the Great Western Divide and the Kaweah Peaks Ridge.

DESCRIPTION (Moderate trip)

1st Hiking Day: Follow the 1st hiking day, Trip 90, to **Upper Cliff Creek**, 8½ miles.

2nd Hiking Day (**Upper Cliff Creek** to **Little Five Lakes**, 7 miles): After crossing the meadows south of Pinto Lake, this day's route begins a grueling 3000-foot ascent to Black Rock Pass. There's no decent campsite before Little Five Lakes, but given an early start, the hiker should be able to make it to the pass before the heat of the day reaches its maximum, and fortunately there is plenty of drinking water except in late season. Scattered foxtail pines dot the mostly open slopes, and in early summer wildflower gardens abound on the slopes above Cliff Creek, with their heather, yampa, larkspur, swamp whiteheads, Bigelow sneezeweed, paintbrush, phlox, wallflower, wild onion, senecio and forget-me-nots. Soon Pinto Lake comes into view below, a very small pond at the base of a talus slope. Past a series of meadows the trail begins the switchbacking slog to the pass, and views of the upper basin of Cliff Creek include the cascades below Spring Lake, Spring Lake itself, Cyclamen Lake, and then Columbine Lake, icebound in early summer. The solitary traveler, moving quietly, will see numerous deer on these subalpine slopes. Finally the rocky path attains Black Rock Pass (11,630'), and a good rest stop affords moments for viewing the vast scene ahead. The companion basins of Little Five Lakes and Big Five Lakes drop off into Big Arroyo, and beyond this chasm rise the multicolored, cliffbound Kaweah Peaks. In the east is the 14,000-foot Whitney crest, backbone of the Sierra.

From the pass, the zigzagging downgrade trends southeast and then angles northeast to pass above the highest of the Little Five Lakes—actually more than one dozen lakes. (When snow obscures the trail in early season, one should keep to the left so as not to get off-route too far to the right and come out onto some cliffs.) There are excellent campsites on the peninsula at the north end of the first lake whose shores the trail touches, and across the bay from these is a summer ranger who could provide emergency services. The grass, sedge and dwarf-bilberry ground cover around the peninsula-tip campsite is beautiful in the early-morning and late-evening light, and an evening meal here may be raised to four-star quality by the alpenglow on the Kaweah Peaks across Big Arroyo.

3rd and 4th Hiking Days: Retrace your steps, 15½ miles.

92 Mineral King to Nine Lake Basin

Trip	From Mineral King to Nine Lake Basin via Timber Gap, Cliff Creek, Black Rock Pass, Little Five Lakes and Big Arroyo
Distance	42 miles
Type	Out and back trip
Best season	Mid or late
Topo maps	**Mineral King, Triple Divide Peak** 15′; Mineral King, Triple Divide Peak 7½′

Grade (hiking days/recommended layover days)

Leisurely	—
Moderate	6/2
Strenuous	4/2
Trailhead	Mineral King (21)

HIGHLIGHTS   Nine Lake Basin offers the seclusion that places not reached by maintained trail always possess. While hundreds tramp the High Sierra Trail, not more than ½ mile away, few detour to enjoy these splendid lakes. Located in a south-facing amphitheater between the towering Great Western Divide and the Kaweah Peaks Ridge, this lake basin is a perfect place to explore, fish, climb, photograph and recover your sense of wonder at nature's bounty.

The trail is easy and the route to the lowest lake of Nine Lake Basin is straightforward though trackless: just follow the outlet stream. Map-and-compass skills and some experience in cross-country travel are needed for exploring the basin's highest lakes.

DESCRIPTION (Moderate trip)

1st and 2nd Hiking Days: Follow Trip 91 to **Little Five Lakes**, 15½ miles.

3rd Hiking Day (**Little Five Lakes** to **Nine Lake Basin**, 6½ miles): Just below the second of the Little Five Lakes, our trail fords the outlet and passes a trail to Big Five Lakes. Continue down beside the tumbling stream past the next lake in the chain, then ford the stream back to its north side. Soon the trail crosses the outlet of the northern cluster of Little Five Lakes, and the trout in this stream promise action to anglers who are willing to sweat their way up to the lakes above.

After an easy rise out of the basin, the trail begins to descend into Big Arroyo, a large west-bank tributary of the Kern River, increasing in steepness where it turns northeast. Beyond the ford of Big Arroyo, an unsigned trail leads down Big Arroyo. We go left (north) on the High Sierra Trail to ascend gently up the broad glacial valley past numerous possible campsites with great views of granitic Lippincott Mountain and Eagle Scout Peak towering in the west, and metamorphic Black Kaweah and Red Kaweah piercing the eastern sky. The trail fords Big Arroyo creek again and then climbs over grassy pockets and granite slabs toward Kaweah Gap, a distinctive low spot on the great Western Divide in the northwest. Where this trail swings west, your unmapped trail takes off north into Nine Lake Basin, and it soon arrives at the horseshoe-shaped first lake (10,450'), with numerous fair-to-good campsites and good fishing for brook trout. A base camp here makes a springboard for excursions to the increasingly secluded and dramatic lakes north and east, and for climbing expeditions to the wealth of steep faces west and east of this fine base camp.

4th, 5th and 6th Hiking Days: Retrace your steps, 22 miles.

Kaweah Peaks Ridge over middle Little Five Lake

93 Mineral King to Hamilton Lakes

Trip	From Mineral King to Hamilton Lakes via Timber Gap, Cliff Creek, Black Rock Pass, Little Five Lakes, Big Arroyo, Nine Lake Basin, Kaweah Gap, Little Bearpaw Meadow and Redwood Meadow
Distance	44 miles
Type	Semiloop trip
Best season	Mid or late
Topo maps	**Mineral King, Triple Divide Peak** 15′; Mineral King, Triple Divide Peak, Lodgepole 7½′

Grade (hiking days/recommended layover days)

Leisurely	—
Moderate	6/3
Strenuous	4/2
Trailhead	Mineral King (21)

HIGHLIGHTS Backpackers who want to sample the multifold attractions of Sequoia National Park will find in this one trip high passes and barren divides, subalpine stream valleys, inviting glacial lake basins, middle-altitude meadows, deep river canyons and remote giant sequoia groves. Many of the finest sequoia groves are reached by road, threaded by trails and full of visitors, so that your visit there is full of noise and exhaust fumes. What a treat it is to be at remote, silent, flowery Redwood Meadow, its patch of bright green grass surrounded by immense ruddy trunks!

The trail is straightforward; exploring off-trail in Nine Lake Basin calls for map-and-compass skills and cross-country experience.

DESCRIPTION (Moderate trip)

1st, 2nd and 3rd Hiking Days: Follow Trip 92 to **Nine Lake Basin**, 22 miles.

4th Hiking Day (**Nine Lake Basin** to **Little Bearpaw Meadow**, 9½ miles): After retracing the steps to the High Sierra Trail, this route turns right (west) and quickly climbs the few hundred feet to Kaweah Gap (10,700'). This pass on the Great Western Divide lies between the waters of the Kern River and those of the Kaweah River, and it affords views of many of the peaks whose snow-clad slopes give birth to these rivers. From the pass, our route drops moderately and then more steeply in granite sand. Early-season hikers are likely to see some gray-crowned rosy finches feeding on aphids and other insects that were blown onto the late-melting snow from lower elevations. The near-vertical faces of Mt. Stewart and Eagle Scout Peak cradle the trail as it passes aptly named Precipice Lake. Beyond the lake, the cirque widens and drops off. This stretch of trail is one of the most spectacular in the range: lush wildflowers and a multitude of cascades cover the valley wall, and the hiker is awe-struck by the immensity of the colorful cliffs that rise from azure-blue lower Hamilton Lake far below to the lofty crags above.

This vertical world will delight photographers, especially early in the day, and few of them will resist the spectacle of a channel for the trail that was blasted out of the canyon wall to create a "tunnel" open on one side—the cliff side. On these cliffs, white-throated swifts twinkle by, giving their mocking, laughlike cry as the trail drops and drops, 2000 feet in about 2 miles. A long switchback leg delivers the weary-kneed hiker to the west shore of upper Hamilton Lake (8235'), where fishing is good for rainbow trout (to 16"). No open fires are allowed here.

The trail crosses Hamilton Creek just below the lake and descends in or near the riparian vegetation along the stream. Below lower Hamilton Lake the descending trail refords the creek and then contours along an increasingly steep rock face that gives a second and equally apt meaning to the name of this trail, the *High* Sierra Trail.

Now off the cliff face, our route climbs shortly as it swings north before descending to the cement bridge crossing of Lone Pine Creek. Below, in the gorge, the collapsed old bridge lies draped over a gigantic chockstone where the old trail crossed. From this creek to Bearpaw Meadow, the trail climbs more than it drops, as it traverses the steep walls high above River Valley. Views back toward the Great Western Divide and the glacier-carved canyons of Eagle Scout, Hamilton and Granite creeks emanating from it are awesome.

As we enter the Bearpaw Meadow area (no open fires), the ranger station appears north of the trail, and south of it the tents of Bearpaw

Meadow camp, where meals, lodging (with reservations) and candy bars can be bought during the summer. Take the first trail to the left through the campground, toward Redwood Meadow. This campground gets heavy use, and it is dirty. More secluded campsites may be found at Little Bearpaw Meadow (6850′), about a mile south on a moderately-to-steeply descending trail that winds down under white fir, incense-cedar and sugar pine.

5th Hiking day (**Little Bearpaw Meadow** to **Cliff Creek**, 6½ miles): Below Little Bearpaw Meadow we pass a marked trail on the right and continue our descent in mid-elevation mixed forest, with the spicy scent of mountain misery heavy in the air. At the bottom of this descent the trail passes a sign that points out the little used trail upstream and then fords the Middle Fork Kaweah River on logs and rocks (difficult in early season). Then our trail climbs the opposite bank and descends gently past a junction with a little-used trail down the Middle Fork, and we continue ahead, soon reaching cascading Eagle Scout Creek.

Rounding the next ridge, we come to Granite Creek, which is a roaring torrent in early season. An easy crossing by bridge and another short climb over a ridge in timber lead us to our last descent before Redwood Meadow. Even before we reach the meadow, we encounter red columnar giants standing tall among the lesser firs and pines in this forest. These are the giant sequoias, Sierra redwoods or Big Trees, earth's largest living things.

Our trail skirts the fenced meadow, where grazing is limited, and arrives at the Redwood Meadow Ranger Station. The building is an impressive two-story log house which is now used only by maintenance crews and park officials' guests. Camping is limited in this very peaceful place, as water is scarce. From here the trail climbs steadily, gradually leaving the Big Trees for mixed pine and fir, with patches of manzanita. Coralroot, a root parasite, grows here along the trail, commonly under firs and pines, where it feeds on living tree roots. Our route undulates through heavy forest for several miles, toward Cliff Creek and then away from it, and finally arrives at tiny Cliff Creek campground (7140′).

6th Hiking Day (**Cliff Creek** to **Mineral King**, 6 miles): Retrace the steps of part of the 1st hiking day.

Mineral King to Spring Lake 94

Trip	From Mineral King to Spring Lake via Glacier Pass, part cross-country
Distance	12 miles
Type	Out and back trip
Best season	Mid
Topo maps	**Mineral King** 15′; Mineral King 7½′
Grade (hiking days/recommended layover days)	
Leisurely	—
Moderate	—
Strenuous	2/0
Trailhead	Mineral King (21)

HIGHLIGHTS   This "weekender" makes a fine exercise for the experienced backpacker in good condition, crossing the Empire Mountain ridge by a little-used pass to beautiful Spring Lake. Rugged peaks, mirror-like tarns, possibilities for exploring old "prospects" and cascading streams are the rewards for making a difficult 3300-foot climb. This trip is only for the hardier breed of hiker with experience in and a liking for the challenges of cross-country travel.

DESCRIPTION (Strenuous trip)

1st Hiking Day (**Mineral King** to **Spring Lake**, 6 miles, part cross country): Beginning from the dirt parking lot on the north side of the road, at the point where the road bends south ("Harry's Bend") our trail jogs north and then turns east on ascending switchbacks. This dusty, eroded trail winds up a dry, brushy slope, offering some views up the Mineral King valley to Farewell Gap. In 1 mile, our trail passes the Timber Gap Trail branching north, and then continues east up the Monarch Creek drainage. Few trees screen this trail section from the sun. Sometimes but not always visible from the trail, Monarch Creek splashes down to the valley in a series of granite-bottomed falls from the "false cirque" just above. This bowl does, at first glance, appear to be a true cirque—the womb of a glacial *mer de glace*—but as you continue you will see that it is merely where the river of ice midway down the slope discovered a schistic weakness in the underlying rock, and ground down on its heel, carving, scraping and sculpting the resulting amphitheater. Early white residents brought their eastern terminology to this country and, in honor of the many marmots that inhabit the rocky fringe of the grassy-bottomed bowl, named it Groundhog Meadow.

At Groundhog Meadow we take the right trail fork across Monarch Creek. The left fork climbs directly up the canyon toward Sawtooth Pass and Glacier Pass. However, this trail is on unstable talus and it is no longer maintained. We pass a fair campsite and begin several miles of long switchbacks which take us through open stands of red fir and western white pine with an understory of chinquapin, currant, gooseberry and lupine. Finally the trail crosses a ridge in timber that now includes some handsome foxtail pines, and just beyond the next hairpin bend is a nice lunch stop, where you can get drinking water by going 100 yards across the hillside. A short way up the trail from this lunch spot, a trail takes off to Crystal Lake.

Our trail, the new Monarch Lakes Trail, then rounds a shoulder, and now we can see the old trail across the canyon below, as well as Timber Gap, the Great Western Divide and Sawtooth Pass. We cross two forks of Monarch Creek and arrive at lower Monarch Lake (10,380'), where camping is fair (toilet). A jumbled trail climbs around the north side of the lake through willows to upper Monarch Lake (10,640'), which is dammed and which lacks any decent campsites.

At the north end of lower Monarch Lake we turn north and soon come to an unsigned trail going left. Keeping to the right, in ¼ mile we meet another junction, and take the right fork. (Many people coming down from Sawtooth Pass take the westbound fork here because it looks to be the more used trail. It connects with the old Sawtooth Pass Trail farther down the canyon.) Soon the trail peters out and we work our way up a sandy hillside. Alternatively, we could pick our way up the sandy "staircase" formed by a vegetated slot in the white granite outcrop north of the second junction. After nearly a mile of cross-country work, we arrive at a west-trending ridge lined with a few foxtail pines. From the top of this ridge we can see many sets of footprints leading north in the granite sand nearly horizontally over to the notch that is Glacier Pass.

Glacier Pass (11,000') is the first significant notch west of the sandy-backed, unnamed peak above us. The exposure at the very top on the north side of Glacier Pass is high Class 2 or even Class 3. Views of the Cliff Creek drainage and barren Mt. Eisen are impressive as you scramble down the north side of the pass.

This side of the pass is frequently covered with late-melting snow. Be sure to keep to the tundra-topped granite ledges east of and above the tarn that is the beginning of the west tributary of Spring Lake. Here the track (sometimes ducked, sometimes worn into the grass) descends steeply to ford a tributary just above its final plunge into Spring Lake (10,040′). The trail then traverses the sparsely timbered west slope of the Spring Lake cirque to the overused campsites (no campfires). Views from the campsites of the sheer, smoothed granite headwall at the south end of the lake fill the viewer with a sense of awe and respect for the glacier's power. Fishing for brook (to 8″) is good.

2nd Hiking Day: Retrace your steps, 6 miles.

Foxtail pines die slowly

95 Mineral King to Lost Canyon

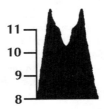

Trip	From Mineral King to Lost Canyon via Sawtooth Pass and Columbine Lake
Distance	15 miles
Type	Out and back trip
Best season	Mid
Topo maps	**Mineral King** 15′; Mineral King 7½′

Grade (hiking days/recommended layover days)

Leisurely	—
Moderate	—
Strenuous	2/1
Trailhead	Mineral King (21)

HIGHLIGHTS This demanding trail traces the Monarch Creek drainage to cross the Great Western Divide at Sawtooth Pass. High alpine scenery climaxed by the cold, often ice-filled waters of Columbine Lake make this a fine route for all who love the High Sierra and are in good shape. The excellent fishing in the upper Lost Canyon drainage will reward anglers who are willing to walk for their suppers.

The 3800-foot elevation gain requires that you be in excellent physical condition.

DESCRIPTION (Strenuous trip)

1st Hiking Day (**Mineral King** to **Upper Lost Canyon**, 7½ miles): Follow the 1st hiking day, Trip 94, to the ridge from where many tracks lead north toward Glacier Pass. From here we go north nearly to the notch, where we double back southeast just below the ridgecrest. Stay high—all lower routes to Sawtooth Pass are difficult, especially with a full pack.

Sawtooth Pass (11,600′) is signed—and you may need the sign to tell you which notch is the pass, for it is not the low point on the ridge. From the summit of this high-ridged pass there are vistas of the surrounding country exceeded only by those from the tops of nearby

Sawtooth Peak and Needham Mountain. One can see the length of the Monarch Creek drainage to the west, and on down into the wooded drainage of the East Fork Kaweah River. Empire Mountain and the ridge to its southeast dominate the view to the north, Sawtooth Peak is on the skyline to the south, and to the east one looks across Columbine Lake, Lost Canyon and Big Arroyo to the timbered reaches of the Chagoopa Plateau. Far on the eastern horizon, one can see the Mt. Whitney complex of peaks, south as far as Mt. Langley and Cirque Peak.

The descent on the east side of Sawtooth Pass, like the western ascent, is a steep, sandy, zigzagging affair that gives the backpacker little chance to look at the spectacular scenery. This route continues down, dropping steeply to the north side of Columbine Lake. Here glacially scoured granite slabs tilt into the lake's usually mirrorlike surface. The reflections of the nearby mineralized, rust-colored rocks blend with the chalkier whites of the lakeside granites to leave an indelible impression—despite the basin's harsh, treeless condition.

After rounding the north side of the lake, our route drops steeply down to the head of Lost Canyon on a rocky surface that does not give way to grass and trees until one is almost due north of the westernmost spire of Needham Mountain. Here good campsites will be found in an open, grassy setting (10,200') amid a sparse forest cover of stunted lodgepole pines. Fishing for brook trout farther downstream is excellent.

2nd Hiking Day: Retrace your steps, 7½ miles.

Looking across Mineral King Valley from the Franklin Pass Trail

96 Mineral King to Upper Rattlesnake Creek

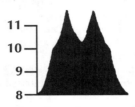

Trip	From Mineral King to Upper Rattlesnake Creek via Franklin Pass
Distance	20 miles
Type	Out and back trip
Best season	Mid or late
Topo maps	**Mineral King** 15′; Mineral King 7½′

Grade (hiking days/recommended layover days)

Leisurely	—
Moderate	—
Strenuous	2/1
Trailhead	Mineral King (21)

HIGHLIGHTS   This trip explores unusually colorful settings, while the 4000-foot climb evokes colorful epithets. The peaks cupping the Franklin Lakes cirque are an artist's canvas of different grays, shades of red, and various tone of green. Across Franklin Pass the fine fishing and beautifully intimate scenery of Rattlesnake Creek beckon to anglers and appreciative naturalists.

This strenuous, taxing trip is a workout for backpackers in top shape.

DESCRIPTION (Strenuous trip)

1st Hiking Day (**Mineral King** to **Upper Rattlesnake Creek**, 10 miles): For this trip you may be able to park at the Sawtooth Pass/ Timber Gap trailhead or you may have to park at the lot about halfway from the ranger station to that lot. You then walk up the road past the Mineral King pack station and go by a locked gate. A rough jeep road continues from this gate for about 1 mile, to an unimproved campground near the junction of Crystal Creek and the East Fork Kaweah River. Looking up-canyon from this point, one can readily make out Farewell Gap at the top of V-shaped upper Farewell canyon. Just west of the trail-road, the hurrying waters of the Kaweah River are hidden by a screen of willows, and the early-morning hiker is very apt to see a marmot surveying its territory. Scattered clumps of juniper and red fir contrast with the ghostly white of cottonwood trunks just below the point where the route fords Crystal Creek and, veering left where the road continues straight, begins an unrelenting ascent of several miles.

Along the shaley trail, the savory odor of sagebrush assails the nostrils, and between the sagebrush and the gooseberry of those lower slopes, spots of wildflower color are provided by purple Indian paintbrush, lavender fleabane, cream cow parsnip and red ipomopsis. Soon the trail fords dashing Franklin Creek (difficult in early season) just below a lovely fall and begins a steep, switchbacking ascent above a section of the Kaweah River that flows through a deep, eroded gash.

About 1¼ miles north of Farewell Gap, our route doubles back north, passes a junction with the trail to Farewell Gap, and begins a long, stuttering traverse around the northwest slopes of Tulare Peak. This traverse provides excellent views back down the Kaweah River canyon to Mineral King and beyond to Timber Gap. The contrast between the green hillside and the red of Vandever Mountain in the south is especially striking in the morning light. Then you enter a sparse forest cover of mature foxtail pines and crosses red-hued rocky slopes dotted with spring flowers and laced with little snow-melt rills as you turn northeast into Franklin Creek's upper canyon.

After descending briefly to ford the creek, the trail rises steeply to the rock-and-concrete-dammed outlet of lower Franklin Lake (10,300′). The colors in this dramatically walled cirque basin are a bizarre conglomeration. To the northeast, the slopes of Rainbow Maintain are a study of gray-white marble whorls set in a sea of pink, red and black metamorphic rocks. To the south, the slate ridge joining Tulare Peak and Florence Peak is a hue of chocolate red that sends color photographers scrambling for viewpoints from which to foreground the contrasting blue of lower Franklin Lake against this colorful headwall. Anglers will find the fishing for brook trout (to 10″) good at the lower lake, and better at the upper lake. Some small, sandy ledges with a few trees well above the northeast shore of the lower lake make pleasant campsites with good lake views. Other campsites, treeless, are near the trail beside the east inlet about 400 feet higher than the lake.

From this lake the trail rises steadily and then steeply on switchbacks. Views of the Franklin Lakes cirque improve with altitude, and it isn't long before both the upper and lower lakes are in view. This ascent leaves the forest cover behind, as it crosses and recrosses a field of coarse granite granules dotted with bedrock outcropping. Despite the sievelike drainage of this slope, flowers abound. High up on the slope two adjacent year-round streamlets nourish gardens of yellow mimulus and lavender shooting stars. At windy Franklin Pass (11,760'), views are panoramic. Landmarks to the northwest include Castle Rocks and Paradise Peak; to the east are the immediate unglaciated plateau about the headwaters of Rattlesnake Creek, and Forester Lake (on the wooded bench just north of Rattlesnake Creek). East of the Kern Trench and plateaus, one can make out Mt. Whitney on the Sierra Crest.

The initial descent from the pass, unlike the west-side ascent, is an ad-lib plunge down a slope mostly covered with a layer of disintegrated quartz sand and oddly dotted with small, wind-sculpted granite domes. After crossing this bench, the trail drops steeply down rocky, rough, blasted switchbacks that twine back and forth over some of the headwaters of Rattlesnake Creek. The trail levels out on the north side of the creek, and enters a friendly forest of young lodgepole pines broken by pleasant meadow patches. Several excellent campsites (10,300') line the creek here. Fishing for brook trout (to 8") is good to excellent, and the stream is ideal for fly fishermen. These streamside campsites are fine base camps for angling side trips to the several nearby lakes situated on the benches on each side of Rattlesnake Creek canyon.

2nd Hiking Day: Retrace your steps, 10 miles.

Mineral King to Little Claire Lake 97

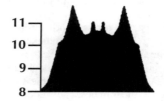

Trip	From Mineral King to Little Claire Lake via Franklin Pass, Rattlesnake Creek and Forester Lake
Distance	26 miles
Type	Out and back trip
Best season	Mid to late
Topo maps	**Mineral King** 15′; Mineral King 7½′

Grade (hiking days/recommended layover days)

Leisurely	—
Moderate	4/0
Strenuous	2/1
Trailhead	Mineral King (21)

HIGHLIGHTS   For fine fishing, superlative scenery and a whole range of side-trip possibilities, this trip is hard to beat. As the opportunities for recreation are varied, so are the watersheds that this trip visits. After crossing Franklin Pass, this route visits the alpine headwaters of two tributaries of the Kern River—Rattlesnake Creek and Soda Creek.

The great elevation changes on this trip require that you be in top shape.

DESCRIPTION (Moderate trip)

1st Hiking Day (**Mineral King** to **Franklin Lakes**, 6 miles): Follow the 1st hiking day, Trip 96, as far as Franklin Lakes.

2nd Hiking Day (**Franklin Lakes** to **Little Claire Lake**, 7 miles): Follow the 1st hiking day, Trip 96, to the campsites on upper Rattlesnake Creek. From the streamside campsites the trail descends moderately through an increasingly dense forest cover of lodgepole pine. In ¼ mile we pass the Shotgun Pass Trail, and in another 0.2 mile reach the Soda Creek Trail, which leads to Forester Lake, Little Claire Lake and Big Arroyo. Leaving Rattlesnake Creek, we fork left here. A short distance beyond the junction, the trail fords a little stream and then ascends gently over a rocky slope. Soon the trail arrives at the charmingly meadowed west side of Forester Lake, where fine campsites look across the azure blue waters to a dense forest fringe, and an occasional dimpling on the surface indicates the presence of brook trout.

Turning northwest, the trail ascends through a moderate forest cover to a meadowed bench, and then makes another ascent to the sandy crown of the ridge dividing the Rattlesnake and Soda Creek drainages. From this rounded summit the crests of Sawtooth Peak and Needham Mountain are easily visible to the north, and they continue to be seen as the trail descends moderately to the south end of Little Claire Lake. The effervescent burble of the Brewer blackbird and the raucous call of the Clark nutcracker frequently are heard as the traveler skirts the east side of Little Claire Lake (10,450′) to the good campsites at the north end of the lake, around the outlet. Fishing for brook trout is excellent (to 11″).

3rd and 4th Hiking Days: Retrace your steps, 13 miles.

Main Franklin Lake

Mineral King to Little Five Lakes

98

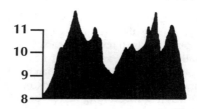

Trip	From Mineral King to Little Five Lakes via Franklin Pass, Little Claire Lake, Lost Canyon, return via Little Five Lakes, Black Rock Pass and Timber Gap
Distance	40½ miles
Type	Loop trip
Best season	Mid or late
Topo maps	**Mineral King** 15'; Mineral King, Chagoopa Falls 7½'

Grade (hiking days/recommended layover days)

Leisurely	—
Moderate	6/1
Strenuous	4/1
Trailhead	Mineral King (21)

HIGHLIGHTS   This is perhaps the best backpacker's route for looping the fine fishing country east of Mineral King. Challenging passes and remote lakes reward the hiker. For the angler, the chance to wet a line in excellent golden-trout waters is added inducement.

All will need to be in excellent condition.

DESCRIPTION (Moderate trip)

1st and 2nd *Hiking Days:* Follow Trip 97 to **Little Claire Lake**, 13 miles.

3rd Hiking Day (**Little Claire Lake** to **Unnamed Lake at 10,000'**, 7 miles): The trail west of the outlet stream from Little Claire Lake follows well-graded switchbacks down a steep, forested slope for over a mile. At the foot of this precipitous duff-and-rock slope, the route fords Soda Creek, descends gently over duff and sand through a moderate forest cover, and then becomes steeper. Marmots on the rocky slopes south of the creek whistle excitedly as unexpected visitors to their domain pass by, but they do not usually stir from their watching posts unless the traveler shows more than passing interest.

During the next several miles of steady descent through lodge-pole forest, somewhat away from Soda Creek, we hop across numerous refreshing tributaries and pass a half-dozen campsites of uneven quality. Among the evergreens one finds an occasional western white pine, and then red fir appears. Clumps of sagebrush space the stands of timber, and nestled next to their aromatic branches are much Douglas phlox and Indian paintbrush.

The appearance of Jeffrey pines heralds our approach to the junction where a trail down into Big Arroyo branches right and our route starts a steep, rocky, exposed ascent to the foot of Lost Canyon. Nearing the creek in this canyon, we double back to the northwest and suddenly leave the dry south slope for a cool, moist, verdant bower at a ford of Lost Canyon creek (difficult in early season). Beyond the ford we veer away from the creek on a steady ascent up a duff-and-sand trail. More than a mile beyond the ford, just before a second ford of Lost Canyon creek, our trail to Big Five Lakes branches right (north) and begins to climb the steep north wall.

This ascent makes a clear series of short, steep switchbacks which afford fine views west to the barren headwaters of Lost Canyon and the cirque holding Columbine Lake. Mostly lodgepole and foxtail pine, the timber cover thickens as the trail approaches a small, unnamed lake (10,000′), due east of a granite spur. Fields of red heather highlight the luxuriant growth of the wildflowers around this lake's meadow fringes, and above the treetops in the north, the barren, massive, brown hulk of Mt. Kaweah rises just barely higher than the serrated Kaweah Peaks Ridge west of it. The excellent campsites at this little lake allow the dusty hiker to have a leisurely swim in water much warmer than can be found most places in the Sierra.

4th Hiking Day (**Unnamed Lake at 10,000′** to **Little Five Lakes**, 5 miles): From the north side of the unnamed lake, our sometimes faint trail crosses a long ridge that is heavily overlaid with fallen snags. Above Big Five Lakes, the trail tops the ridge and we have views of Black Rock Pass to the west, and the lowest of the Big Five Lakes (9840′) immediately below. The descent to the good camp-sites near the outlet and along the north side of this lake is a rocky, steep downgrade.

Beyond the log-jammed outlet of the lake, the trail leads west toward a reed-filled bay. At a junction we take the right fork and embark upon a steep, rocky, switchbacking climb of ½ mile. Just before the top of this climb, at a **T** junction, the left fork leads to another of the Big Five Lakes, and we fork right on the Little Five Lakes Trail. Topping the ridge, we proceed to undulate for a dry mile, with periodic great views of Mt. Kaweah, the Kaweah Peaks Ridge and, at the ridge's west end, Red Kaweah and Black Kaweah.

The dry stretch ends when the trail dips into a small, intimate valley where a stream flows at least until late summer. From this brook we ascend for several hundred vertical feet in a moderate lodgepole forest, level off, and then gain sight of the main Little Five Lake (10,550′) and its large bordering meadow. In a few minutes our trail reaches the base of the lake's north-end peninsula, which contains many good-to-excellent campsites. The one nearest the peninsula's tip is surrounded by a wonderful carpet of grass, sedge and dwarf bilberry which shimmers in the delicate light of late afternoon, and an evening meal here may be raised to four-star quality by the alpenglow on the Kaweah Peaks across Big Arroyo. Across the bay here is a summer ranger station where emergency services are usually available.

5th and 6th Hiking Days: Reverse the 2nd and 1st hiking days of Trip 91, 15½ miles.

Unnamed lake at 10,000 feet

99

Mineral King to Big Five Lakes

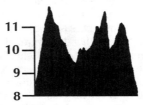

Trip   From Mineral King to Big Five Lakes via Sawtooth
                  Pass, Lost Canyon, return via Little Five Lakes,
                  Black Rock Pass, Spring Lake and Glacier Pass, part
                  cross-country

Distance   24½ miles

Type   Semiloop trip

Best season   Mid or late

Topo maps   **Mineral King** 15′; Mineral King, Chagoopa Falls
                  7½′

Grade (hiking days/recommended layover days)

    Leisurely   —

    Moderate   4/2

    Strenuous —

Trailhead   Mineral King (21)

HIGHLIGHTS   This fine, short, looping trip is a delight for
                  anglers in top condition. The route, part cross
country, passes 15 lakes, providing a variety of both trout water and
trout. The cross-country route to and beyond Spring Lake requires
mountaineering skills.

DESCRIPTION (Moderate trip)

1st Hiking Day: Follow Trip 95 to **Upper Lost Canyon**, 7½
miles.

2nd Hiking Day (**Upper Lost Canyon** to **lower Big Five Lake**,
4½ miles): From the alpine-meadowed bench below Columbine
Lake, the trail enters forest cover (sparse lodgepole and foxtail) and
then drops steeply over broken granite and meadowy sections. This
stepladdering descent keeps to the north side of Lost Canyon creek
for about 1 mile, and then fords the creek twice in the space of the
next mile. The second ford returns to the north side of the creek,

where our route branches north, away from Lost Canyon, on the poorly signed Big Five Lakes Trail. The trail ascent of the steep north wall makes a clear series of short, steep switchbacks which afford excellent views west to the barren headwaters of Lost Canyon and the cirque holding Columbine Lake. Mostly lodgepole and foxtail pine, the tree cover thickens as the trail approaches a small, unnamed lake (10,000′) due east of a granite spur. Fields of red heather highlight the luxuriant growth of the wildflowers around this lake's meadowy fringes, and above the treetops in the north, the barren, massive brown hulk of Mt. Kaweah rises just barely higher than the serrated Kaweah Peaks Ridge west of it. At this little lake, the dusty hiker can have a leisurely swim in water much warmer than is found most places in the Sierra.

From the north side of the unnamed lake, our sometimes faint trail crosses a long ridge that is heavily overlain with fallen snags. Above Big Five Lakes, the trail tops a ridge and we have views of Black Rock Pass to the west and the lowest of the Big Five Lakes (9830′) immediately below. The descent to the good campsites near the outlet and along the north side of this lake is a rocky, steep downgrade.

3rd Hiking Day (**Lower Big Five Lake** to **Spring Lake**, 5½ miles, part cross-country): Beyond the log-jammed outlet of the lake, the trail leads west on the lake's north side toward a reed-filled bay. From a junction near the bay, the trail ascends along the north side of the inlet through rank growths of ferns and moderate stands of foxtail pine. This moderately ascending trail fords the stream ¼ mile below the outlet of the largest lake in the Big Five chain, and climbs over glacially smoothed granite to the lake's east shore. There you ford the outlet stream again and pass several campsites before crossing the swampy area around the north inlet of the late. Just west of this inlet, your trail passes a trail to Little Five Lakes branching right and continues west up the Big Five Lakes basin. Anglers will find the fishing for golden trout good to excellent in all the lakes of the upper basin except the highest.

The ascent to the third lake we pass is gentle over grass and swampy areas, and, near the outlet of this lake, the trail passes two primitive, exposed campsites. We follow the grassy trail about three-fourths of the way around this lake before turning sharply right (northwest) to begin a cross-country ascent of the steep granite ridge separating the Big Five Lakes and Little Five Lakes drainages. After thrashing through a little brush, we head for the forested area and pick out a route that ascends by grass-topped ledges to the saddle just south of the uppermost lake of the Little Five Lakes chain.

From this ridge one can see across Big Arroyo to the Kaweah Peaks and Red Spur. To the west, aptly named Black Rock Pass stands out in startling relief from the surrounding white granite. The steep, difficult, rocky descent on the north side of the ridge may be ducked, but some scrambling is required to bring one to the edge of the uppermost Little Five lake. (Fishing for golden in the two lower lakes of this chain is good.) Crossing the outlet stream from this lake, our route meets and turns left onto the Black Rock Pass Trail.

First ascending across alpine meadows, the trail veers north and then climbs a steep, very rocky series of switchbacks to the fine viewpoint at Black Rock Pass (11,630'). Looking east one can see the Kaweah Peaks Ridge, the wooded flats of Chagoopa Plateau, a considerable length of Big Arroyo, and both the Little and the Big Five Lakes basins. On the south side of the pass, there are heart-stopping panoramas of the deep Cliff Creek drainage and towering Empire Mountain, seeming to be almost at fingertip distance.

Descending on the west side of the pass, the rocky trail makes one long traverse and then drops by steady and steep zigzags toward the grass-bottomed basin just north of Spring Lake. Where we almost touch a year-round stream at a hairpin bend in the trail, a route of use takes off for Spring Lake, visible in the distance, and we take this route. This unducked, rough route crosses several talus fans. Do not try to stay high as the route drops, or you will find yourself confronting steep, water-slick slabs with much exposure. After crossing the last of the talus, we are below Spring Lake. Ford the tributary northeast of the lake and work your way upward through meadows and willows to Spring Lake (10,050'). There are good campsites (somewhat exposed) on the east side of the outlet and in the sparse timber cover of the northwest shore. Views from these campsites of the massive cirque headwall and the ribboned waterfall inlets are satisfying, and fishing for brook trout (to 8") is good. (Less experienced backpackers should not go via Spring Lake but should stay on the trail from Black Rock Pass down Cliff Creek to the Timber Gap Trail and return via it. See the 1st hiking day, Trip 90.)

4th Hiking Day (**Spring Lake** to **Mineral King**, 6 miles, part cross country): Reverse the 1st hiking day, Trip 94. Note that Glacier Pass is the third saddle to the left of Empire Mountain.

Mineral King to Crescent Meadow **100**

Trip	From Mineral King to Crescent Meadow via Franklin Lakes, Franklin Pass, Rattlesnake Creek, Kern Canyon, Moraine Lake, Chagoopa Plateau, Big Arroyo, Kaweah Gap, River Valley and Bearpaw Meadow
Distance	56 miles
Type	Shuttle trip
Best season	Mid or late
Topo maps	**Mineral King, Triple Divide Peak** 15'; Mineral King, Chagoopa Falls, Mt. Kaweah, Triple Divide Peak, Lodgepole 7½'

Grade (hiking days/recommended layover days)

Leisurely	—
Moderate	8/2
Strenuous	6/1
Trailhead	Start at Mineral King (21), end at Crescent Meadow (20)

HIGHLIGHTS   This remarkable shuttle trip, partly on the famed High Sierra Trail, should be taken by all who would say, "I know the Great Western Divide country" or "I know the Kern Trench and its wooded plateaus." This route surveys a 5000-foot range of Sierran biota, and the scope of the glaciated terrain one travels over reads like the synopsis of a geology textbook. Hikers with time to spare will want to visit Nine Lake Basin along the way, while anglers will want to try their luck at Rattlesnake Creek and the Kern River.

Exploring off-trail, as in Nine Lake Basin, calls for map-and-compass skills and cross-country experience. Bears are a serious problem on the High Sierra Trail part; store food properly at all times.

DESCRIPTION (Strenuous trip)

1st Hiking Day: Follow Trip 96 to the campsites on **Upper Rattlesnake Creek**, 10½ miles.

2nd Hiking Day (**Upper Rattlesnake Creek** to **Rattlesnake Creek/ Kern River**, 8 miles): Traveling down through the upper reaches of Rattlesnake Creek is a delightful study in intimate meadows, dense stands of lodgepole pine and a classic, murmuring mountain creek. About ¼ mile from the timberline campsites, our trail passes the Shotgun Pass Trail leading south across the creek, and in another 0.2 mile passes the Soda Creek Trail. Then it fords the winding meadow stream, only to return to the north side a few hundred yards downstream. Soon we pass the Upper Rattlesnake Creek drift fence, the first of four seasonal stock fences in the canyon. The creek picks up speed as its meandering course is constricted by narrowing canyon walls, and the trail stays fairly close to its swiftly tumbling waters as you descend on a long, steady, rocky traverse of the canyon wall. After rounding the fractured granite nose of a ridge, you descend steeply to ford an unnamed tributary cascading down from the north wall, and then rejoin Rattlesnake Creek in the level stretches at Cow Camp Meadows.

This green grassland is frequented by the many mule deer in the vicinity and an occasional bear. Reflecting the lower altitude, the meadow's fringes show a forest cover of lodgepole, fir and some juniper, and as the trail continues to descend steadily Jeffrey pine and aspen begin to make their predictable appearance.

Just above the final descent into the Kern Trench, our trail passes a trail to Big Arroyo, branching north, and then switchbacks down to the good campsites just south of the junction with the Kern River Trail (6590'). Fishing for rainbow in the Kern is excellent (to 20").

3rd Hiking Day (**Rattlesnake Creek/Kern River** to **Moraine Lake**, 7½ miles: This day begins with 2½ miles of easy ascent beside the youthful Kern River, deep in the gorge that the weak zone of rocks along the Kern Canyon fault has allowed the stream to cut. Almost as deep is the canyon of Big Arroyo creek, which we cross on a steel cantilever bridge. Beyond a drift fence, your trail crosses the site of an old burn. In the wetter stretches above, thick patches of bracken fern sometimes inhibit the going. Passing through a moderate-to-dense forest of white fir, Jeffrey and sugar pine, and some black oak, birch and aspen, we reach Upper Funston Meadow and then ford Funston Creek (difficult in early season). Just beyond is a junction with the High Sierra Trail, and you turn left up it. From here to Moraine Lake, reverse the steps of the first part of the 4th hiking day, Trip 79.

4th, 5th and 6th Hiking Days: Reverse the first three hiking days, Trip 79, 30 miles.

Trip Cross-Reference Table

Trip No.	Hiking Days*	Pace*			Season			Trip Type			
		Leis	Mod	Str	Early	Mid	Late	O&B	Shut	Loop	Semi
1	2	•			•		•	•			
2	4	•			•		•	•			
3	3		•		•		•			•	
4	6	•				•	•	•			
5	6		•			•	•				•
6	3			•		•	•	•			
7	4		•			•	•			•	
8	7		•			•	•				•
9	7		•				•				•
10	2	•				•	•	•			
11	2		•			•	•	•			
12	5		•			•	•	•			
13	2		•			•		•			
14	4	•				•		•			
15	4		•			•	•	•			
16	6			•		•	•				•
17	2	•				•	•	•			
18	4	•				•	•	•			
19	5	•				•	•	•			
20	2		•			•		•			
21	2	•				•	•	•			
22	3	•			•			•			
23	2	•				•	•	•			
24	2	•				•	•			•	
25	2	•				•	•	•			
26	2		•		•	•		•			
27	2			•	•	•				•	
28	2	•			•	•		•			
29	4	•			•	•		•			
30	4	•				•	•	•			
31	6	•				•	•				•
32	6	•				•	•	•			
33	7		•			•	•				•
34	6	•				•	•	•			
35	5		•			•	•			•	

*Number of hiking days reflects the pace described in the trip's text. You can take most trips at another pace by taking more or fewer days.

Trip No.	Hiking Days	Pace			Season			Trip Type			
		Leis	Mod	Str	Early	Mid	Late	O&B	Shut	Loop	Semi
36	6			•		•	•			•	
37	4	•			•	•		•			
38	6	•				•		•			
39	4	•			•	•					•
40	2	•			•			•			
41	4	•			•	•		•			
42	7	•				•	•	•			
43	2	•				•	•	•			
44	2		•			•	•				•
45	2		•			•	•	•			
46	2	•				•		•			
47	6			•		•	•				•
48	7		•			•	•			•	
49	2	•			•		•				•
50	4	•				•	•				•
51	2			•	•			•			
52	4			•		•	•	•			
53	4			•		•	•			•	
54	4			•		•				•	
55	4			•		•	•	•			
56	4			•		•	•			•	
57	3		•		•		•	•			
58	5		•			•	•	•			
59	6			•		•	•			•	
60	3		•		•	•		•			
61	5	•				•	•	•			
62	7		•			•	•	•		•*	
63	6		•				•			•	
64	4		•			•	•	•			
65	6			•			•				•
66	2	•			•	•		•			
67	3	•				•	•	•			
68	5	•				•	•	•			
69	7		•			•	•			•	
70	2	•				•	•	•			

*Optional loop trip possible.

Trip No.	Hiking Days	Pace			Season			Trip Type			
		Leis	Mod	Str	Early	Mid	Late	O&B	Shut	Loop	Semi
71	4			•		•	•	•			
72	6			•		•	•	•			
73	8			•		•	•	•			
74	8			•		•	•	•			
75	5			•		•	•		•		
76	2	•				•	•	•			
77	6	•				•	•	•			
78	6	•					•		•	•*	
79	6		•			•	•			•	
80	14	•				•	•				•
81	2	•				•	•			•	
82	4	•				•	•	•			
83	4	•				•	•			•	
84	5		•			•	•			•	
85	7			•		•	•			•	
86	8	•			•		•		•		
87	4	•			•			•			
88	11	•					•			•	
89	5	•				•	•			•	
90	2	•			•			•			
91	4	•				•	•	•			
92	6	•				•	•	•			
93	6	•				•	•				•
94	2			•		•		•			
95	2			•		•		•			
96	2			•		•	•	•			
97	4	•				•	•	•			
98	6	•				•	•			•	
99	4	•				•	•				•
100	6			•		•	•			•	

*Optional loop trip possible.

Thomas Winnett

Jason Winnett

Co-authors

Kathy Morey

Lyn Haber

Index

altitude sickness 8
Anvil Camp 211–12, 229–30, 265
Arctic Lake 220, 240
Arrowhead Lake 194
Aspen Meadow 118
Avalanche Pass 185

Baboon Lakes 93
Baker Lake 154
Barigan Stringer 259, 267
Barrett Lakes 143
Baxter Lakes 167–68
Baxter Pass 168–69, 194
Bear Creek 32, 36–57, 75
——, East Fork 46
——, West Fork 49
Bear Dam Junction 29 *See next*
——, trips from 36–59
Bear Diversion Dam 37
bear boxes 13–14
——, locations of 16–17
bear problem, the 12–18
bearbagging, how to 14–15
Bearpaw Lake 46
Bearpaw Lodge 237, 240
Bearpaw Meadow 236–38, 240, 283–84, 301
Bearpaw Ranger Station 240
bearproof food canisters 14
Bench Lake (Independence Creek) 204
Bench Lake (South Fork Kings River) 164–65
Bench Valley 110–12, 115
Beville Lake 232
Big Arroyo 239–42, 245, 271, 280–82, 296, 301–02
Big Arroyo Creek 241
Big Bear Lake 46, 55
Big Bird Lake 236
Big Five Lakes 281, 296–99
Bighorn Plateau 211, 229
Big Maxon Meadow 111, 114–15, 124
Big Pete Meadow 146–47
Big Pine Creek 30, 99 *See below*
——, North Fork 153, 155–58
——, South Fork 153, 155
——, trips from 153–58

Big Shot Lake 113
Big Whitney Meadow 258–59, 266–67, 269–70
Birchim Lake 68
Bird, W. 101
Bishop Creek 84
——, Middle Fork 86
——, North Fork 32, 78
——, South Fork 134, 137, 140
Bishop Lake 139
Bishop Pass 100, 136, 139, 182
Blackcap Basin 97, 106, 109, 114–15, 120, 123
Black Lake 157
Black Rock Pass 241, 277–80, 282, 295, 298, 300
Blackrock sawmill, flume (site) 160
Blayney Hot Springs 50–52, 118, 152
Blayney Meadows 50, 75
Blue Canyon 120, 131–33
Blue Canyon Cabinsite 132
Blue Canyon Creek 120, 132–33
Blue Canyon Pass 120
Blue Lake 87, 93
boat taxi *See* Edison, Lake *and* Florence Lake
Bob Creek 130
boiling, to purify water 8–9
Boreal Plateau 252, 268
Boulder Creek 53, 95
Box Lake 61–62
Brewer Creek 234
Brewer Survey (Party) 33, 101
Brown Bear Lake 75
Brownstone Mine (site) 68
Bubbs Creek 98, 184–88, 190, 195–96, 200, 210, 214
Buck Creek 240
Bullfrog Lake 186, 188, 195, 205–06
Bullfrog Meadow 259
Bull Lake 138, 140
Burnt Corral Creek, West Fork 97
Burnt Corral Meadows 102

Cabin Creek 127–29
cables, for bearbagging 15
Cahoon Meadow 232

campfires 5–7
campsites, how to choose 5
cars at trailheads 18
Cartridge Creek 181
Castle Domes Meadow 192
Cathedral Lake 120
Cedar Grove (Roadend) 30 *See next*
——, trips from 175–202
Center Basin 200, 210
Chagoopa Creek 242
Chagoopa Falls 242
Chagoopa Plateau 239
Chagrin Lake 117
Chain Lakes 129
Chamberlain's Camp 97
Chaney, Lon 154
Charlotte Creek 184–85, 196, 202
Charlotte Lake 187–89, 195, 205–07
chemicals to purify water 8–9
Chickenfoot Lake 61
Chicken Spring Lake 253–54, 269, 272–75
Chocolate Lakes 137–38, 140–41
Chuck Pass 122–26
Cienega Mirth 154
Cirque Lake 250
Cirque Pass 144
Cliff Creek 276–80, 282, 284, 300
Cloud Canyon 233
Clover Creek, East Fork 232
Clyde, Norman 153–54
co–authors 306
Colby Meadow 150–51
Colby Pass 227
Cold Creek 41
Colt Lake 112
Columbine Lake 288–89, 298
Comanche Meadow 233–34
Comb Creek 171
Copper Creek 175–76
Cotter, Richard 229
Cottonwood (Lakes) Basin 250, 253, 255
Cottonwood Creek 250, 252
——, South Fork 249–50
Cottonwood Lakes 250
Cottonwood Lakes Trailhead 31, 273 *See next*
——, trips from 249–65
Cottonwood Pass 214, 266–67, 269,
272–74
counterbalance bearbagging *See* bearbagging, how to
Courtright Reservoir 30, 96–98 *See next*
——, trips from 102–120
Cow Camp Meadows 302
Cow Meadow 129
Crabtree Lakes 257
Crabtree Meadow(s) 217, 252, 255, 257, 263–64, 271–72, 274
Crabtree Pass 252
Crabtree Ranger Station 218–21, 223, 226, 229, 238, 244–46, 256–57, 271
Crescent Meadow 31, 237, 301 *See next*
——, trips from 238–48
criteria for rating trips 1–3
Crown Basin 115
Crown Creek 129–31
Crown Lake 123, 125
Crown Pass 123
Crown Valley 130
Crown Valley Guard Station 129
Crown Valley Ranch 130
Crown Valley Trailhead 30, 119 *See next*
——, trips from 127–33
Cryptosporidium 8–9
Crystal Creek 290–91
Crystal Lake 286

Darwin Canyon 89, 150–51
Deadman Canyon 233, 235
Deadman Canyon Creek 234, 236
Deer Creek 130
Deer Meadow 144–45
Desolation Lake(s) 80–82
Devils Punchbowl 108–09, 112–13, 116
Devils Washbowl 181
Dingleberry Lake 87
Disappointment Lake 117
Dollar Lake 168, 194
Donkey Lake 87, 93
Double Meadow 53
Dougherty Creek 178, 180
——, Middle Fork 178
Dragon Lake 194, 208
Dusy, Frank 101, 131

Dusy Basin 138, 142–43, 145–47, 183
Dusy Branch (Creek) 182–83

Eagle Scout Creek 284
East Creek 196–98, 202
East Kennedy Lake 174
East Lake 186, 198, 201–02
East Pinnacles Creek 76
East Twin Buck Lake 113
Edison, Lake 41
——, boat taxi on 41
Elba Lake 71, 76
Elizabeth Pass 236–37, 240
Emerald Lakes 86–87
Emerson Lake 79
Evolution Creek 118, 150–51
Evolution Lake 150
Evolution Meadow 151
Evolution Valley 84, 150–51

Fall Creek 110–11
Farewell Gap 291
Ferguson Creek 234
Filly Lake 113
filters to purify water 8–9
First Falls 154–55
First Lake 154, 157–58
Fish Camp 58, 65–66
Fleming Creek 105–08, 117
——, East Fork 109
Fleming Lake 107
Florence Lake 29–30, 52–53, 116, 118 *See below*
——, boat taxi on 53, 94
——, trips from 94–96
Flower Lake 203–05
food storage in backcountry 13–17
fool(s) 100
Forester Lake 294
Forester Pass 200, 209–10
Fourth Lake 157
Fourth Lake Lodge (site) 157
Fourth Recess 62, 65
Fourth Recess Lake 63–64
Franklin Creek 291
Franklin Lake(s) 291, 293, 301
Franklin Meadow 117
Franklin Pass 258, 290, 292–93, 295, 301
Frémont, John C. 101, 104–05

French Canyon 70–71, 76, 81, 83
Frypan Meadow 170–71
Funston Creek 242, 271, 302
Funston Lake 268
Funston Meadow *see* Upper Funston Meadow *and* Lower Funston Meadow

Gabbot Pass 58
Gallats Lake 227
Gardiner Basin 190
Gem Lakes 60–61
George Lake 86, 90–91
Geraldine Lakes 129
Giant Forest 222
Giardia lamblia, giardiasis 8–9
Gilbert Lake 204
glacial erosion 33, 43–44, 46
Glacier Creek 144
Glacier Lodge 153
Glacier Pass 285–86, 288, 298, 300
Glacier Valley 178
Glen Pass 190, 194, 207–08
Goddard Canyon 151–52
Goddard Creek 181
Golden Bear Lake 210
Golden Creek 63
Golden Lake 202
Golden Trout Camp 249
Golden Trout Creek 259–60, 267, 270
Golden Trout Lake(s) 81
Golden Trout Wilderness 246, 259, 261, 266, 272
Goodale Pass 41
Granite Basin 175–76
Granite Creek (South Fork Kings River) 176
Granite Creek (Middle Fork Kaweah River) 284
Granite Lake 173–77
Granite Park 72–73
Granite Pass 174, 177
Grass Lake 84
Great Western Divide 214, 239, 298, 301
Grinnell Lakes 66
Grizzly Lakes 171
Groundhog Meadow 286
group size, limits on 21–23
Grouse Meadows 145, 181–82

Guest Lake 110–12
Guitar Lake 220, 246, 257, 271–72
Guyot Creek 256, 269, 272
Guyot Pass 272

Halfmoon Lake 115, 121–23
Hamilton Creek 240
Hamilton Lakes 238, 240–41, 245,
   282–83
Harrison Pass 199, 201
hazards 8–11
Heart Lake (northern Rock Creek)
   61
Heart Lake (South Fork San Joaquin)
   51
Helen Lake 148–49
Hell Diver Lakes 88
Hell for Sure Lake 117
Hell for Sure Pass 101, 106–08,
   117, 152
Helm, Bill 101
High Lake 251
High Sierra Trail 222–24, 226, 237,
   248, 271, 281, 283, 301–02
——, classic trip on 238–44
Hilgard Branch 43–44, 47–48, 75
Hilgard Lake 43, 75
Hilgard Meadow 42–44, 75
Hobler Lake 97
Honeymoon Lake 67, 69, 72
Hopkins Lakes 65
Hopkins Pass 65
Horsehead Lake 112–13
Horseshoe Lakes 180
Horseshoe Meadow 31, 99, 214,
   253–54 See next
——, trips from 266–75
Hot Springs Pass 94
Hotel Creek 171
Humphreys Basin 80–82
Hungry Packer Lake 88
Hutchinson Meadow 75–76, 81–83,
   152
hypothermia 9

Independence Creek 203
Indian Springs 125–26
insect repellent See mosquitoes
Italy, Lake 42–45, 55–56, 57–58,
   72–73
Italy Pass 35, 42, 68, 70, 72–73

JO Pass 232
John Muir Trail throughout
John Muir Wilderness 32, 27, 41,
   52, 68, 94, 97. 103, 118, 127, 154,
   203, 216
Johnson Creek 260
Johnson Lake 268
Jumble Lake 44,–46, 55, 73
Junction Meadow (Bubbs Creek)
   185, 188, 196, 200
Junction Meadow (Kern River)
   226–27, 238, 243, 245, 247–48,
   269, 271
Junction Pass 200, 210, 212, 230

Kanawyer Gap 234
Kaweah Gap 238–39, 241, 245,
   281–82, 301
Kaweah River 214, 291
——, East Fork 290
——, Marble Fork 231
——, Middle Fork 238–39, 284
Kearsarge Lakes 205
Kearsarge Pass 100, 195, 205, 207,
   209
Kennedy Creek 174
Kennedy Creek Canyon 171–72
——, tarns on upper 172–74
Kennedy Lakes 170
Kennedy Pass 170–72, 174, 178
Kern Canyon (Trench) 224, 242–
   43, 248, 261, 270–71, 301
Kern Canyon Ranger Station 261
Kern Hot Spring 238–39, 243, 269–
   71
Kern Plateau 270
Kern River 201, 214–15, 223–27,
   242–43, 247–48, 260–61, 264–65,
   270, 301–02
——, South Fork 259
Kern–Kaweah Pass 227
Kern–Kaweah River 226–27
King, Clarence 32, 229
Kings Canyon National Park
   throughout
Kings-Kern Divide 200, 202, 214,
   229
Kings River 100
——, Middle Fork 98, 132, 145,
   147–48, 180–82
——, North Fork 104–05, 109,

110–11, 114–15, 124
——, South Fork 98
Knapsack Pass 143

L Lake 71, 76
Lamarck Col 84
Lamarck Lake(s) 84
Laurel Creek 261–62
LeConte Canyon 145, 147–48
LeConte Ranger Station 182
Lewis Creek 30 *See next*
——, trips from 170–74
lightning 9–10
Little Bear Lake 46–47, 55
Little Bearpaw Meadow 282–84
Little Claire Lake 214, 293–95
Little Five Lake(s) 241, 278–82, 295–300
Little Lakes Valley 60, 62, 65
Little Pete Meadow 148
Little Pothole Lake 204
Little Rancheria Creek 127
Little Shot Lake 113
Little Whitney Cow Camp 260
Little Whitney Meadow 259–60, 269–70
Loch Leven 79
Lodgepole Campground 31 *See next*
——, trips from 231–37
Lone Pine Canyon 237
Lone Pine Creek (Middle Fork Kaweah River) 240, 283
Lone Pine Creek (Mt. Whitney) 216, 218
——, Middle Fork 219
——, North Fork 216
Lone Pine Lake 216
Long Lake (Bishop Creek) 137–38
Long Lake (Cottonwood Creek) 250–51
Long Lake (northern Rock Creek) 61
Long Meadow 97, 102
Lost Canyon 242, 288–89, 296, 298–99
Lost Lake (South Fork San Joaquin River) 94–96
Lost Lake (Sugarloaf Creek) 232–33
Lou Beverly Lake 49
Lovelace, Shorty 193, 200

Lower Crabtree Meadow 220
Lower Desolation Lake 81
Lower Funston Meadow 261, 269–70
Lower Goddard Canyon 116–18
Lower Lamarck Lake 84
Lower Mills Creek Lake 58, 66
Lower Rock Creek Ford 256, 272, 275
Lower Tent Meadow 175–76
Lower Vidette Meadow 195
Lucys Foot Pass 202

Mack Lake 60
Malpais Lava 260
Map Center, The 20
maps 19–20
Margaret Lake 137
Marie Lake 50–51
Marjorie, Lake 164
marmots, protecting against 10, 15
Marsh Lake 60–61
Marvin Pass 234
Mary Louise Lakes 137–38
Matlock Lake 204
Maxon Lake 124
Maxon Meadows 102
McClure Meadow 151
McDermand, Lake 149
McGuire Lake 111
Meadow Brook 108–10
Medley Lakes 48–50, 54, 74–75
Mehrten Creek Crossing 237
Midnight Lake 88–89
Midway Lake 120
Milestone Basin 224–25, 247, 263–65
Milestone Bowl 227
Milestone Creek 201, 211, 225
Mineral King 31, 214, 258, 262 *See next*
——, trips from 276–302
Mirror Lake 219
Mist Falls 192
Miter Basin 252, 253, 255, 274–75
Monarch Creek 285–86, 288
Monarch Lake(s) 286
Moniere, Alfred 236
Mono Creek 32, 35–36, 40, 58–59, 66
Mono Pass 35, 60, 63, 65

Moon Lake 70–71, 76
Moore Boys Camp 121–22, 125
Moraga, Gabriel 101
Moraine Lake 238–39, 241–42, 301–02
Morgan Pass 60–62
Mosquito Flat 29 *See next*
——, trips from 60–66
mosquitoes 10–11
Mountain Meadow 130
Muir Pass 148–49
Muir Trail Ranch 52, 94
Muir, John 100, 128, 149, 246, 250
Mule Lake 160

Natural Bridge 260–61
New Army Pass 251–53, 255, 258, 273
Nichols Canyon 123
Nine Lake Basin 241, 280–83, 301
North Lake 29, 146, 152 *See next*
——, trips from 78–85

Oak Creek Roadend 30, 166, 168–69
Oak Creek, North Fork 169
Old Army Pass 252
Old Kip Camp 39
Onion Valley 30, 99 *See next*
——, trips from 203–13
Outpost Camp 216–18, 238, 255, 274

Pacific Crest Trail 42, 47–48, 51, 221, 243–44, 252, 254, 257, 259, 265, 267, 271–73, 275
Packsaddle Lake 80
Palisade Basin 143
Palisade Creek 144–45, 181–82
Palisade Lakes 144
Paradise Valley 167, 185, 191–92
Parcher, A. 137
Parcher, W.C. 137
permit application form 27
permit reservations 21–22
permits 21–28
permits on demand 24–27
permits, applying for by mail 23–24
Pinchot Pass 164
Pine Creek 32, 61, 67–68, 71, 77, 118

——, North Fork 77
Pine Creek Pass 68–71, 76
Pine Creek Roadend 29 *See next*
——, trips from 67–78
Pine Lake 68
Pinto Lake 276–77, 279
Pioneer Basin 63–65
Pioneer Basin Lakes 63–65
Piute Canyon 75–76
Piute Creek 76, 83, 118
Piute Lake 78–80
Piute Pass 35, 80, 83, 100
Portal Lake 114–15, 119–20, 124
Post Corral Creek 103–04, 106
Post Corral Meadows 102–04, 106, 114
Pothole, The 212
Potluck Pass 143–44
Precipice Lake 241, 283
profiles 19, *throughout*

Quail Meadows 40–41, 58–59
quota periods 21–24
quotas 21

Rae Lake (north) 106–08, 116
Rae Lake(s) (south) 168, 190–91, 193–94, 207–08
Ramshaw Meadows 260
Randle Corral 131–32
Ranger Lake 231–33, 235
Ranger Meadow 236
Rattlesnake Creek 258, 260–61, 271, 292–94, 301–02
rattlesnakes 10
Red Mountain Basin 109, 113, 117
Redwood Meadow 277, 282, 284
Redwood Meadow Ranger Station 284
Reflection, Lake 196, 198
River Valley 240, 283, 301
Roaring River 214, 233–36
Roaring River Ranger Station 234
Rock Creek (north) 32, 60–61, 99
Rock Creek (south) 220, 243, 252, 256, 272, 274–75
Rockslide Lake 227
Rocky Basin Lakes 259, 266–68
Roman Four Lake 113
roof pendants 51–52
Rosemarie Meadow 49

Ruby Lake 63
Ruwau Lake 137, 139

Sabrina, Lake 29 *See next*
——, trips from 86–93
Saddlerock Lake 139
Sallie Keyes Lakes 51, 75
Salt Lick Meadow 260
Sandpiper Lake 49–51
Sandy Meadow 222, 271
sanitation 5
San Joaquin River 100
——, South Fork 35, 51, 53, 75,
98, 117–18, 151
Sapphire Lake 150
Sawmill Canyon 160
Sawmill Creek 160
Sawmill Creek Roadend 30 *See
next*
——, trips from 159–69
Sawmill Lake 159–160, 162, 166
Sawmill Meadow 160
Sawmill Pass 160–62
Sawtooth Pass 276, 286, 288–90,
298
Scaffold Meadows 234
Scepter Creek 126
Scepter Lake 126
Schoolmarm Lake 113
Second Falls 154
Second Lake 157
Second Recess 65–66
Senger Creek 52, 75
sequoia, giant 284
Sequoia National Park *throughout*
Seven Gables Lakes 47
Seville Lake 233–34
Shepherd Creek 212, 230
Shepherd Creek Canyon 212
Shepherd Pass 211–12, 228–29,
263, 265
Shotgun Pass 293, 302
Siberian Outpost 259
Siberian Pass 252, 254, 258, 267,
275
Siberian Pass Creek 275
Sierra Club 48, 149
Silliman Creek 232
Silliman Pass 231–33, 235
Simpson Meadow 100, 178, 180–81
Sixth Lake 156–57

Sixty Lake Basin 168, 189–90, 194,
208
Sky Parlor Meadow 242
Smith, Jedediah 101
snow bridges, cornices 11
Snowslide Camp 115
Soda Creek 242, 293–96, 302
Soldier Lakes 252
South America, Lake 201, 211,
247, 265
South Fork Lakes 249–51, 253,
255, 273
South Lake 30, 183 *See next*
——, trips from 134–52
South Lake Road (trailhead) 31, 92
Spanish Lake 127, 129
Sphinx Creek 185
Spring Lake 285, 287, 298, 300
stash-in-a-crack 15
State Lakes(s) 177–80
Statham Meadow 129
Stokes Stringer 266–67
stoves, backpacking 5–6
stream crossings 11
stream erosion 33, 43–44
Sugarloaf Creek 234
Sugarloaf Meadow 234
Sugarloaf Valley 233
Summit Lake (Mono Pass) 63
Summit Lake (Piute Pass) 81
Summit Meadow 129
Symmes Creek 212
Symmes Creek Trailhead 31, 209,
212–13, 228, 230, 263, 265

Taboose Canyon 164
Taboose Creek 165
Taboose Creek Roadend 30, 163,
165
Taboose Pass 163, 165
Talbot, Theodore 101
Tamarack Lake 237, 240
Teddy Bear Lake 44, 75
Tehipite Valley 100–01, 180–81
Third Lake 157
Thompson *see also* Thomson
Thompson Lake 53
Thomson *see also* Thompson
Thomson Lake 94–95
Thomson Pass 96
Three Springs 127

Thunderbolt Pass 143
Timber Gap 276, 280, 282, 285, 290, 295, 300
Timber Gap Creek 276
Timberline Lake 220, 271
Toe Lake 58
Trail Camp (Big Pine Creek) 154
Trail Camp (Mt. Whitney) 217, 219
Trail Crest 218–19, 228, 238
Trail Lakes 63
trailheads, the 29–31
trash in backcountry 5
Treasure Lake(s) (South Fork Bishop Creek) 134–38
Treasure Lakes (northern Rock Creek) 61
trip cross–reference table 303–05
tungsten mill, mines 61, 67–68
Tunnel Ranger Station 259–60
Turret Creek 76
Turtle Island 53
Twin Falls 36–38, 40, 48
Twin Lakes (Clover Creek) 232
Twin Lakes (South Fork Kings River) 161–64
Tyee Lakes 91–92
Tyndall Creek 201, 224, 228–29, 246–47, 265
Tyndall Frog Ponds 229

Union Carbide tungsten mill 67
Upper Cliff Creek 276–78
Upper Crabtree Meadow 220
Upper Funston Meadow 248, 302
Upper Golden Trout Lake 81
Upper Kern River 245–46, 264
Upper Lamarck Lake 84
Upper Lost Canyon 288–89
Upper Mills Creek Lake 58
Upper Pine Lake 68, 70, 77
Upper Ranger Meadow 236–37
Upper Rattlesnake Creek 262, 290, 302
Upper Rock Creek 258, 264, 272–73
Upper Rock Creek Lake 251–53, 255, 263, 269
Ursa Lake 46

Vee Lake 45–47, 54–55
Vermilion Campground, Trailhead 29, 40–41
Vermilion Valley 41
Vermilion Valley Resort 41
Vidette Meadow 184–87, 194–95, 200, 209–10
Volcanic Lakes 173–74
Volcano Falls 261
Volcano Meadow 260

Wales Lake 222
Walker, Joseph 101
Wallace Creek 222–24, 238, 243, 269, 271
Wallace Lake 211, 221–22
Wanda Lake 148–50
Warm Lake 52
water, pollution/purification of 7–9
West Pinnacles Creek 76
West Twin Buck Lake 113
Wet Meadow see Summit Meadow
White Bear Lake 46, 55
Whitney, Mt. 46, 217, 219, 245–46, 255, 269–72, 274
Whitney Creek 220–21, 243–44, 246, 257, 269, 271
Whitney Portal 31, 238, 244, 255, 274 See next
——, trips from 216–30
Willow Creek 130
Windy Canyon 181
Windy Canyon Creek 181
Wishon Reservoir 30, 98 See next
——, trips from 121–26
Wolverine Lake see Rae Lake (north)
Wolverton Corral 239
Wolverton Cutoff 237
Wonder Lakes 84
Woodchuck Country 99, 122
Woodchuck Creek 122, 126
Woodchuck Lake 122
Woods Creek 161–62, 167, 192
——, North Fork 162
——, South Fork 167, 194
——, White Fork 167
Woods Creek Crossing 166–67, 185, 192–93
Woods Lake 162
Wright Lakes 209, 211

Zumwalt Meadow 100